Mystical Poems
of Rumi

Untitled
Sadegh Tabrizi, 100 x 100 cm, ink on parchment

Mystical Poems
of Rumi

Translated from the Persian by
A. J. Arberry

Annotated and prepared by
Hasan Javadi

Foreword to the new and corrected edition by
Franklin D. Lewis

General Editor,
Ehsan Yarshater

The University of Chicago Press ∴ Chicago & London

The translations in this volume were originally published in two books. The first volume, including the first 200 poems, or ghazals, appeared in 1968 under the title *Mystical Poems of Rūmī 1, First Selection, Poems 1–200*. It was part of a UNESCO Collection of Representative Works and was accepted in the translation series of Persian works jointly sponsored by the Royal Institute of Translation of Teheran and United Nations Educational, Scientific, and Cultural Organization (UNESCO). The second selection, prepared by Hasan Javadi, was published in 1979 by Bibliotheca Persica as number 23 in their Persian Heritage Series, edited by Ehsan Yarshater with the assistance of the Center for Iranian Studies at Columbia University. It was reprinted in 1991 by the University of Chicago Press under the title *The Mystical Poems of Rūmī 2, Second Selection, Poems 201–400*. This combined and corrected edition contains the text and notes from those two books as well as significant revisions based on a new reading of Arberry's original handscript and some new notes and a new foreword by Franklin D. Lewis.

Published by arrangement with Bibliotheca Persica.
The University of Chicago Press, Chicago 60637
Poems 1–200 and notes to poems 1–200 © 1968 by A. J. Arberry
Poems 201–400 and notes to poems 201–400 © 1979 by Ehsan Yarshater
Combined and Corrected edition with a new Foreword by Franklin D. Lewis © 2009 by The University of Chicago
All rights reserved.
Originally published in two volumes. Poems 201–400 originally published in 1979 as No. 23 in the Persian Heritage Series, Bibliotheca Persica.
University of Chicago Press edition 2009
Printed in the United States of America

18 17 16 15 14 13 12 11 10 09   1 2 3 4 5

ISBN-13: 978-0-226-73162-9 (paper)
ISBN-10: 0-226-73162-6 (paper)
Library of Congress Cataloging-in-Publication Data

Jalal al-Din Rumi, Maulana, 1207–1273.
      [Divan-i Shams-i Tabrizi. English. Selections]
      Mystical poems of Rumi / translated from the Persian by A.J. Arberry ; annotated and prepared by Hasan Javadi; foreword to the new and corrected edition by Franklin D. Lewis ; general editor, Ehsan Yarshater.
      p. cm.
      Includes bibliographical references.
      ISBN-13: 978-0-226-73162-9 (pbk. : alk. paper)
      ISBN-10: 0-226-73162-6 (pbk. : alk. paper)   1. Jalal al-Din Rumi, Maulana, 1207–1273—Translations into English.   2. Sufi poetry, Persian—Translations into English.   I. Arberry, A. J. (Arthur John), 1905–1969.   II. Javadi, Hasan.   III. Lewis, Franklin, 1961–   IV. Yar-Shater, Ehsan.   V. Title.
      PK6480.E5A72   2008
      891'.551—dc22   2008034071

Contents

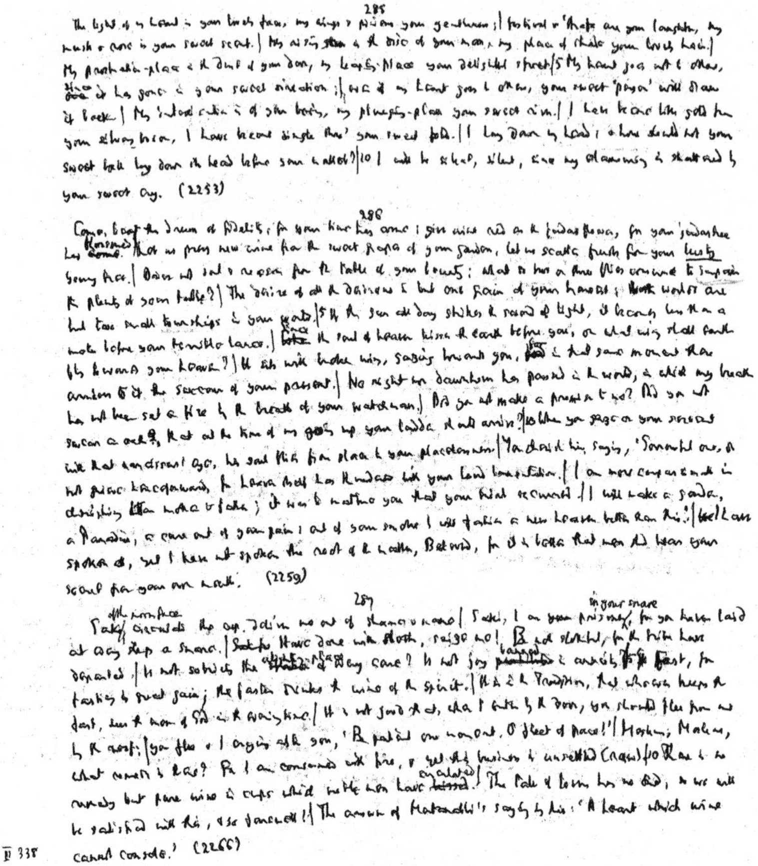

A page from A. J. Arberry; translation of *Mystical Poems of Rumi*, in his own handwriting, showing poems 285–287. (Courtesy of Hasan Javadi).

Foreword

A professorship of Arabic at Cambridge University was established in 1632 and endowed by Thomas Adams, who had made his fortune as a draper and haberdasher, and later went on to become the Lord Mayor of London. As its name implies, the Sir Thomas Adams's Professorship of Arabic was to be devoted to the study of Arabic—it is the oldest endowed professorship for this purpose in the English-speaking world. Several of the professors who occupied the Sir Thomas Adams chair at Cambridge in the twentieth century—E. G. Browne, C. A. Storey, R. A. Nicholson, and A. J. Arberry—were, however, equally or even more renowned as Persianists. Indeed, the latter two especially distinguished themselves as scholars of the Persian mystical poet Maulānā Jalāl al-Dīn Rūmī, now known in English simply as Rumi, or in Turkey as Mevlana.

While Edward Granville Browne (1862–1926) was perhaps not as enamored of Rumi (Jalálu'd-Dín Rúmí, as the scholarly conventions were then spelling his name) as two of his successors to the Sir Thomas Adams's Professorship of Arabic would be, he nevertheless passed on to his students a deep and abiding love for the poet he described as "without doubt the most eminent Ṣūfī poet whom Persia has produced, while his mystical *Mathnawí* deserves to rank amongst the great poems of all time."[1] In 1898, Browne's student Reynold Alleyne Nicholson (1868–1945) published a selection of forty-eight of Rumi's Persian ghazals with facing-page translation in English, accompanied by scholarly notes.[2] Nicholson would later go on to edit and translate Rumi's great narrative poem the *Maṣnavi* (also transliterated as *Mathnavī* or *Mathnawí*), a project to which he devoted a large part of his scholarly career. Although attempts had been made to translate parts of Rumi's *Maṣnavi* into English before Nicholson did so, his selection from Rumi's *Dīvān-i Shams-i Tabrīz*, or "great Dīvān" (*Dīvān-i kabīr*), was the first work in English devoted to Rumi's ghazals, of which Nicholson remarked, they "reach the utmost heights of which a poetry inspired by vision and rapture is capable."

Arthur J. Arberry (1905–69), the translator of the present work, had attended the funeral of Professor E. G. Browne in 1926 and in 1927 received the scholarship for Cambridge students Browne had established in his will. Arberry used this scholarship to pursue his studies in Persian and Arabic, becoming a student of R. A. Nicholson and obtaining his doctorate at Cambridge in 1936. In 1944, after some time spent in Cairo, A. J. Arberry succeeded Vladimir Minorsky as Chair of Persian at the School of Oriental and African Studies at the University of London. Meanwhile, back in Cambridge, C. A. Storey had succeeded Nicholson as Thomas Adams Professor of Arabic.

1. E. G. Browne, *A Literary History of Persia, vol. II: From Firdawsí to Saʼdí* (London: T. Fisher Unwin and New York: C. Scribner's Sons, 1906; reissued: Cambridge: The University Press, 1928 and several reprints. Reissued Bethesda, Maryland: Iranbooks, 1997), 515.

2. *Selected Poems from the Dīvāni Shamsi Tabrīz*, trans. R. A. Nicholson (Cambridge University Press, 1898, reissued in 1952, paperback edition 1977; reissued by Ibex publishers in 2002)

FRANKLIN D. LEWIS

But when Storey retired in 1947, Arberry returned to Cambridge to himself assume the position of his former teacher, Nicholson, and his benefactor, Browne, as Sir Thomas Adams Professor.

Though Arberry did not publish on Rumi while Nicholson was still alive, during his twenty-year career at Cambridge he devoted much of his scholarly efforts to building upon his mentor's project of translation and introduction of Rumi to the West. Arberry's voluminous scholarly output included translations of some poems of Rumi in his *Immortal Rose: An Anthology of Persian Lyrics* (London: Luzac, 1948), verse translations of Rumi's quatrains (*rubāʿiyāt*, 1949), his translation of Rumi's lectures and discourses (*Fīhi mā fīh*, 1961), two volumes of prose translations of selected stories from Rumi's *Maṣnavī* (1961 and 1963), selections from the spiritual diaries of Rumi's father, Bahāʾ al-Dīn-i Valad (*Maʿārif*, 1964), and an extended selection of Rumi's mystical lyrics (1968 and, posthumously, 1979). We may also note that during these years Arberry also translated two works tangentially related to Rumi: both the Qurʾān itself, which figures so prominently in Rumi's poetry, as well as the famous modern Persian poem by Muhammad Iqbal, in which Rumi features as a character, guiding Iqbal (just as Virgil guided Dante) through the heavens.[3] Beyond all this, Arberry had announced in 1961 a hope to publish a "full study of the life, writings and teachings of Rumi" which was to include an "extended analysis of the contents, pattern and doctrine of the *Masnavi*," which, sadly, he did not live long enough to complete.[4]

---

3. *The Koran Interpreted*, trans. A. J. Arberry (London: Allen and Unwin; New York: MacMillan, 1955), which has served as a standard source for quotations of the Qurʾān in English. And Muhammad Iqbal, *Jāvīd-nāma*, trans. A. J. Arberry (London: Allen and Unwin, 1966).

4. The following chronological capsule summarizes Arberry's great contribution to the study of Rumi:

1949 *The Rubāʿiyât of Jalâl al-Dîn Rûmî* (London: E. Walker)
1961 *Discourses of Rumi* (London: J. Murray)
1961 *Tales from the Masnavi* (London: Allen and Unwin)

Arberry and Nicholson together thus provided the major portal to the poetry of Rumi for English-language readers. In the decades since their death, many poets and modern interpreters have introduced new contemporary English versions that have popularized Rumi's poetry. Yet many who claim to "translate" Rumi in English do not know Persian at all; their glimpse of Rumi, and the inspiration they receive from him, in fact often relies upon the pages of Nicholson and Arberry, or on English translations of Turkish translations of the Persian of Rumi. Without the scholarly translations of Nicholson and Arberry, it would have been impossible for poets like Robert Bly and Coleman Barks to recognize Rumi's potential appeal and reimagine him as a new-age American poet. Because Nicholson and Arberry were interested primarily in conveying the ideas and expressions of Rumi, their translations may lack the popular and literary appeal of subsequent English retranslations (or re-versions), but they are both more precise and much more informative about the particulars of Rumi's thought than the widely known popular versions.[5]

1963 *More Tales from the Masnavi* (London: Allen and Unwin)
1964 *Aspects of Islamic Civilization: As Depicted in the Original Texts* (London: Allen and Unwin) [includes selected translations from the spiritual diary of Rumi's father]
1968 *Mystical Poems of Rūmī 1* (Chicago: University of Chicago Press)
1979 *Mystical Poems of Rūmī 2* (Chicago: University of Chicago Press)

5. Other Persian scholars have since published direct translations of Rumi's ghazals from the Persian, including William Chittick in *The Sufi Path of Love: The Spiritual Teachings of Rumi* (Albany: The State University of New York Press, 1983); Talat Halman and Metin And in *Mevlana Celaleddin Rumi and the Whirling Dervishes* (Istanbul: Dost Yayınları, 1983); Annemarie Schimmel in *Look! This is Love* (Boston: Shambala, 1991), and myself in *Rumi: Past and Present, East and West* (Oxford: Oneworld, 2000) and *Rumi: Swallowing the Sun* (Oxford: Oneworld, 2008). In German there is J. Christoph Bürgel, *Licht und Reigen: Gedichte aus dem Diwan der größten mystischen Dichters persischer Zunge* (Bern: Herbert Lang and Frankfurt: Peter Lang, 1974) and a revised, expanded edition of that, published as *Rumi: Gedichte aus dem Diwan* (Munich: Beck, 2003); and in French, Leili Anvar Chenderoff in *Rûmî* (Paris: Entrelac, 2004).

Indeed, Nicholson's translations of selected poems of the *Dīvān-i Shams* are still in print 110 years later, and Arberry's two volumes of *Mystical Poems of Rumi*, containing four hundred poems from the *Dīvān-i Shams*, continue to inspire popular re-translations (including some by Colin Stuart, Coleman Barks, Kabir Helminski, and Raficq Abdulla, etc.). The two volumes of Arberry's *Mystical Poems of Rumi* have even been reprinted several times in Iran, presumably so that Persian-speakers can either share their favorite ghazals from Rumi with their non-Persophone friends and relatives, or use Arberry's English as a gloss, where the meaning of the Persian may be not quite transparent to modern Iranians![6]

It was the summer after my freshman year in college—a little over a year after the revolution in Iran—when I bought my own copy of volume one of A. J. Arberry's *Mystical Poems of Rumi*. As the receipt has remained in my copy, I can be precise: it was purchased on July 18, 1980, at Cody's Books (an influential institution, sadly now defunct) on 2454 Telegraph Avenue in Berkeley, California. It cost only $3.95, a grand total of $4.21 after tax: a most rewarding purchase, one that I have frequently had occasion to consult over the three intervening decades.

This translation of 200 of Rumi's ghazals had first been published as *Mystical Poems of Rūmī* in 1968, the year before Arberry's untimely death. It appeared as part of UNESCO's Collection of Representative Works, jointly sponsored by UNESCO and the Royal Institute of Translation in Tehran, and

---

6. These Iranian reprints of Arberry's *Mystical Poems of Rumi* include one done in Isfahan (Ibrāhīm Sipāhānī) in 2001; a parallel Persian and English text, *Guzīda-yi ghazalīyāt-i ʿirfānī-yi Maulānā: mushtamil bar 400 ghazal hamrāh bā tarjama-yi Ingilīsī* (Tehran: Nashr-i Būta, 2002); and *Kalām-i khāmūsh: guzīda-yi shiʿr va naṣr-e Jalāl al-Dīn Muḥammad bin Muḥammad Maulavī-yi Rūmī* (Tehran: Hermes Publishers, 2004), a project of the International Centre for Dialogue among Civilisations in Tehran in the form of a handy volume with the Persian text of Rumi facing Nicholson's translations of the *Maṣnavī*, and Arberry's translations of *Mystical Poems of Rumi*, the *Rubāʿiyāt*, and the *Discourses*.

published by the University of Chicago Press.[7] It was Professor Ehsan Yarshater of Columbia University who had originally suggested to Arberry in the early 1960s the important project of translating Rumi's ghazals. Arberry began to work on this project, probably in 1964, along with his assistant, Hasan Javadi, then a Lector at Cambridge, who had come from Tabriz as a Ph.D. student in 1960. Javadi would visit Arberry at his Cambridge home once a week in 1964–65, during which time they read through Rumi's *Dīvān-i Shams* and discussed Arberry's translations. Arberry would often have a first draft of the poems he wished to translate, which together they would then compare to the very literal Turkish translation of Gölpınarlı. Javadi, a bilingual native speaker of both Azeri Turkish and Persian, would orally translate this for Arberry, who did not work with Turkish. Arberry had at his disposal the Chester Beatty Library manuscript of Rumi's *Dīvān* (one of the earliest and most complete manuscripts, which Arberry had cataloged), which he consulted alongside Badī' al-Zamān Furūzānfar's newly published critical edition of the text.[8]

The corpus of Rumi's ghazals is huge (3229 poems); Arberry culled through them, selecting 400 poems for the variety of their themes, and excluding those he thought would not translate well owing to repetition or other factors. By 1965, the initial translations were nearly complete, and Javadi, now back in Iran, was hired to do annotations to accompany the text. Arberry lived to see the first volume (poems 1–200 in the present collection) through the press, culling an abbreviated selection

7. In that same year, 1968, the Shah of Iran visited the University of Chicago and dedicated the cornerstone for a proposed center of Iranian Studies, to which the Iranian government had pledged generous financial support; unfortunately, this project was not pursued expeditiously, and the Iranian offer was eventually withdrawn. My own copy of *Mystical Poems of Rumi* was actually a paperback reprint issued as a Phoenix Book by the University of Chicago Press in 1974.

8. *Kullīyāt-i Shams, yā Dīvān-i kabīr*, ed. Badī' al-Zamān Furūzānfar, 8 vols. (Tehran: University of Tehran Press, 1957–66.)

FRANKLIN D. LEWIS

of the notes that Javadi had prepared. Arberry had completed
work on the translations for the second volume (poems 201–
400) before he passed away in the early autumn of 1969, leaving
behind a handwritten manuscript of his translations. Arberry
had suffered from Parkinson's disease, which made his small
handwriting quite difficult to make out (see the facsimile page
of poems 285–87, reproduced here on page 6). These transla-
tions were written out in blue ink on both sides of white un-
ruled paper with few corrections, though from time to time
a phrase is crossed out and replaced with a different wording,
either in the space just above it or in the margins. This is some-
times done in the same blue ink and sometimes, evidently at a
later time, in red ink. Arberry included frequent marginal nota-
tions about wordplay in Rumi's Persian, usually indicating this
in the margins of his handscript by the word *jinās* in Persian
script (جناس). These occurrences of paronomasia are sometimes
mentioned in the notes published with Arberry's translations,
and sometimes not. The marginal notes also include occasional
notation of places where Arberry preferred the reading of the
Chester Beatty manuscript to the reading of Furūzānfar's criti-
cal edition.

Several individuals, including Arberry's daughter and various
of his colleagues, including Javadi, collaborated in the effort to
decipher these handwritten translations. Hasan Javadi was com-
missioned to prepare a typescript for publication, including the
addition, as before, of Javadi's annotations to Arberry's trans-
lations. *Mystical Poems of Rūmī 2* was published eleven years
after volume one, and by that time, a revolution in Iran had
swept away both the Shah and the Royal Institute of Transla-
tion, which institute had sponsored publication. Volume 2 ap-
peared through Bibliotheca Persica with the imprimatur of the
Persian Heritage Series, under the general editorship of Ehsan
Yarshater.[9]

9. Published as *Mystical Poems of Rūmī. Second Selection, Poems 201–400*.
Persian Heritage Series, no. 23 (Boulder, Colorado: Westview Press, 1979). It

Over the years, as I consulted Arberry's translations, I had noted some errors, and others who had noticed errors over the years have also kindly provided their lists of corrections to me.[10] These have now been checked and corrected against Arberry's original handscript, the partial fair copy prepared after Arberry's death, as well as Professor Javadi's typescript,[11] and the Persian text of the poems as they appear in Furūzānfar's critical edition. I did not, however, have the Chester Beatty manuscript at my disposal while correcting the text and could not always tell whether Arberry might have been looking at a variant reading not in the Furūzānfar edition.

The present, new edition of *Mystical Poems of Rumi*, then, appears in a corrected and consistent format, closer to what Arberry apparently envisioned. The two separate volumes have been combined into one, standardizing the format, the transliterations, and the notes. Numerous errors of reading (well over a hundred of them, many of them impacting the meaning) have been corrected, some of them resulting from the difficulty of deciphering Arberry's handwriting and others introduced during typesetting or copyediting. The numerals indicating the line numbers in each poem (in intervals of five: 5, 10, 15, etc.), which appear in Arberry's own handscript and in Professor Javadi's typescript, but which were left out when the second volume was prepared for print, have been restored. The notes, which in volume one had been keyed to the sequential number of the poem in the translation (1–200) and the line number of the relevant poem, but which were signaled instead by sequential footnotes

was reprinted by the University of Chicago Press in 1991. I acquired my copy of this from the Seminary Co-op Bookstore in Chicago in 1992 for $10.95.

10. I am grateful to Ibrahim Gamard and Susan Friedman for their assistance, but most especially to Steven Johnson, who took great pains to go through all the poems in volume two, collating them to the text of Furūzānfar, and uncovering many other potential errors.

11. I am extremely grateful to Professor Javadi for inviting me to his home to consult Arberry's original handwritten translations, which have remained in his possession since he worked on the manuscript in the 1970s.

FRANKLIN D. LEWIS

in volume two, have been regularized, now all uniformly presented, keyed to the poem number and line number. The original wording of Arberry's translations remains unchanged, except to correct errors in rendering Arberry's intention.[12]

Eight hundred years have now passed since the birth of Rumi in 1207, yet his poems remain vibrant and revelatory to contemporary readers. Indeed, in collaboration with Afghanistan, the Islamic Republic of Iran, and Turkey, UNESCO celebrated the anniversary of Rumi's birth at its Paris headquarters in September 2007, quoting from one line in his ghazals ("I do not distinguish between the relative and the stranger") as evidence of his "especially good relations with people of diverse social, cultural, and religious backgrounds."

All English renderings will pale before the sheer beauty and sonorous intensity of Rumi's original Persian. Still, whether in Persian or in English translation, his poems continue to be richly rewarding, revealing more of themselves with each rereading, or with each well-informed interpretive translation. Arberry not only chose an interesting and representative sample of Rumi's ghazals, but also explained many obscure passages in the Persian that have baffled other readers. It seems fitting that his influential translations of 400 of Rumi's ghazals now be presented in this consistent and corrected format.

Franklin D. Lewis
University of Chicago, 2008

---

12. There are some archaicisms in Arberry's English; for example, he uniformly translated the word *khumār* as the now very obsolete "crop-sickness." This should be understood as hangover, or the more technical crapulence. In a very few places, Arberry's interpretation might be questioned. However, his wording has not been changed, except that an occasional addition has been made to the notes, to suggest an alternative reading to the one he has adopted. Words appearing in pointed brackets {} indicate additions which I have made to the published text of Arberry's *Mystical Poems of Rumi* after consulting the original Persian.

Foreword

TO VOLUME 2,
Mystical Poems of Rumi

In 1963, I suggested to the late Professor Arberry that he un-
dertake the translation of a representative selection of Rūmī's
lyrics from the *Dīvān-i Shams,* to be published in the Persian
Heritage Series. Rūmī's *Dīvān,* despite its somewhat uneven
texture, contains some of the most inspiring poems written
in the Persian language and has certainly not been surpassed
in the sheer depth and exuberance of feeling by the work of any
other Persian poet. And yet the *Dīvān* had remained largely un-
translated into English. R. A. Nicholson's *Selected Poems from
the Dīvāni Shamsi Tabrīzī* (Cambridge University Press, 1898),
which contained the translation of forty-eight lyrics, was the
most extensive work to represent the *Dīvān* in English.

Professor Arberry, with his exemplary knowledge of Persian
literature, his vast experience in translating literary works, and
his personal affinities with mystical thought of the poet, was
the outstanding choice for the handling of this most difficult
task. Rūmī, although easy to enjoy in Persian, is far from easy to

translate. Much of the appeal of his poetry depends on the musicality of his verse, which is bound to be lost in translation. The force of his passion and the subtlety of his mystical sentiments, expressed in a somewhat unorthodox diction, is also a constant challenge to the translator.

Professor Arberry's translation of the first two hundred poems was ready in 1965 and was published jointly by Allen and Unwin and the University of Chicago Press in 1968 under the title of *Mystical Poems of Rūmī, I*.[1]

After the publication of the first volume, Professor Arberry, afflicted with failing health, nevertheless was able to complete, though with great difficulty, the preparation of the present volume, which contains translations of another two hundred poems. His untimely death in 1969, which dealt a serious blow to Persian and Arabic studies, came before he was able to send me his manuscript and it was only through the diligence and kindness of his daughter that the manuscript was located and placed at my disposal.

The reading of Professor Arberry's once fine and legible handwriting, however, proved a major task. Fortunately Dr. Hasan Javadi, a former and loyal student of his and now Professor and Chairman of the English Department at the University of Tehran, kindly agreed to prepare the manuscript for typing, collate it with the original, and also annotate the translation, following the pattern set by Professor Arberry in the first volume. Without his dedicated assistance the publication of this volume could not have been accomplished.

This volume is prefaced by what is perhaps the most intimate writing of Professor Arberry on his training, his spiritual journey, and his intellectual outlook. It throws light on the inner thought and sentiments of a distinguished humanist and scholar.

---

1. A paperback edition of the same was published by the University of Chicago Press in 1972.

It is my pleasant task to thank Mr. M. Kasheff and Dr. D. Bishop of Columbia University, and Professor Gh. Youssefi of the University of Mashhad for their assistance in resolving some of the ambiguous points in the translation. The editors, however, have not allowed themselves, except in a few necessary cases, to alter the text of the translation, which remains basically the same as left by the translator.

It is hoped that the two volumes, now made available, will prove of assistance to the students of Rūmī and an incentive to them for a complete translation of his *Dīvān*.

Ehsan Yarshater
Columbia University, 1978

An Autobiographical sketch

BY THE LATE PROFESSOR A. J. ARBERRY[*]

I was born the child of Victorian parents, strict believers of the Christian evangelical school. My early religious education was therefore of the same pattern: family prayers, church three times every Sunday, a severe puritanical attitude to pleasure, especially on the Lord's Day. My parents were virtuous and, according to their lights, deeply sincere in their conformity; they were poor, but being industrious and thrifty they spared their children the full rigors of poverty only too prevalent in England at the beginning of the present century. They were also ambitious for their children, determined that they should benefit to the full from the rapidly improving educational opportunities of those times. I attended elementary school from the age of three, won a scholarship to the local grammar school, and from there proceeded in due course to Cambridge. My education had cost my parents only the expense of feeding and clothing me; but that

[*]This *Apologia Spiritualis* was found among Professor Arberry's papers.

was a sufficiently large sacrifice to the poor of their generation, and I cannot adequately express my thankfulness to them for their love and devotion and unfailing encouragement.

When the first war broke out I was nine years old: my father served in the Royal Navy, and saw his brother's ship go down with all hands at the Battle of Jutland. The years 1914–18 were terribly anxious years for naval families; they were also fearful years for children as the technique for bombing civilians advanced, but they were incomparably easier than the years 1939–45 in which my own child grew up. The early 1920s were a time of disillusionment and doubt. For us in Britain the war had been won, but the peace was obviously lost: many thousands of heroes returned to unemployment; the poor became poorer still. These were the years in which, along with perhaps the majority of my contemporaries, I lost faith—the faith, that is, which I had been taught by my parents. Being what is called a clever boy, I read voraciously the rationalists, the agnostics, the atheists; I was persuaded that the mind was the measure of all things; I applied my reason to the dogmas of Christianity, and my reason rejected them. Having at one time seriously thought of the priesthood, I now abandoned worship entirely and resolved to become an academic scholar, abstract truth being the only altar before which I would kneel.

By a paradox which would have delighted Shaw whose writings had done so much to destroy my childhood beliefs, it was this resolution which ultimately led to the restoration of my faith. I graduated in classics, and then, disappointed at the narrow field of research offered by those ancient studies, I decided in a hasty moment to become an orientalist and chose for my particular course Arabic and Persian. I suppose it amused the unbeliever in me that I would henceforward be devoting my mind to a critical examination of Islam, no doubt as fallacious as Christianity. It certainly never occurred to me that that examination would have the effect of bringing me back to a belief in God.

In 1926, while still an undergraduate, I had attended the funeral of Edward Granville Browne. It was a studentship established under his will that enabled me in 1927 to embark on my new studies. My teachers were Anthony Ashley Bevan, a Victorian agnostic who was a splendid philologist and a most kindly man, and Reynold Alleyne Nicholson, the eminent authority on Islamic mysticism. My encounter with Nicholson was the turning point in my life. He was at that time engaged on his last and greatest work, the editing and translating of the *Maṣnavī* of Jalāl al-Dīn Rūmī; and when I was ready to undertake research in Arabic and Persian, he persuaded me to follow in his footsteps and to explore the rich literature of the Sufis. My first labor was to edit and translate the *Mavāqif* of al-Niffārī, and this led to my first journey to the East and three years' residence in the lands of Islam. In those years I married and became a father.

Nicholson was a very shy and retiring man, painfully diffident—a scholar of the study who never traveled out of Europe, yet he achieved a deeper penetration of the mind and spirit of Islam than any other man I have ever known. He rarely spoke of his personal beliefs, and in twenty-five years of close friendship I learned little of his own spiritual formation. But the impression I gained was that he too had lost his faith as a young man, and had regained it through his intellectual communion with the mystics of Islam. In his old age he composed a poem in which he revealed for the first time his inner thoughts. These thoughts had obviously been profoundly influenced by his long studies of Rūmī.

> Deep in our hearts the Light of Heaven is shining
>   Upon a soundless Sea without a shore.
> Oh, happy they who found it in resigning
>   The images of all that men adore.
> Blind eyes, to dote on shadows of things fair
>   Only at last to curse their fatal lure,
> Like Harut and Marut, that Angel-pair
>   Who deemed themselves the purest of the pure.
> Our ignorance and self-will and vicious pride
>   Destroy the harmony of part and whole.

In vain we seek with lusts unmortified
    A vision of the One Eternal Soul.
Love, Love alone can kill what seemed so dead,
    The frozen snake of passion. Love alone,
By tearful prayer and fiery longing fed,
    Reveals a knowledge schools have never known.
God's lovers learn from Him the secret ways
    Of Providence, the universal plan.
Living in Him, they ever sing His praise
    Who made the myriad worlds of Time for Man.
Evil they knew not, for in Him there's none;
    Yet without evil how should good be seen?
Love answers: "Feel with me, with me be one;
    Where I am nought stands up to come between."
There are degrees of heavenly light in souls;
    Prophets and Saints have shown the path they trod,
Its starting points and stages, halts and goals,
    All leading to the single end in God.
Love will not let his faithful servants tire,
    Immortal Beauty draws them on and on
From glory unto glory drawing nigher
    At each remove and loving to be drawn.
When Truth shines out words fail and nothing tell;
Now hear the Voice within your hearts. Farewell.

I have spoken at this length of my old friend, whom I saw
last very shortly before his death in 1945, because I am con-
scious of a debt to Nicholson which I can never hope to re-
pay. He was the perfect scholar, so devoted to his books that he
blinded himself by reading, so modest and humble that he was
totally unaware of his greatness. It was an old man with failing
sight who penned these lines which for me contain the surest
revelations and the most moving of last men's eyes:

    When Truth shines out words fail and nothing tell;
    Now hear the Voice within your hearts. Farewell.

It was of that serene vision of Truth that al-Ḥallāj, the great
Muslim mystic, spoke shortly before his crucifixion in 922:

A. J. ARBERRY

Now stands no more between the Truth and me
Or reasoned demonstration,
Or proof or revelation;
Now, brightly blazing full, Truth's luminary,
That drives out of sight
Each flickering, lesser light.

"What is Truth?" asked jesting Pilate of the Man whom he would presently give on a like Cross, the Man who said, "I am the Way, the Truth and the Life." I have said earlier that as a young man, having abandoned formal worship, I resolved to become an academic scholar, abstract truth being the only altar before which I would kneel. In those days I supposed truth to be a thing intellectually attainable, a quest for reason, far removed from the emotions. But the mystical affinity of truth with light was evidently already apprehended by Sir William Jones, that greatest of British orientalists who died in 1794 and whose example has always been my chief inspiration. Jones wrote:

Before thy mystic altar, heavenly Truth,
I kneel in manhood, as I knelt in youth.
There let me kneel, till this dull form decay,
And life's last shade be brightened by thy day;
Then shall my soul, now lost in clouds below,
Without consuming glow.

Truth, then, is Light—a light that shines into the heart. And what is light? The answer seems to be given in that sublime verse of the Koran:

God is the light of the heavens and the earth;
    the likeness of His Light is as a niche
        wherein is a lamp
        (the lamp in a glass,
    the glass as it were a glittering star)
        kindled by a Blessed Tree,

an olive that is neither of the East nor of the West
whose oil well-nigh would shine, even if no fire touched it.
     Light upon Light,
God guides to His Light whom He will.

Once this light has shone into the heart, no darkness can
ever overcome it. I believe that light to be a reality, because I
have myself experienced it. I believe it also to be the Truth, and
I think it not inappropriate to call it God. I am an academic
scholar, but I have come to realize that pure reason is unquali-
fied to penetrate the mystery of God's light, and may, indeed, if
too fondly indulged, interpose an impenetrable veil between the
heart and God. The world in which we live is certainly full of
shadows. I have had my full share of personal sorrows and anxi-
eties, and I am as acutely aware as the next man of the appalling
dangers threatening mankind. But because I have experienced
the Divine Light, I need not wish for any higher grace.

I have now for some years resumed my Christian worship,
in which I find great comfort, being no longer troubled by the
intellectual doubts generated by too great a concern for dogma.
I know that Jew, Muslim, Hindu, Buddhist, Parsi—all sorts and
conditions of men—have been, are and will always be irradiated
by that Light "kindled by a Blessed Tree, an olive that is neither
of the East nor of the West"—the universal tree of the Truth
and Goodness of God. For God, being the One Universal, has
an infinite solicitude and love of each particular, and suffers His
Light to shine into every human heart open to receive it.

A. J. ARBERRY

[26]

Introduction

TO VOLUME I,
Mystical Poems of Rumi

Jalāl al-Dīn Rūmī, author of a vast collection of Persian odes
and lyrics, of which a selection is here offered in translation, was
born in A.D. 1207 at Balkh, which now lies within the frontiers
of Afghanistan, and died in 1273 at Konya, in Asiatic Turkey.
For an account of his life and times, the reader is invited to pe-
ruse the preface to my version of Rūmī's *Fīhi mā fīhi,* published
by John Murray in 1961 under the title *Discourses of Rumi;* there
is nothing I wish to add to what is written there, except by way
of stressing the curious circumstances which attended Rūmī's
transformation from sober theologian and preacher into ecstatic
dancer and enraptured poet.

Rūmī's father, Bahā' al-Dīn Valad, had attained eminence in
religious circles in Khorasan before his headlong flight to Saljūq
Turkey on the eve of the Mongol invasions; in Konya, where
he died in 1230, he enjoyed royal patronage and popular esteem
as preacher and teacher. From 1240 to 1244, having completed
his long formal education in Aleppo and Damascus, Rūmī in his

own turn taught and preached in Konya. Then, in 1244, when Rūmī was already thirty-seven years of age and seemingly set in his ways as a conventional mullah, a wandering dervish named Shams al-Dīn, a native of Tabriz apparently of artisan origin, suddenly arrived in the Saljūq capital and attracted attention by the wildness of his demeanour.

"Jalāl al-Dīn," wrote R. A. Nicholson in his *Rumi, Poet and Mystic*,[13] "found in the stranger that perfect image of the Divine Beloved which he had long been seeking. He took him away to his house, and for a year or two they remained inseparable. Sulṭān Valad (Rūmī's son and biographer) likens his father's all-absorbing communion with this 'hidden saint' to the celebrated journey of Moses in company with Khaḍir (Koran, XVIII 64–80), the sage whom Sufis regard as the supreme hierophant and guide of travellers on the Way to God. Rūmī's pupils resented their teacher's preoccupation with the eccentric stranger, and vilified and intrigued against him until Shams al-Dīn fled to Damascus. Rūmī sent his son to bring him back; but the tongues of his jealous traducers soon wagged again, and presently, perhaps in 1247, the man of mystery vanished without leaving a trace behind."

The intense excitement of these adventures transformed Jalāl al-Dīn from the sober divine into an ecstatic wholly incapable of controlling the torrent of poetry which now poured forth from him. To symbolize, it is said, the search for the lost Beloved, now identified with Shams al-Dīn, he invented the famous whirling and circling dance of his Mevlevi dervishes, performed to the accompaniment of the lamenting reed pipe and the pacing drum. Night was turned into day in the long mystical orgy, and from time to time under the impact of the passionate moment Jalāl al-Dīn uttered extempore brief quatrains or extended lyrics, which his disciples hastily transcribed and committed to memory. To confess the human source of his inspiration, he very often introduced into his lyrics the name of Shams al-Dīn;

13. *Rūmī, Poet and Mystic* (London, George Allen & Unwin, 1950), 19.

later he similarly commemorated Shams al-Dīn's successor in his spiritual affection, Ṣalāḥ al-Dīn Zarkūb. At other times Rūmī signed his verses with the soubriquet Khāmūsh, the Silent, a reference to the ineffable nature of the mysteries.

Though no manuscript copy of these poems has survived which had been compiled during Rūmī's lifetime, it is certain (as the learned editor Professor Badīʿ al-Zamān Furūzānfar has pointed out) that such a collection was made, and was available to the scribe of one of the existing codices, dated 723/1323. Nor is this all; it is equally certain that the copyist of another, undated but very ancient, codex had access to material in the autograph of Rūmī himself. Fortunately, several manuscripts have been preserved dating from within fifty years or so from the poet's death, and these have all been collated to serve as a very solid basis for Professor Furūzānfar's edition.[14] The total output, excluding stanza-poems, quatrains, and other minor pieces, amounts to 3,229 separate odes, in 34,662 couplets. In the course of making the present versions, I have collated once more with the printed text the magnificent Chester Beatty codex, used by the editor in a microfilm which I caused to be made for him; I have noted numerous places where the readings of this codex, sometimes superior to the printed text, have been overlooked by the editor.

The Chester Beatty codex, besides being close to the poet's lifetime and on the whole very correct, exhibits a unique feature to which attention may be once more drawn. The Persian ode (Qaṣīda), like its shorter derivative the lyric (Ghazal), was composed in monorhyme, each couplet terminating in the same vowel+consonant as that chosen to end the opening line. The poet was free to choose between some dozen or so metres, but having made his choice he was required to keep strictly to it throughout the length of the individual composition. Medieval editors and copyists, when they came to publish the collected works (dīvān) of a poet, arranged the pieces not

14. *Kullīyāt-i Shams.* 8 vols. (Tehran, 1336–45/1957–66).

chronologically, nor according to style or subject, but alphabetically according to rhyme, ignoring differences of metre.
Now in the Chester Beatty manuscript of Rūmī's *Dīvān,* the
poems have been arranged group by group according to metre;
then, within each group, alphabetically by rhyme. Moreover,
the opening couplet of each separate poem has been inscribed
in red ink, to facilitate speedy identification. The resulting impression is of a gigantic hymnbook; and this indeed may well
have been the intention. When it is remembered that these
poems were originally composed, and were thereafter chanted,
as accompaniment to the sacred dance of the Mevlevi dervishes,
it does not seem too fantastic to conclude that the Chester
Beatty codex, which once belonged to a Mevlevi monastery in
Cairo, was compiled after this fashion as a service book, to help
the cantor to choose speedily the poem appropriate in rhythm
to the particular phase of the dance.

Rūmī was by no means the first Persian to compose mystical
poetry.[15] He had not a few predecessors (and they had predecessors who wrote in Arabic) who gradually established conventions of language, imagery and rhetoric. The most eminent and
influential of these pioneers were Sanā'ī, who died *circa* A.D.
1150, and Farīd al-Dīn 'Aṭṭār, whom Rūmī met in his youth.

> Attar was the spirit,
> Sana'i his eyes twain,
> And in time thereafter
> Came we in their train.

So Rūmī acknowledged his debt to these great masters, each
of whom left behind a large quantity of mystical odes, as well
as didactic, epic verse. But he did not confine his reading and

15. For a brief account of the history of Persian mystical poetry prior to
Rūmī, see my *Muslim Saints and Mystics* (the first volume in the Persian Heritage Series, Chicago and London, 1966), pp. 5–11. It is hoped to go into more
detail in the introduction to a second volume of translations of Rūmī's poems,
now being prepared.

admiration to the mystical poets. We know, for instance, that he particularly appreciated the work of the great Arab heroic poet al-Mutanabbī (d. A.D. 955), from whom he quotes in his *Discourses*, as also occasionally in his *Dīvān*. His many nature-poems, especially those on the glories of spring, recall many models amongst the secular Arab and Persian poets. From these and other clues we are able to build up a picture of a man deeply immersed in the poetic traditions of Islam. Yet poetry was very far from being the centre of Rūmī's life; before everything he was a learned theologian after the finest pattern of medieval Islam, very familiar with the Koran and its exegesis, the traditional sayings of the Prophet Muhammad, the sacred law and its erudite expositors, the wranglings of the "Two-and-Seventy jarring sects," not to mention the "foreign sciences" including philosophy, and the lives and dicta of the saints and mystics. All this various learning is reflected in Rūmī's poetry; and it is this fact, coupled with abstruseness of thought and exotic convention of expression, that stands in the way of easy understanding and ready appreciation.

Whereas the interpreter of the *Mathnavī*, Rūmī's massive epic poem on the mystical life, can have recourse to a number of medieval commentaries to assist him in his task, no such aid is available to the student of the *Dīvān*. On the other hand we are very fortunate in possessing R. A. Nicholson's magnificent eight-volume edition, translation, and commentary of the *Mathnavī*, as well as his remarkable primitias, the *Selected Poems from the Dīvāni Shamsi Tabrīz*, with its astonishingly mature and luminous introduction, together with his many other writings on Islamic mysticism, and the precious memory of his personal teaching. (The *Selected Poems* contains only forty-eight pieces, and even so includes a number of poems not found in the oldest manuscripts, and therefore of very doubtful authenticity.) We can also draw upon the erudite writings of Professor Furūzānfar, who has dedicated a lifetime of arduous and unremitting labour to the study of Rūmī. From the medieval period we can rely, albeit cautiously, on the *Manāqib al-'ārifīn* of

Shams al-Dīn Aflākī, completed in 1353, a hagiography of Rūmī and his circle which purports to give the circumstances under which a number of the poems were composed. We are also grateful to have Rūmī's "table-talk" in the *Fīhi mā fīhi*, probably compiled by his son Sulṭān Valad, in the excellent edition of Professor Furūzānfar. Finally, I have had the good fortune to read all the poems chosen for translation with my learned friend and colleague Dr. Ḥasan Javādī-Tabrīzī, who has made numerous corrections and suggestions for the improvement of this interpretation.

These versions, being in the vast majority the first renderings into a western language (and the modern Turkish translation has been fully consulted), and intended primarily for non-specialists, have been made as literal as possible, with a minimal concession to readability. Short notes have been appended, to clarify obscurities and to explain unfamiliar allusions. For the rest, the reader is earnestly advised to make himself familiar with the *Mathnavī* in Nicholson's translation, and with the *Fīhi mā fīhi* in my own *Discourses of Rumi*. The poet is always consistent in his thought, and often repetitive in his expression, so that all his writings shed an abundance of mutually clarifying light. When all is said and done, however, it must be admitted that a number of passages in these poems still baffle the understanding, which is hardly surprising, considering the occasional nature of some of the references (for these poems were the spontaneous utterances of an ecstatic, unpremeditated and unrevised). There is also the further difficulty, that the language of the poems, though of course greatly influenced by literary style, is basically colloquial. It incorporates many Khorasanian idioms, affected by long residence in Arabic-speaking and Turkish-speaking lands, all from seven hundred years ago, so that the colloquial usages of the present day are not always a reliable guide. Rūmī himself appears to have been conscious of the elusive, evanescent nature of his utterances, as when he says (in poem 125 of this selection), "My verse resembles the bread of Egypt—night passes over it, and you cannot eat it any more."

A. J. ARBERRY

Rūmī affected an astonishing contempt for his own poetry. On one occasion he remarked, "I am affectionate to such a degree that when these friends come to me, for fear that they may be wearied I speak poetry so that they may be occupied with that. Otherwise, what have I to do with poetry? By Allah, I care nothing for poetry, and there is nothing worse in my eyes than that. It has become incumbent upon me, as when a man plunges his hands into tripe and washes it out for the sake of a guest's appetite, because the guest's appetite is for tripe." The poet's modesty, rooted in a puritanical scrupulosity, does not need to affect our judgment. In Rūmī we encounter one of the world's greatest poets. In profundity of thought, inventiveness of image, and triumphant mastery of language, he stands out as the supreme genius of Islamic mysticism. He invites and deserves the most attentive and intensive study, by a succession of devoted scholars, whose combined explorations will vastly improve upon our first halting attempt. Future generations, as his poetry becomes wider known and more perfectly understood, will enjoy and applaud with increasing insight and enthusiasm the poems of this wisest, most penetrating, and saintliest of men.

The poems that follow are not a continuous cycle, but a careful selection from the first 1,500 odes and lyrics. They thus represent a planned selection, my purpose being to include poems of various styles and degrees of difficulty. The numbering 1–200 is my own, but in the notes I have in every case given the reference to the corresponding number in the Tehran edition.

Mystical Poems
of Rumi

I

What excuses have you to offer, my heart, for so many short-comings? Such constancy on the part of the Beloved, such un-faithfulness on your own!

So much generosity on his side, on yours such niggling con-trariness! So many graces from him, so many faults committed by you!

Such envy, such evil imaginings and dark thoughts in your heart, such drawing, such tasting, such munificence by him!

Why all this tasting? That your bitter soul may become sweet. Why all this drawing? That you may join the company of the saints.

5   You are repentant of your sins, you have the name of God on your lips; in that moment he draws you on, so that he may deliver you alive.

You are fearful at last of your wrongdoings, you seek desper-ately a way to salvation; in that instant why do you not see by your side him who is putting such fear into your heart?

If he has bound up your eyes, you are like a pebble in his hand; now he rolls you along like this, now he tosses you in the air.

Now he implants in your nature a passion for silver and gold and women; now he implants in your soul the light of the form of Muṣṭafā.

On this side drawing you towards the lovely ones, on that side drawing you to the unlovely; amid these whirlpools the ship can only pass through or founder.

10   Offer up so many prayers, weep so sorely in the night season, that the echo may reach your ears from the sphere of the seven heavens.

When Shuʿaib's groaning and lamentation and tears like hailstones passed beyond all bounds, in the morning a proclamation came to him from heaven:

"If you are a sinner, I have forgiven you and granted you pardon for your sins. Is it paradise you seek? Lo, I have given it to you; be silent, cease these petitions!"

Shuʿaib retorted, "I seek neither this nor that. What I desire is to see God face to face; though the seven seas all turn to fire, I will plunge therein if only I may encounter Him.

But if I am banished from that spectacle, if my tear-stained eyes are shut against that vision, I am more fit to dwell in hell-fire; paradise becomes me not.

15   Without His countenance, paradise for me is hateful hell. I am consumed by this hue and scent of mortality; where is the splendour of the lights of immortality?"

They said, "At least moderate your weeping, lest your sight be diminished, for the eye becomes blind when weeping passes beyond bounds."

He said, "If my two eyes in the end should be seeing after that fashion, every part of me will become an eye: why then should I grieve over blindness?

But if in the end this eye of mine should be deprived forever, let that sight indeed become blind which is unworthy to behold the Beloved!"

In this world, every man would become a ransom for his beloved; one man's beloved is a bag of blood, another's the sun in splendour.

20 Since every man has chosen a beloved, good or bad, as suits his own nature, it would be a pity if we should annihilate ourselves for the sake of nothing!

One day a traveller was accompanying Bā Yazīd on a certain road. Presently Bā Yazīd said to him, "What trade have you chosen, you rogue?"

The man replied, "I am an ass-driver." Bā Yazīd exclaimed, "Be gone from me!—Lord, grant that his ass may die, that he may become the slave of God!"

2

O lovers, lovers, this day you and we are fallen into a whirl-pool: who knows how to swim?

Though the world's torrent should overflow and every wave become like a dromedary, why shall the waterfowl worry? It is the bird of the air that should be anxious.

Our faces are lighted up with gratitude, schooled as we are in wave and sea, inasmuch as ocean and flood are life-increasing to the fish.

Elder, hand us a towel; water, let us plunge into you; Moses son of 'Imrān, come, smite the water of the sea with your staff!

5 This wind concocts in every head a different passion; let my passion be for yonder cupbearer, and you may have all the rest!

Yesterday yon saki on the way snatched the caps of the drunkards; today he is giving yet more wine, preparing to strip us of our robes.

O envy of the Moon and of Jupiter, with us, yet hidden from sight like a peri, gently, gently you are drawing me on—will you not say whither?

Wherever you go, you are with me still, you who are my eyes and my brightness; if you will, draw me to drunkenness, if you will, transport me to annihilation.

Know that the world is like Mount Sinai, and we like Moses are seekers; every moment an epiphany arrives and cleaves the mountain asunder.

10   One portion becomes green, one portion becomes narcissus-white; one portion becomes a pearl, one portion ruby and amber.

You who seek to behold Him, gaze upon this mountainchain of His. O mountain, what wind has blown upon you? We have become intoxicated with the echo.

O gardener, gardener, why have you come to grapple with us? If we have carried off your grapes, you have carried off our purse!

3

Today I beheld the beloved, that ornament of every affair; he went off departing to heaven like the spirit of Muṣṭafā.

The sun is put to shame by his countenance, heaven's sphere is as confused as the heart; through his glow, water and clay are more resplendent than fire.

I said, "Show me the ladder, that I may mount up to heaven." He said, "Your head is the ladder; bring your head down under your feet."

When you place your feet on your head, you will place your feet on the head of the stars; when you cleave through the air, set your foot on the air, so, and come!

5   A hundred ways to heaven's air become manifest to you; you go flying up to heaven every dawning like a prayer.

4

Every instant a revelation from heaven comes to men's innermost souls: "How long like dregs do you remain upon earth? Come up!"

Whoever is heavy of soul in the end proves to be dregs; only then does he mount to the top of the vat when his dregs are clarified.

Do not stir the clay every moment, so that your water may become clear, so that your dregs may be illumined, so that your pains may be cured.

It is spiritual, like a torch, only its smoke is greater than its light; when its smoke passes beyond bounds, it no longer displays radiance in the house.

5   If you diminish the smoke, you will enjoy the light of the torch; both this abode and that will become illumined by your light.

If you look into muddy water, you see neither the moon nor the sky; sun and moon both disappear when darkness possesses the air.

A northern breeze is blowing, through which the air becomes clarified; it is for the sake of this burnishing that at dawn the zephyr breathes.

The spiritual breeze burnishes the breast of all sorrow; let the breath be stopped but for a moment, and annihilation will come upon the spirit.

The soul, a stranger in the world, is yearning for the city of placelessness; why, O why does the bestial spirit continue so long to graze?

10   Pure, goodly soul, how long will you journey on? You are the King's falcon; fly back toward the Emperor's whistle!

5

O lovers, lovers, the time of union and encounter has come. The proclamation from heaven has come: "Moon-faced beauties, welcome hither!"

Joyous hearts, joyous hearts, joy has come skirt a-trailing; we have seized its chain, it has seized our skirts.

The fiery potion has come; demon sorrow, sit in a corner; death-anxious soul, depart; immortal saki, enter in!

The seven spheres of heaven are drunk with passion for you; we are as counters in your hand; our being through your being is a myriad times at ease.

5   Sweet-breathed minstrel, every instant shake the bell; O gladness, saddle your steed; O zephyr, blow upon our souls!

O sound of the sweet-conversing reed, in your note is the taste of sugar; your note brings me night and morning the scent of fidelity.

Make beginning again, play those airs once more; O sun lovely of presence, glory over all the lovely ones!

Be silent, do not rend the veil; drain the flagon of the silent ones; be a veiler, be a veiler, habituate yourself to the clemency of God.

6

How sweet it is to give speech and head, to converse with his lip, especially when he opens the door and says, "Good sir, come in!"

To the dry lip he tells the story of the fountain of Khidar; according to the stature of the man the tailor of his love cuts the gown.

The fountains become drunken through the intoxication of his eye; the trees are dancing before the gentle breeze of dawn.

The nightingale says to the rosebush, "What is in your

heart? Declare it this instant. No other is near; only you and I."

5   The rosebush answers, "So long as you are with yourself, entertain not this ambition. Make a special effort to transport the burden of your selfhood out of this earthly abode."

The eye of the needle of passion is narrow; know for a certainty that it will not admit any thread when it perceives it to be of double strand.

Behold how the sun is up to the throat in fire, so that through its face the face of the earth may become full of light.

When Moses proceeded towards the burning bush, the bush said, "I am the water of Kauthar; take off your shoes, and come!

Do not fear my fire, for I am water and sweet at that; you have come to prosperity; the seat of honour is yours, welcome!

10   You are a pearl of pure lustre, a ruby of the mine, the soul of place and placelessness; you are the nonpareil of the age; where are other creatures beside you?"

Through love's hand, every hand becomes the royal court of munificence; through you, the faithless world becomes the factory of fidelity.

At the first hour of day you came, in your hand the royal bowl; you are drawing my soul towards the feast, saying, "Welcome!"

What becomes of the heart, when the heart's hand grasps the hand of a sweetheart? What becomes of the dross copper, when it hears the welcoming voice of the philosopher's stone?

A wondrous darling came, in his hand a lance, like a bedouin. I said, "What service can I render?" He said, "Come up to me!"

15   My heart leaped, saying, "Shall I run?" My reason said, "Shall I go?" Generously he signaled, saying, "Yes, both of you!"

Since the table has come down from heaven, wash your hands and your mouth too, that there may not proceed from your palms the odour of onions and chives.

The mine of salt has arrived; take heed, if you are goodly and a lover. Seize the bowl, and give the cup; choose riot, not broth!

Now I close these two lips, so that the lamp of day and night even with the flame of the tongue may tell you the whole story.

7

The king has come, the king has come; adorn the palace-hall; cut your forearms in honour of the fair one of Canaan.

Since the Soul of the soul of the soul has come, it is not meet to mention the soul; in his presence of what use is the soul, save as a sacrifice?

Without love I was one who had lost the way; of a sudden love entered. I was a mountain; I became a straw for the horse of the king.

Whether he be Turk or Tajik, this slave is near to him even as soul to body; only the body does not behold the soul.

Ho, my friends, good luck has arrived; the time has come for offering up the load; a Solomon has come to the throne, to depose Satan.

Leap from your place; why do you tarry? Why are you so helpless? If you know it not, seek from the hoopoe the way to Solomon's palace.

There make your litanies, there utter your secrets and your needs; Solomon indeed knows the speech of all the birds.

Speech is a wind, O slave, and distracts the heart; but he commands it, "Gather together the scattered ones!"

8

Have you ever seen any lover who was satiated with this passion? Have you ever seen any fish that had become satiated with this sea?

Have you ever seen any image that was fleeing from the engraver? Have you ever seen any Vāmiq asking pardon of 'Adhrā?

In separation, the lover is like a name empty of meaning; but a meaning such as belovedness has no need of names.

You are the sea, I am a fish—hold me as you desire; show compassion, exercise kingly power—without you, I remain alone.

5   Puissant emperor, what dearth of compassion is this then? The moment you are not present, the fire rages so high.

If the fire beholds you, it withdraws to a corner; for whoever plucks a rose from the fire, the fire bestows a lovely rose.

Without you, the world is a torment; may it not be without you for a single instant; by your life I implore this, for life without you is a torture and an agony to me.

Your image like a sultan was parading within my heart, even as a Solomon entering the Temple of Jerusalem;

Thousands of lanterns sprang into flame, all the temple was illumined; paradise and the Pool of Kauthar thronged with Riḍwān and houris.

10   Exalted be God, exalted be God! Within heaven so many moons! This tabernacle is full of houris, only they are hidden from the eyes of the blind.

Splendid, happy bird that has found a dwelling in love! How should any but the 'Anqā find place and lodging in Mount Qāf?

Splendid, lordly 'Anqā, Emperor Shams-i Tabrīz! For he is the Sun neither of the east nor of the west, nor of any place.

9

How would it be, if my fair love should take my hand tomorrow, hang his head through the window like the lovely-featured moon?

If my life-augmenter enters, loosens my hands and feet?—For my hands and feet too are bound fast by the hand of fixed banishment.

Then I would say to him, "By your life I swear that without you, O life of my soul, gay company makes me not happy, neither does wine intoxicate me."

Then if he replies coquettishly, "Be gone! What do you want of me? I fear that your melancholy may make me melancholic!"—

5   I would bring sword and windingsheet and bow my neck as a sacrificial offering, saying, "Your head is aching because of me; strike deliberately!

You know that I desire not to live without you; better for me is death than banishment, by God who brings the dead to life.

I never could believe that you would turn away from your servant; I ever said, the words spoken by my enemies are lying inventions.

You are my soul, and without my soul I know not how to live; you are my eyes, and without you I have not a seeing eye."

Let go these words; minstrel, strike up an air; bring forward rebeck and tambourine, if you do not have a reed pipe.

10

Today give in full measure that pure wine; strike in utter confusion this hasty wheel of heaven.

Even granted that the unseen bowl has come hidden from the eyes, it is not possible to conceal drunkenness and depravity.

Love, whose trade is joy, sweet of speech and sweet of thought, snatch now the veil from the face of that veiled king;

Auspicious one, that cries of exultation may arise from this side and that, ho, fill up, rosy of cheek, flagon and bowl.

5   If you do not wish the rosebower to be disclosed, why did you open the rosewater shop?

Having robbed us of our senses and set this river flowing, fling into the water with all speed the water-duckling.

O soul, we are as corn sprung in this expanse, dry of lip and seeking with our lives the cloud-borne rain.

On every side a new messenger declares, "You will never find; depart!" Cry "God forfend" against that ill-omened crow.

Riot-provoker of every spirit, purse-robber of every Goha,
filching the rebeck from the hand of Bū Bakr the Lutanist,

10   Today I desire that you should intoxicate and craze this chat-
terbox soul, that wordy reason.

Water of life to us, become manifest as the resurrection, what
though the milk of the scabby camel is life to the bedouin.

Very lovely is your majesty and beauty; be silent and hold
your breath, make not aware of us every heedless one drowned
in slumber.

II

Like the rose I am laughing with all my body, not only with
my mouth, because I am without myself, alone with the king of
the world.

You who came with torch and at dawn ravished my heart,
dispatch my soul after my heart, do not seize my heart alone.

Do not in rage and envy make my soul a stranger to my
heart; do not leave the former here, and do not summon the
latter alone.

Send a royal message, issue a general invitation; how long,
O sultan, shall the one be with you and the other alone?

5   If you do not come tonight as yesterday and close my lips,
I will make a hundred uproars, my soul, I will not lament alone.

12

Come, you who have given new life to the world, put out of
action cunning reason.

Until you flight me like an arrow, I cannot fly; come, fill
once more the bow.

Because of your love, the bowl has fallen again from the roof;
once more send down from the roof that ladder.

Men ask me, "In which direction is His roof?" In that direction whence the soul was brought;

5   In that direction whither every night the soul departs, then in the time of dawn He brings back the soul;

In that direction whence spring comes to the earth, and at dawn He bestows a new lamp upon the heavens;

In that direction whence a staff became a serpent, and He bore off Pharaoh's host to hell;

In that direction whence arose this quest in you—itself a token, it seeks a token.

You are that man who is seated upon an ass, and keeps asking of the ass this and that.

10   Be silent; for out of jealous regard He desires not to bring all and sundry into the sea.

13

Do you break our harp, exalted one; thousands of other harps are here.

Since we have fallen into the clutches of love, what matters it if we lose harp or reed pipe?

If the whole world's rebeck and harp should be consumed, many a hidden harp there is, my friend;

The twanging and strumming mounts to the skies, even if it does not enter the ears of the deaf.

5   If the whole world's lamp and candle should flicker out, what cause for sorrow is that, since flint and steel still remain?

Songs are spindrift on the face of the sea; no pearl comes on the surface of the sea;

Yet know that the grace of the spindrift derives from the pearl, the reflection of the reflection of whose gleam is upon us.

Songs are all but a branch of the yearning for union; branch and root are never comparable.

Close your lips, and open the window of the heart; by that way be conversant with the spirits.

14

O soul and stay of every soul, who bestow wings and set the
spirits in motion,
    With you, what fear have we of loss, you who convert all
losses to gain?
    Alas for the arrows of the glances and the brows curved like
bows!
    You have sugared the ruby lips of fair idols, you have opened
those mouths in desire.
5   You who have put a key in our hand and therewith opened
the door of the worlds,
    If you be not in the midst of us, then why are those waists
close-girdled?
    And if yours is not the wine without token, of what are these
tokens testimony?
    And if you are beyond our surmise, yet through whom are
these surmises living?
    And if you are hidden from our world, from whom do the
hidden things become manifest?
10   Let go the tales of this world; we have grown aweary of them.
    The soul that has fallen into the sugar-sprinkler—how
should such things be contained in its heart?
    He who has become the earth for your feet, how should he
be mindful of the heavens?
    Bind up our tongue with your protection; cast us not forth
into the midst of these tongues.

15

I beheld the lovely rosebower face, that eye and lamp of all
brightness,
    That altar before which the soul prostrates, that gladness and
place of security.

The heart said, "I will yield up my soul there, I will let go of being and selfhood."

The soul also joined in the concert and began to clap hands.

5   Reason came and said, "What shall I say regarding this good fortune and sublime felicity,

This scent of a rose that made upright as a cypress every back that was curved and bent double?"

In love all things are transformed; Armenian is changed to Turk.

Soul, you have attained to the Soul of the soul; body, you have abandoned bodihood.

The ruby is the alms of our Beloved; the dervish eats the gold of the Rich;

10   That Mary in anguish discovers anew dates fresh and ripe.

Lest the eye of a stranger should fall upon it, do not show off your good deed to men;

If your desire from faith is security, seek your security in seclusion.

What is the place of seclusion? The house of the heart; become habituated to dwell in the heart;

In the heart's house is delivered that bowl of wholesome and everlasting wine.

15   Be silent, and practise the art of silence; let go all artful bragging;

For the heart is the place of faith, there in the heart hold fast to faithfulness.

16

Love has rosebowers amid the veil of blood; lovers have affairs to transact with the beauty of incomparable Love.

Reason says, "The six directions are the boundary, and there is no way out"; Love says, "There is a way, and I have many times travelled it."

Reason beheld a bazaar, and began trading; Love has beheld many bazaars beyond Reason's bazaar.

Many a hidden Manṣūr there is who, confiding in the soul of Love, abandoned the pulpit and mounted the scaffold.

5   Dreg-sucking lovers possess ecstatic perceptions inwardly; men of reason, dark of heart, entertain denials within them.

Reason says, "Set not your foot down, for in the courtyard there is naught but thorns"; Love says, "These thorns belong to the reason which is within you."

Beware, be silent; pluck the thorn of being out of the heart's foot, that you may behold the rosebowers within you.

Shams-i Tabrīzī, you are the sun within the cloud of words; when your sun arose, all speech was obliterated.

17

Yesterday I gave a star a message for you; I said to it, "Deliver my compliments to that one fair as the moon."

Prostrating myself, I said, "Convey this prostration to that sun who by his burning glow converts hard rocks to gold."

I opened my breast and showed it the wounds; I said to it, "Bear tidings of me to the Beloved who delights in drinking blood."

I rocked to and fro to hush the infant of my heart; the infant sleeps when the cradle is rocked.

5   Give milk to the infant of my heart, deliver us from turning about, you who every moment succour a hundred helpless ones like me.

After all, in the first place the heart's abode was the city of union; how long will you keep in exile this vagrant heart?

I have relapsed into silence; but to ward off crop-sickness turn about, O saki of the lovers, your vintner eye!

18

Go forth, my comrades, draw along our beloved, at last bring to me the fugitive idol;

With sweet melodies and golden pretexts draw to the house that moon sweet of presence.

And if he promises, "I will come in another moment," all his promises are but cunning to beguile you.

He possesses a flaming breath, by enchantment and wizardry knotting the water and tying up the air.

5   When in blessedness and joy my darling enters, sit you down and behold the marvels of God!

When his beauty shines forth, what shall be the beauty of the comely ones? For his sun-bright face extinguishes all lamps.

Go, fleet-paced heart, to Yemen, to my heart's beloved, convey my greetings and service to that ruby beyond price.

19

A garden—may its roses bloom till resurrection-day; an idol—may the two worlds be scattered over its beauty!

At daybreak the prince of the fair ones stalks forth to the chase—may our hearts be the quarry for the arrows of his glances!

What messages are momently flashing from his eyes to mine—may my eyes be gladdened and intoxicated by his message!

I broke down the door of an ascetic; with an imprecation he banned me: "Be gone! May your days all be without peace!"

5   Thanks to his curse, the beloved has left me neither peace nor heart, that beloved who thirsts for my blood—may God befriend him!

My body is like the moon, melting away out of love; my heart is like Venus' harp—may its strings be snapped!

Regard not the moon's melting, Venus' broken estate;

behold rather the sweetness of his sorrow—may it increase a thousand-fold!

What a bride is in the soul! Through the reflection of her face may the world be fresh and figured as the hands of the newly-wedded!

Regard not the fleshly cheek, which corrupts and decays; regard the spiritual cheek—may it be fair and lovely for ever!

10   The dark body is like a raven, and the physical world is winter—despite these two unlovelies, may there be spring eternal!

For these two unlovelies subsist through the four elements; may your servants subsist through other than these four!

20

When you display that rosy cheek, you set the stones a-spinning for joy.

Once again put forth your head from the veil, for the sake of the dumbstruck lovers,

That learning may lose the way, that the man of reason may break his science to pieces;

That water through your reflection may convert to a pearl, that fire may abandon warfare.

5   With your beauty, I desire not the moon, neither those two or three hanging little lanterns.

With your face, I do not call the ancient, rusty heavens a mirror.

You breathed, and created anew in another shape this narrow world.

In desire for his Mars-like eye, play, Venus, again that harp!

21

The heart is like a grain of corn, we are like a mill; how does the mill know why this turning?

The body is like a stone, and the water its thoughts; the

stone says, "The water knows what is toward."

The water says, "Ask the miller, for it was he who flung this water down."

The miller says to you, "Bread-eater, if this does not turn, how shall the crumb-broth be?"

5 Much business is in the making; silence, ask God, that He may tell you.

22

Here someone is hidden; suppose not that you are alone. She has very sharp ears; do not open your tongue to evil.

That peri has taken lodging by the fountain of your heart; thereby every form of image has become manifest to you.

Wherever a fountain is, there is a place for peris; you must act cautiously there.

Since these five fountains of the senses are flowing over your body, know that it is by the superintendence of that fairy that sometimes they are stopped up, sometimes set flowing.

5 Know also that those five inward senses, such as imagination and conception, are likewise five fountains running towards the pasture.

Every fountain has two superintendents and fifty controllers; they disclose their forms to you in the time of burnishing.

The peris smite you if you are unmannerly, for this kind of famous peri is impetuous and shows no favour.

Determinism beguiles deliberation, saying, "Now leap into action"; its cunning has snatched the blanket from a hundred thousand such as we.

Behold the birds in the cage, behold the fishes in the net, behold the hearts lamenting on account of that knowing trickster.

10 Open not your eye surreptitiously on any idol out of treachery, lest that all-seeing prince cast you from his regard.

Several verses still remain, but this fountain has sunk into the ground; that will bubble up from the fountain when we leap up tomorrow.

23

Bring into motion your amber-scattering tress; bring into dancing the souls of the Sufis.

Sun, moon and stars dancing around the circle, we dancing in the midst—set that midst a-dancing.

Your grace minstrelwise with the smallest melody brings into the wheel the Sufi of heaven.

The breeze of spring comes hurrying, uttering a melody; it sets the world a-laughing, raises autumn from the dead.

5   Many a snake becomes a friend, rose partners thorn; the season of scattering largesse is come to the king of the orchard.

Every moment a perfume wafts from the garden like a message some whither, as if to say, "Cry welcome today to the friends!"

The orchard, departed into its secret heart, is speaking to you; do you depart into your own secret, that life may come to your soul,

That the lily's bud may open its secret to the cypress, that the tulip may bring good tidings to willow and judas-tree,

That the secret of every young shoot may emerge from the depths, the ascensionists having set up a ladder in the garden.

10   The songbirds and nightingales are seated in the branches, like the guardian enjoying his stipend from the treasury;

These leaves are like tongues, these fruits like hearts—when the hearts show their faces, they give worth to the tongue.

24

You who are my soul's repose in the time of pain, you who are my spirit's treasure in the bitterness of poverty,

That which imagination never conceived, reason and understanding never perceived, has entered my soul from you; therefore to you alone I turn in worship.

Through your grace I gaze boldly upon eternal life; O king, how should a perishing empire beguile me?

The melody of that person who brings me glad tidings of you, even if it be in sleep, is better than all poets' songs to me.

5   In the genuflections of prayer your image, O king, is as necessary and obligatory to me as the seven oft-repeated verses.

When unbelievers sin, you are all compassion and intercession; to me you are the chief and leader of the stonyhearted.

If everlasting bounty should offer all kingdoms and place before me every hidden treasure,

I would prostrate myself with all my soul and lay my face on the earth, I would say, "Out of all these, the love of a certain one for me!"

For me the time of union is eternal life, for in that moment no time contains me.

10   Life is a vessel, and in it union is a pure wine; without you, of what avail to me is the labour of the vessels?

Before this, twenty thousand desires were mine; in my passion for him, not one single aspiration has remained to me.

Through the succour of his grace, I have become secure from the Monarch of the Unseen saying to me, *Thou shalt not see me*.

The essence of the meaning of "He" my heart and soul has filled; he is—even though he said he is not—the third and the second to me.

Union with him transported my spirit; my body paid not attention, though disengaged from the body he became visible to me.

15   I have become old in grief for him; but when you name
Tabriz, all my youth returns.

25

Again the violet bent double has arrived beside the lily, again
the ruby-clad rose is tearing her gown to shreds;

Again our green-gowned ones have gaily arrived from be-
yond the world swift as the wind, drunken and stalking and
joyous.

The standard-bearing cypress went off and consumed au-
tumn with rage, and from the mountaintop the sweet-featured
anemone showed its face.

The hyacinth said to the jasmine, "Peace be upon you";
the latter replied, "Upon you be peace; come, lad, into the
meadow!"

5   A Sufi on every side, having attained some favour, clapping
hands like the plane-tree, dancing like the zephyr;

The bud, concealing its face like veiled ladies—the breeze
draws aside its chaddur saying, "Unveil your face, good friend!"

The friend is in this quarter of ours, water in this our stream;
lotus in your finery, why are you athirst and pale?

Sour-faced winter has departed, that joy-slayer has been
slain; swift-footed jasmine, long may you live!

The busy narcissus winked at the verdure; the verdure under-
stood its words and said, "Yours is the command."

10   The clove said to the willow, "I am in hope of you"; the
willow answered, "My bachelor apartment is your private
chamber—welcome!"

The apple said, "Orange, why are you puckered?" The or-
ange replied, "I do not show myself off for fear of the evil eye."

The ringdove came cooing, "Where is that friend?" The
sweet-noted nightingale pointed him to the rose.

Beside the world's springtide there is a secret spring; moon-
cheeked and sweet of mouth, give wine, O saki!

Moon rising in the shadows of darkness, the light of whose
lamp vanquishes the sun at noon!

15 Several words yet remain unsaid, but it is unseasonably late;
whatever was omitted in the night I will complete tomorrow.

26

If you are Love's lover and in quest of Love, take a sharp
dagger and cut the throat of bashfulness.

Know that reputation is a great barrier in the path; what I say
is disinterested—accept it with a tranquil mind.

Why did that madman work a thousand kinds of madness,
that chosen wild one invent a thousand wiles?

Now he rent his robe, now he ran over the mountains, now
he quaffed poison, now he elected annihilation;

5 Since the spider seized such huge prey, consider what prey
the snare of *My Lord the Most High* will take!

Since the love of Lailā's face had all that worth, how will it be
with *He carried His servant by night?*

Have you not seen the *Dīvāns* of Vīsa and Rāmīn? Have you
not read the stories of Vāmiq and 'Adhrā?

You gather up your garment lest the water should wet it; you
must dive a thousand times into the sea.

Love's path has proved all drunkenness and abasement, for
the torrent flows downwards; how should it run upwards?

10 You will be as a bezel in the lovers' ring, if you are the ear-
ringed slave of the king, my master;

Just as this earth is thrall to the sky, just as the body is thrall
to the spirit.

Come, say, what loss did earth suffer from this bond? What
kindnesses has not reason done to the members?

My son, it behoves not to beat the drum under a blanket;
plant your flag like a brave warrior in the midst of the plain.

With your spirit's ear listen to the thousand tumults echoing
in the green dome's air from the clamour of the passionate ones!

15 When the cords of your robe are loosened by Love's intox-
ication, behold then the angel's rapture, the houri's amaze-
ment!

How all the world trembles, on high and below, because of
Love, which transcends all below and on high!

When the sun has arisen, where then remains night? When
the army of grace has come, where then remains affliction?

I fell silent; Soul of the soul, do you speak, for every atom
has grown articulate out of love for your face.

27

You have seized me by the ear—whither are you drawing
me? Declare what is in your heart, and what your purpose is.

Prince, what cauldron did you cook for me last night? God
knows what melancholy madness there is in Love!

Since the ears of heaven and earth and the stars are all in your
hand, whither are they going? Even to that place whither you
said, "Come!"

The rest you seized only by one ear, me you seized by two;
from the roots of each ear I say, "Long may you endure!"

5 When a slave grows old, his master sets him free; when I be-
came old, He enslaved me over again.

Shall not children rise up white of hair at the resurrection?
But your resurrection has turned the old men's hair black.

Since you bring the dead to life and make the old men
young, I have fallen silent, and occupy myself with prayer.

28

If you do not know Love, question the nights, ask of the pale
cheek and the dryness of the lips.

Just as the water relates about the stars and the moon, even
so the physical forms relate about intellect and spirit.

From Love the soul learns a thousand manners of culture, such culture as cannot be found from schools.

Amongst a hundred persons, the lover stands out as plain as the shining moon in heaven amid the stars.

5   The mind, though it be apprised of all the doctrines of the sects, knows nothing and is bewildered by the doctrine of Love.

The man who has a heart like Khiḍar, who has quaffed the water of life of Love—to such a one the most limpid fountains are nothing worth.

Toil not in the garden; behold within the soul of the lover Damascus and Ghūṭa, rosebowers and all Nairab.

What is Damascus? For that is a paradise full of angels and houris; minds are amazed at those cheeks and rounded chins.

Its delectable wine does not produce vomiting and crop-sickness, the sweetness of its halva does not give rise to boils and fevers.

10   All men, from king to beggar, are in the tug of appetite; Love delivers the soul out of all appetites and desires.

What pride does Love take in its purchasers? What sort of a prop are foxes to the lion?

Upon the datepalm of the world I do not discover one ripe date, for all my teeth have been blunted by unripe dates.

Fly on the wings of Love in the air and to the skies, be exempt like the sun from the need of all riding-beasts.

Lovers' hearts do not experience loneliness like simples, they have no fear of severance and separation like compounds.

15   Providence chose Love for the sake of the souls, the Cause purchased Love out of all things caused.

Love's deputy entered the breast of the Cadi of Kāb, so that his heart should shy from giving judgment and such prattle.

What a world! What rare arrangement and ordering, that casts a thousand confusions into well-ordered things!

Beggar of Love, for all the joys that the world contains, reckon that Love is the gold-mine, and those things but gilded.

Love, you have filched my heart by trickery and cunning; you lied—God forfend!—but sweetly and charmingly.

20   I desire to mention you, Love, with gratitude; but I am distraught with you, and my thought and reason are confused.

Were I to praise Love in a hundred thousand languages, Love's beauty far surpasses all such stammerings.

29

Our desert has no bounds, our hearts and souls know no rest.

World upon world took shape and form; which of these shapes is ours?

When you see on the road a severed head which goes rolling towards our arena,

Ask of it, ask of it our secrets, for from it you will hear our hidden mystery.

5   How would it be, if but one ear showed itself, familiar with the tongues of our birds?

How would it be if one bird took wing, having on its neck the collar of our Solomon's secret?

What am I to say, what suppose? For this tale transcends our bounds and possibilities.

Yet how shall I keep silence? For every moment this distraction of ours becomes yet more distraught.

What partridges and falcons are flying with wings outspread amidst the air of our mountainland,

10   Amidst the air, which is the seventh atmosphere, on the summit whereof is our portico!

Leave this tale; ask not of us, for our tale is broken entirely;

Ṣalāḥ al-Ḥaqq wa'l-Dīn will display to you the beauty of our Emperor and Ruler.

30

A hundred drums are being beaten within our hearts, the roar of which we shall hear tomorrow.

Cotton wool in the ear, hair in the eye—that is the anxiety for tomorrow, the subtle whisper of grief;

Fling Love's flame into this cotton wool, like Ḥallāj and like the people of purity.

Why do you keep fire and cotton wool together? These two are opposites, and the opposite never survived.

5   Since the encounter of Love is near, be joyous of presence for the day of meeting.

For us, death is gladness and encounter; if for you it is an occasion of mourning, depart hence!

Inasmuch as this present world is our prison, the ruining of prisons is surely a cause for joy.

He whose prison was so delightful—how shall be the court of Him who adorned the world?

Look not for constancy in this prison, for herein constancy itself never kept faith.

31

Hark, for I am at the door! Open the door; to bar the door is not the sign of good pleasure.

In the heart of every atom is a courtyard for You; until You unbar it, it will remain in concealment.

You are the Splitter of Dawn, the Lord of the Daybreak; You open a hundred doors and say, "Come in!"

It is not I at the door, but You; grant access, open the door to Yourself.

5   Sulphur came to a fire; it said, "Come out to me, beloved!

My form is not your form, but I am all you, my form is as a veil.

I become you in form and reality when you arrive, my form is blotted out in the encounter."

The fire replied, "I have come forth; why should I veil my face from my very self?"

Hark, receive from me and deliver my message to all the companions and all the kinsmen.

10   If it is a mountain, draw it like a straw; I have given you the quality of amber.

My amber draws the mountain; did I not bring forth Mount Ḥirā out of nonexistence?

I am wholly and completely within your heart; {come toward your own heart—Welcome!

I am the heart-stealer and I take the heart,} for the pearl of the heart was born of my ocean.

I move my shadow, otherwise how is it that my shadow is apart from me?

15   But I transport it from its place so that, at the time of unveiling, its union may become manifest,

So that it may realize that it is a branch of me, so that it may become separated from all other.

Go to the saki and hear the rest of it, that he may tell you it with the tongue of immortality.

32

The wheel of heaven, with all its pomp and splendour, circles around God like a mill.

My soul, circumambulate around such a Kaaba; beggar, circle about such a table.

Travel like a ball around in His polo-field, inasmuch as you have become happy and helpless.

Your knight and rook are circumambulating about the king, even though you move from place to place on this chessboard.

5   He set on your finger the royal signet so that you might become a ruler having authority.

Whoever circumambulates about the heart becomes the soul of the world, heart-ravishing.

The heart-forlorn becomes companion to the moth, he circles about the tip of the candle,

Because his body is earthy and his heart of fire—congener has an inclination towards congener.

Every star circles about the sky, because purity is the congener of purity.

10 The mystic's soul circles about annihilation, even as iron about a magnet,

Because annihilation is true existence in his sight, his eyes having been washed clean of squinting and error;

The drunkard made ablution in urine, saying, "O Lord, deliver me out of impurity."

God answered, "First realize what impurity is; it is not meet to pray crookedly and topsy-turvy.

For prayer is a key; and when the key is crooked, you will not attain the favour of opening the lock."

15 I fall silent; all of you, leap up! The cypress-like stature of my idol cries come!

Emperor of Tabriz, my King, Shams-i Dīn, I have closed my lips; do you come, and open!

33

The water has been cut off from this world's river; O springtide, return and bring back the water!—

Of that water whose like the fountain of Khiḍar and Ilyās never saw and will never see.

Glorious fountain, through the splendour of whose gushing every moment water bubbles up from the well of the soul.

When waters exist, loaves grow; but never, my soul, did water grow from loaf.

5 O guest, do not beggarlike shed the water from the face of poverty for the sake of a morsel of bread.

The entire world from end to end is but half a morsel; because of greed for half a morsel, the water vanished.

Earth and heaven are bucket and pitcher; water is outside earth and heaven.

Do you also speed forth from heaven and earth, that you may behold water flowing from placelessness,

That the fish of your soul may escape from this pool, and sip water from the boundless sea.

10   In that sea whose fishes are all Khiḍars, therein the fish is immortal, immortal the water.

From that vision came the light of the eye, from that roof is the water in the spout;

From that garden are these roses of the cheeks, from that waterwheel the rosebower obtains water;

From that date-tree are the dates of Mary. That water derives not from secondary causes and suchlike things.

Your soul and spirit will then become truly happy, when the water comes flowing towards you from hence.

15   Shake no more your rattle like a nightwatchman, for the water itself is the guardian of these fishes.

34

Do you not know what the rebeck says concerning tears of the eyes and burning hearts?

"I am a skin far sundered from the flesh; how should I not lament in separation and torment?"

The stick also says, "I was once a green branch; that cavalcade broke and tore to pieces my saddle."

We are exiles in separation; O kings, give ear to us—"To God is the returning."

5   From God in the first place we sprang in the world; to Him likewise we revert from the revolution.

Our cry is like the bell in the caravan, or as thunder when the clouds travel the sky.

Wayfarer, set not your heart upon a lodging-place, becoming weary at the time of attraction;

For you have departed from many a stage, from the sperm until the season of youth.

Take it lightly, that you may escape easily; give up readily, and so find the reward.

10 Take hold of Him firmly, for He has taken firm hold on you; first He and last He—go, discover Him.

Gently He draws the bow, for that arrow of His quivers in the hearts of the lovers.

Be the lover Turk or Greek or Arab, this cry right enough is fellow-tongue with him.

The wind is lamenting and calling to you, "Come in my wake, even to the river of water.

I was water; I became wind; I have come to deliver the thirsty ones from this mirage."

15 Speech is that wind which was formerly water; it becomes water when it casts off the veil.

This shout arose from without the six directions: "Flee from direction, and turn not your face from Us."

O lover, you are not less than the moth; when does the moth ever avoid the flame?

The King is in the city; for the sake of the owl how should I abandon the city and occupy the ruin?

If an ass has gone mad, strike the ox-whip upon its head until its senses return.

20 If I seek his heart, his worthlessness increases still more; God said regarding the unbelievers, *Strike their necks.*

35

That moon has returned, whose like the sky never saw even in dreams; he has brought a fire which no water can extinguish.

Behold the body's tenement, and behold my soul—Love's cup has intoxicated the one and ruined the other.

When the master of the tavern became my heart's compan-
ion, my blood turned to wine out of love, my heart to roast.

When the eye is filled with his image, a voice proclaims,
"Well done, goblet, and bravo, wine!"

5 My heart suddenly descried the ocean of Love; it leaped away
from me, saying, "Come, find me now!"

The sun of the countenance of Shams-i Dīn, Pride of
Tabriz—in its track like clouds all hearts are running.

36

You who possess not Love, it is lawful to you—sleep on; be
gone, for Love and Love's sorrow is our portion—sleep on.

We have become motes of the sun of sorrow for the Beloved;
you in whose heart this passion has never arisen, sleep on.

In endless quest of union with Him we hurry like a river; you
who are not anguished by the question "Where is He?"—sleep
on.

Love's path is outside the two and seventy sects; since your
love and way is mere trickery and hypocrisy, sleep on.

5 His dawn-cup is our sunrise, his crepuscule our supper; you
whose yearning is for viands and whose passion is for supper,
sleep on.

In quest of the philosopher's stone we are melting like cop-
per; you whose philosopher's stone is the bolster and the bed-
fellow, sleep on.

Like a drunkard you are falling and rising on every side, for
night is past and now is the time for prayer; sleep on.

Since fate has barred slumber to me, young man, be gone;
for sleep has passed you by and you can now fulfil slumber;
sleep on.

We have fallen into Love's hand—what will Love do? Since
you are in your own hand, depart to the right hand—sleep on.

10 I am the one who drinks blood; my soul, you are the one who
eats viands; since viands for a certainty demand slumber, sleep on.

I have abandoned hope for my brain and my head too; you aspire to a fresh and juicy brain—sleep on.

I have rent the garment of speech and let words go; you, who are not naked, possess a robe—sleep on.

37

Since midnight sickness has manifested itself in that Master; till daybreak he has been beating his head uncontrollably against our wall.

Heaven and earth weep and lament because of his lamentation; his breaths have become fiery—you might say he is a fire-temple.

He has a strange sickness—no headache, no feverish pain—no remedy is to be found for it on earth, for it came upon him out of heaven.

When Galen beheld him he took his pulse; and he said, "Let go my hand and examine my heart; my pain is beyond the rules."

5   He suffers neither from yellow nor black bile, neither colic nor dropsy; a hundred tumults have arisen in every corner of our city because of this untoward happening.

He neither eats nor sleeps; he receives his nourishment from Love, for this Love is now both nurse and mother to the Master.

I said, "O God, grant compassion, that he may find rest for a brief hour; he has spilled no man's blood, he has seized no man's property."

The answer came from heaven, "Let him be as he is, for medicine and remedy are useless in lovers' suffering.

Seek no cure for this Master; do not bind him, do not counsel him, for where he has fallen is neither transgression nor piety.

10   When did you ever see Love? You have never heard from lovers; keep silent, chant no spells; this is not a case for magic or jugglery!"

Come, Shams-i Tabrīzī, source of light and radiance, for this illustrious spirit without your splendour is frozen and congealed.

38

I have come so that, tugging your ear, I may draw you to me, unheart and unself you, plant you in my heart and soul.

Rosebush, I have come a sweet springtide unto you, to seize you very gently in my embrace and squeeze you.

I have come to adorn you in this worldly abode, to convey you above the skies like lovers' prayers.

I have come because you stole a kiss from an idol fair; give it back with a glad heart, master, for I will seize you back.

5   What is a mere rose? You are the All, you are the speaker of the command *Say*. If no one else knows you, since you are I, I know you.

You are my soul and spirit, you are my *Fātiḥa*-chanter; become altogether the *Fātiḥa,* so that I may chant you in my heart.

You are my quarry and game, though you have sprung from the snare; return back to the snare, and if you go not, I will drive you.

The lion said to me, "You are a wondrous deer; be gone! Why do you run in my wake so swiftly? I will tear you to pieces."

Accept my blow, and advance forward like a hero's shield; give your ear to naught but the bowstring, that I may bend you like a bow.

10   So many thousand stages there are from earth's bounds to man; I have brought you from city to city, I will not leave you by the roadside.

Say nothing, froth not, do not raise the lid of the cauldron; simmer well, and be patient, for I am cooking you.

No, for you are a lion's whelp hidden in a deer's body: I will cause you suddenly to transcend the deer's veil.

You are my ball, and you run in the curved mallet of my de-
cree; though I am making you to run, I am still running in your
track.

39

Come, come, for the rosebower has blossomed; come, come,
for the beloved has arrived.

Bring at once altogether soul and world; deliver over to the
sun, for the sun has drawn a fine blade.

Laugh at that ugly one showing off airs; weep for that friend
who is severed from the Friend.

The whole city seethed when the rumour ran abroad that the
madman had once again escaped from his chains.

5   What day is it, what day is it, such a day of uprising?—
Perchance the scroll of men's deeds has already fluttered from
the skies.

Beat the drums, and speak no more; what place is there for
heart and mind? For the soul too has fled.

40

This house wherein continually rings the sound of the bell-
staff—ask of the master what house this house is.

What is this idol-form, if it is the house of the Kaaba? And
what is this light of God, if it is the Magian temple?

In this house is a treasure which the whole of being cannot
contain; this house and this master are all a fiction and a pretence.

Lay not hand upon this house, for this house is a talisman;
speak not to the master, for he is drunk since last night.

5   The dust and rubbish of this house is all ambergris and musk;
the noise of the door of this house is all verse and melody.

In short, whoever enters this house has found a way to the
King of the world, the Solomon of the time.

Master, bend down your head once from this roof, for in your fair face is the token of fortune.

I swear by your life that, but for beholding your countenance, though it be the kingdom of the earth, all is mere fantasy and fable.

The garden is baffled as to which is the leaf, which the blossom; the birds are distraught as to which is the snare, which the bait.

10   This is the Master of heaven, who is like unto Venus and the moon, and this is the house of Love, which is without bound and end.

The soul, like a mirror, has received your image in its heart; the heart has sunk like a comb into the tip of your tress.

Since in Joseph's presence the women cut their hands, come to me, my soul, for the Soul is there in the midst.

The whole household is drunk, and nobody is aware who enters the threshold, whether it be X or Y.

It is inauspicious; do not sit on the threshold, enter the house at once; he whose place is the threshold keeps all in darkness.

15   Though God's drunkards are thousands, yet they are one; the drunkards of lust are all double and treble.

Enter the lions' thicket and do not be anxious for the wounding, for the anxiety of fear is the figments of women;

For there no wounding is, there all is mercy and love, but your imagination is like a bolt behind the door.

Set not fire to the thicket, and keep silence, my heart; draw in your tongue, for your tongue is a flame.

41

Come, for today is for us a day of festival; henceforward joy and pleasure are on the increase.

Clap hands, say, "Today is all happiness"; from the beginning it was manifestly a fine day.

Who is there in this world like our Friend? Who has seen such a festival in a hundred cycles?

Earth and heaven are filled with sugar; in every direction sugarcane has sprouted.

5   The roar of that pearl-scattering sea has arrived; the world is full of waves, and the sea is invisible.

Muhammad has returned from the Ascension; Jesus has arrived from the fourth heaven.

Every coin which is not of this place is counterfeit; every wine which is not of the cup of the Soul is impure.

What a splendid assembly, where the saki is good fortune, and his companions are Junaid and Bā Yazīd!

Crop-sickness afflicted me when I was desirous; I did not know that God Himself desires us.

10   Now I have fallen asleep and stretched out my feet, since I have realised that good fortune has drawn me on.

42

In this river the heart is like a ruined waterwheel; in whichever direction it turns, there is water before it;

And even if you turn your back to the water, the water runs hurrying before you.

How shall the shadow save its soul from the sun, seeing that its soul is in the hand of the sun?

If the shadow stretches forth its neck, the sun's face that instant is shrouded.

5   Brave Sun, before which this sun in heaven quivers with fear like quicksilver!

The moon is like quicksilver on a palsied palm—one night only, and for the rest it is poured forth;

In every thirty nights, two nights it is united and lean, for the rest it endures separation, and separation is torture.

Though it is wretched, it is fresh of face; laughter is the habit and wont of lovers.

It lives laughing, and likewise dies laughing, for its return is to laughing fortune.

10 Keep silent, for the faults of vision always come from question and answer.

43

So long as the form of the Beloved's image is with us, for us the whole of life is a joyful parade.

Where friends unite together, there in the midst of the house, by Allah, is a spreading plain;

And where the heart's desire comes true, there one thorn is better than a thousand dates.

When we are sleeping at the head of the Beloved's lane, our pillow and blankets are the Pleiades;

5   When we are twisted into the tip of the Beloved's tress on the Night of Power, power belongs to us.

When the reflexion of His beauty shines forth, mountainland and earth are silk and brocade.

When we ask of the breeze the scent of Him, in the breeze is the echo of lute and reedpipe.

When we write His name in the dust, every particle of dust is a dark-eyed houri.

We chant a spell of Him over the fire; thereby the raging fire becomes water-cool.

10 Why shall I tell a long tale? For when we mention His name to nonbeing too, it increases being.

That subtlety in which Love is contained is fuller of pith than a thousand walnuts.

That instant when Love showed its face, all these things vanished from the midst.

Silence! For the sealing has been completed; the totality of desire is God Most High.

44

Today a new madness has arrived, it has dragged the chains
of a thousand hearts;
Today it has rent the sides of the bags of white sugar candy.
Again that bedouin has purchased the Joseph of beauty for
eighteen base pieces.
All night the souls in glory and felicity pastured amidst nar-
cissus and jasmine,
5   Until with the dawn of course every spirit leaped forth nim-
ble and sprightly.
Today narcissus-bed and anemone have blossomed out of
stones and clods,
The tree has bloomed in the midst of winter, in January the
fruits have ripened.
You might say that God has created a new world in this an-
cient world.
Lover-gnostic, recite this ode, for Love has chosen you out
of all the lovers.
10   On your golden cheek there is a toothmark—has that silvery-
breasted one perchance bitten you?
It is right that He should cherish that heart which has
throbbed much in anguish for Him.
Silence! Go sauntering through the meadow for today it is
the turn for the eyes to behold.

45

Which is the road by which I came? I would return, for it
likes me not here;
One moment's absence from the Beloved's lane is unlawful
according to the doctrine of lovers.
If only in all the village there is someone—by Allah, a sign
would be completely sufficient.

How shall the finch escape? For even the simurgh is footfast in this stout snare.

5   My heart, do not come wandering in this direction; sit there, for it is a pleasant station.

Choose that dessert which augments life, seek that wine which is full-bodied;

The rest is all scent and image and colour, the rest is all war and shame and opprobrium;

Be silent, and sit down, for you are drunk, and this is the edge of the roof.

46

Be gathered together, comrades, for this is not the time to sleep; by Allah, every comrade who sleeps is not of the true companions.

Whoever is not turning about and weeping after the fashion of a waterwheel shall not see the face of the garden, he will lose the way to the garden.

You who have sought the heart's desire in the world of water and clay, you are running towards that river in which there is no water.

O moon, come forth from the heart's sky and turn our night to day, that no night-traveller may say, "Tonight is not a night of moonshine."

5   May my heart be unapprised of where the Beloved is, if my heart is not quivering like the heart of quicksilver for the love of Him.

47

Love resides not in science and learning, scrolls and pages; whatever men chatter about, that way is not the lovers' way.

Know that the branch of Love is in pre-eternity and its roots in post-eternity; this tree rests not upon heaven and earth, upon legs.

We have deposed reason and circumscribed passion, for such majesty is not appropriate to this reason and these habits.

So long as you are desirous, know that this desire of yours is an idol; when you have become beloved, after that there is no existence for the desirous.

5 The mariner is always upon the planks of fear and hope; once planks and mariner have passed away, nothing remains but drowning.

Shams-i Tabrīzī, you are at once sea and pearl, for your being entirely is naught but the secret of the Creator.

48

Mind you do not slip, for the road behind and ahead is wet with blood; man-robbers are nowadays more numerous than gold-robbers.

If they are intent on robbing people of reason and awareness, what then will they make of him who is unaware of himself?

Do not consider yourself's self so worthless and without antagonist; the world is in quest of gold, and your self is the mine of gold.

The prophet of God said, "Men are as mines"; the self is a mine of silver and gold and is truly full of gems.

5 You find a treasure, and therein you find not life for all the treasure; discover yourself, for this worldly treasure passes away from you.

Discover yourself, and be wary; yet what are you to do? For there is a wakeful, quickhanded thief on this way.

Though the dawn is dark, day is to be reckoned at hand; whoever's face is turned towards the sun is as the dawn.

The spirits become intoxicated through the breath of day-break, inasmuch as the face of daybreak is towards the sun and is the companion of vision.

You fling down the counter so many times upon "haply" and "perchance," for you are very bankrupt, and heaven's wheel carries off everything.

10   Brain-sieved and aware of nothing, you have fallen asleep— one might say your morsel of daily bread is the brain of an ass.

Labour more, and collect gold, and be joyful, for all your silver and gold and wealth is the serpent of hell.

For God's sake, live one night without eating and sleeping; a hundred nights because of lust your carnal soul is sleepless and foodless.

Out of agony and grief, from behind every atom of dust comes sighing and lamentation, but your ear is deaf.

Sprinkle the heart's blood on your cheek at dawn, for your provision for the way is heart's blood and the sigh of morn.

15   Fill your heart with hope, and polish it well and clear, for your pure heart is the mirror of the sun of splendour.

Say, who is the companion of Aḥmad the Apostle in this world? Shams-i Tabrīz the Emperor, who is *one of the greatest things*.

49

Has perchance this instant the tip of that tress become scattered? For such a Tartar musk has become amber-diffusing.

Has perchance the dawn breeze lifted the veil from His face? For thousands of unseen moons have begun to shine.

Is there any soul which is not happy through His sweet perfume? Though the soul has no clue as to the source of its happiness.

Many a happy rose is laughing through the breath of God, yet every soul does not know whence it has become laughing.

5   How fairly the sun of His cheek has shone today, through which thousands of hearts have become rubies of Badakhshān.

Yet why should not the lover set his heart upon Him through whose grace the body has become wholly soul?

Did the heart perchance one morning behold Him as He is, so that from that vision of Him it has today become after this wise?

Ever since the heart beheld that peri-born beauty of mine, it has taken the glass into its hand and become an exorcist.

If His sweet breeze blows upon the tree of the body, how a-tremble two hundred leaves and two hundred branches have become!

10   If there is not an immortal soul for every one slain by Him, why has it become so easy for the lover to yield up his soul?

Even the aware ones are unaware of His life and activities, for His life and activities have become their veil.

If the minstrel of Love has not breathed upon the reed of a heart, why has every tip of the hair become lamenting like the reed pipe?

If Shams-i Tabrīz does not fling clods from the roof against the heart, then why have the souls become as it were his door-keepers?

50

He said, "Who is at the door?" I said, "Your humble slave." He said, "What is your business?" I said, "Lord, to greet you."

He said, "How long will you drive?" I said, "Until you call." He said, "How long will you boil?" I said, "Till the resurrection."

I laid claim to love, I swore many oaths that for love's sake I had lost kingship and nobility.

He said, "For a claim the cadi requires witness." I said, "My witness is my tears, my sign the pallor of my cheeks."

5   He said, "Your witness is invalid; your eye is wet-skirted." I said, "By the splendour of your justice, they are just and without fault."

He said, "Who was your companion?" I said, "Your fantasy, O King." He said, "Who summoned you hither?" I said, "The scent of your cup."

He said, "What is your intention?" I said, "Fidelity and friendship." He said, "What do you desire of me?" I said, "Your universal grace."

He said, "Where is it most agreeable?" I said, "Caesar's palace." He said, "What did you see there?" I said, "A hundred miracles."

He said, "Why is it desolate?" I said, "For fear of the highwayman." He said, "Who is the highwayman?" I said, "This blame."

He said, "Where is safety?" I said, "In abstinence and godliness." He said, "What is abstinence?" I said, "The way of salvation."

He said, "Where is calamity?" I said, "In the street of your love." He said, "How fare you there?" I said, "In perfect rectitude."

Silence! For if I were to utter his subtleties you would come forth from yourself, neither door nor roof would remain to you.

51

Show your face, for the orchard and rosegarden are my desire; open your lips, for abundant sugar is my desire.

Sun of beauty, come forth one moment out of the cloud, for that glittering, glowing countenance is my desire.

Out of your air I heard the sound of the falcon-drum; I returned, for the sultan's forearm is my desire.

You said capriciously, "Trouble me no more; be gone!" That saying of yours, "Trouble me no more," is my desire,

And your repulse, "Be gone, the king is not at home," and those mighty airs and brusqueness of the doorkeeper, are my desire.

In the hand of every one who exists there are filings of beauty; that quarry of elegance and that mine are my desire.

This bread and water of heaven's wheel are like a treacherous torrent; I am a fish, a leviathan, Oman is my desire.

Like Jacob I am crying alas, alas; the fair visage of Joseph of Canaan is my desire.

By Allah, without you the city is a prison for me; I wander abroad, mountain and desert are my desire.

10 My heart is weary of these weak-spirited fellow-travellers; the Lion of God and Rustam-i Dastān are my desire.

My soul is sick of Pharaoh and his tyranny; that light of the countenance of Moses son of 'Imrăn is my desire.

I am aweary of these tearful people so full of complaining; that ranting and roaring of the drunkards is my desire.

I am more eloquent than the nightingale, but because of vulgar envy a seal is on my tongue, and lamentation is my desire.

Last night the shaikh went all about the city, lamp in hand, crying, "I am weary of beast and devil, a man is my desire."

15 They said, "He is not to be found, we too have searched." He answered, "He who is not to be found is my desire."

Though I am penniless, I will not accept a small carnelian, for that rare, precious carnelian is my desire.

Hidden from every eye, and all things seen are from Him— that hidden One manifest in works is my desire.

My state has gone beyond every desire and yearning; from mine and place to the elements is my desire.

My ear heard the tale of faith and became drunk; where is the portion of sight? The form of faith is my desire.

20 In one hand the winecup, in the other the Beloved's curl—to dance so in the midst of the arena is my desire.

That rebeck says, "I am dead of expectation; the hand and bosom and plectrum of 'Uthmān are my desire."

I am at once Love's rebeck, and Love is my rebeck-player; those favours of the plucking of the All-merciful are my desire.

Cunning minstrel, number the rest of this ode after this fashion, for it is after this fashion I desire.

Show your face from the east, Sun of the Pride of Tabriz; I am the hoopoe, the presence of Solomon is my desire.

52

Though from left and right there is useless criticism and vilification, that man who has lost his heart turns not away from Love.

The moon scatters light, and the dog barks at it; what harm does that do to the moon? Such is a dog's speciality.

The lover is a mountain, not a straw to be blown away by the wind; it is a flock of flies that the wind has waylaid.

If it is the rule that blame should arise from Love, it is also the rule for Love to be deaf to it.

5   Desolation of both worlds on this road is true cultivation; to eschew all benefits is a benefit in Love.

Jesus from the fourth sphere calls, "Welcome! Wash your hands and mouth, for now is the time for the Table."

Go, become effaced in the Friend in the tavern of not-being; wherever two drunkards are together, there is bound to be a brawl.

You enter the devil's court crying, "Justice, justice!" Seek justice from God, for here is nothing but wild beasts.

The Prophet said, "Take not counsel from a woman"; this carnal soul of ours is a woman, even though it be an abstinent.

10   Drink so much wine that you cease to chatter; after all, are you not a lover? And is not this love a tavern?

Though you should utter verse and prose like Ja'farī gold, there where Ja'far is it is all worthless tales.

53

My soul, spiritual beauty is passing fair and glorious, yet your own beauty and loveliness is something beside.

You who spend years describing spirit, show one quality that is equal to his essence.

Through his phantasm the light of the eye increases, yet for all that in the presence of union with him it is clouded.

I stand open-mouthed in reverence for that beauty; every moment "God is greater" is on my tongue and in my heart.

5 The heart has acquired an eye constant in desire of you; ah, how that desire nourishes the heart and eye!

Speak not of houris and moon, spirit and peri, for these resemble Him not; He is something other.

Slave-caressing it is that your love has practised, else where is the heart that is worthy of that love?

Every heart that has been sleepless for one night in desire for you is bright as day, and the air by it is illumined.

Every one who has become without object is as your disciple; his object is realized without the form of object.

10 Every limb of hell who has burned and fallen into this love, has fallen into Kauthar, for your love is Kauthar.

My foot does not reach the ground out of hope for union, withal through separation from you my hand is on my head.

My heart, be not sorrowful at this oppression of foes, and meditate on this, that the Sweetheart is judge.

If my enemy is glad because of my saffron-pale face, is not my saffron-pale face derived from the red rose?

Since my Beloved's beauty surpasses description, how fat is my grief, and how lean my praise!

15 Yes, since it is the rule that the more the pain of the wretched sufferer is, the less is his lament.

Shams-i Dīn shone moonlike from Tabriz; no, what is the moon indeed? That face outshines the moon.

54

That spirit which wears not true love as a garment is better not to have been; its being is nothing but a disgrace.

Be drunk in love, for love is all that exists; without the commerce of love there is no admittance to the Beloved.

They say, "What is love?" Say, "The abandonment of free will." He who has not escaped out of free will, no free will has he.

The lover is an emperor; the two worlds are scattered over him; the king pays no heed to the scattering.

5   Love it is and the lover that remain till all eternity; set not your heart on aught but this, for it is merely borrowed.

How long will you embrace a dead beloved? Embrace the soul which naught embraces.

What was born of spring dies in the season of autumn; love's rosebower receives no replenishment from spring.

The rose that comes of spring, the thorn is its companion; the wine that comes of pressed grapes is not exempt from crop-sickness.

Be not an expectant spectator on this path; for by Allah, there is no death worse than expectancy.

10   Set your heart on the true coin, if you are not counterfeit; give ear to this subtlety, if you lack an earring.

Tremble not on the body's steed; fare lighter afoot; God gives wings to him who rides not on the body.

Let go care and become wholly clear of heart, like the face of a mirror without image and picture—

When it has become clear of images, all images are contained in it; that clear-faced one is not ashamed of any man's face.

Would you have your self clear of blemish? Gaze upon Him, for He is not ashamed or afraid of the truth.

15   Since the steely face gained this skill from purity, what shall the heart's face, which is without dust, discover?

I said, "What shall it discover?" No, I will not say; silence is better, lest the heart-ravisher should say, "He cannot keep a secret."

55

Every moment the voice of Love is arriving from left and right; we are departing for the skies—who has a mind for sightseeing?

We were once in heaven, we were friends of the angels; let us all return thither, for that is our city.

We are even higher than the heavens, we are greater than angels; why should we not transcend both? Our lodging-place is Majesty.

How far is the world of dust from the pure substance! Upon what have you alighted? Load up—what place is this?

5   Young luck is our friend, to yield up the soul is our business; the leader of our caravan is Muṣṭafā, Pride of the World.

At his moon the moon was split, it could not endure to behold him; the moon attained such luck—she, a humble beggar.

The sweet scent of the breeze is from the curl of his tress, the glitter of this phantasm is from that cheek like the forenoon.

Behold in our hearts every moment a splitting of the moon, for why does your eye soar beyond the vision of that vision?

Mankind, like waterfowl, are sprung from the sea of the soul; how should the bird that has risen from that sea make its dwelling here?

10   Nay rather, we are pearls in that sea, we are all present therein; else, why does wave upon wave surge from the sea of the heart?

The wave of Alast came along and caulked the body's ship; when the ship is wrecked once more, the turn of union and encounter will come.

56

My being is but a goblet in the Beloved's hand—look at my eyes, if you do not believe it.

I am like a goblet, heart full of blood and body slender, in the hand of Love, which is neither pale nor lean nor slender.

This Love consumes nothing but Moslem blood; come, I will tell it in your ear—amazing, it is not an infidel.

A thousand forms like Adam and Eve are born; the world is full of His image, but He is not endowed with form.

5   He knows what is salutary for the desert sand-grain and the drop of the ocean, and brings replenishment, for His knowledge is not deaf.

Every moment He binds and releases our hearts; why should the heart not know Him by His actions, if it is not an ass?

Through being bound and released by the hand of the ass-driver the ass has become a gnostic, and knows that he is, and none beside;

Seeing him, it moves its head and ear assishly; it recognises his call, for it is not disguised.

From his hand it has consumed sweet provender and water—amazing! Do you not receive such provision from God?

10 A thousand times He has fettered you in pain, and you have cried out; why do you disapprove? God is not constrained to release you.

Like the infidel you bow your head only in time of affliction; not worth half a grain is the head that belongs not yonder.

A thousand spiritual forms are flying in the air like Ja'far-i Ṭaiyār, although they are not Ja'far;

But how should the cage-bird know about the air? It supposes gloomily, "I have no wings."

Every moment it puts its head out of the fissure of the cage; there is room for its head, but not its body, for the head is not the whole.

15 The fissure of your five senses is the fissure of that cage; you see a thousand prospects, but there is no way to the prospect.

Your body is dry tinder, and that vision is fire; when you look well into the matter, all is nothing but flame.

Not tinder is it, for it has become fire in burning; know that the tinder is light, although it is not shining.

For the sake of the ears of those who shall come after me I speak and set down; our life is not postponed;

For Love has seized them by the ear and is bringing them by secret ways where reason is no guide.

20 Muhammad's eye has closed in sleep, and the rebeck has become feeble; sleep not—these words are a treasure of gold, even if they are not gold in truth.

Mankind are stars, and Shams-i Tabrīzī is the sun; which star is there that is not illumined by his sun?

57

What pearl are you? For in no man's hand is the price of you. What does the world possess that is not your gift?

Is there a worse punishment than his who lives exiled from your face? Do not punish your servant, for all that he is unworthy of you.

Every moment I would scatter my heart and soul in your dust; dust be on the head of the soul that is not the dust of your feet!

Blessed to all birds is your air; how unblest is the bird that is not in your air!

5   Amidst the billows of contingencies even the master shall not escape by swimming, if he is not familiar with you.

The world has no permanence, and if it has, count it as perishing, since it is not intimate with your permanence.

How happy is the king that is mated by your rook! How fair of presence is he who is never without your presence!

I will not flee from your blow, for very raw indeed is the heart that is not roasted in the fire of your trial.

The heart that has not been naughted turns its face to place; from placelessness you drive it, saying, "Begone! This is no place for you."

10   There is no end to your praise and praisers; what atom is there that is not reeling with your praise?

As Niẓāmī expresses it in verse, "Tyrannise not, for I cannot endure your tyranny."

58

Three days it is now since my fair one has become changed; sugar is never bitter—how is it that that sugar is sour?

I dipped my pitcher into the fountain that contained the Water of Life, and I saw that the fountain was full of blood.

In the garden where two hundred thousand roses grew, in place of fruit and blossom there are thorns and stones and desert.

I chant a spell and whisper it over the face of that peri—for incantation is always the business of the exorcist—

5 Yet for all my incantations my peri came not back into the bottle, since his activities transcend chants and spells.

Between his brow there are ancient angers; the frown on the brow of Lailā is destruction to Majnūn.

Come, come, for without you I have no life; see, see, for without you my eyes are a veritable flood.

By the right of your moonlike countenance, brighten my eye, though my sins are greater than the whole of mankind's.

My heart turns about itself, saying, "What is my sin? For every cause is conjoined with a consequence."

10 A proclamation comes to me from the Marshal of eternal judgment: "Seek not about your own self, for this cause belongs not to now."

God gives and seizes, brings and carries away; His business is not to be measured by reason's scales.

Come, come, for even now by the grace of *Be and it is* paradise opens its gate which is *ungrudging*.

Of the essence of the thorn you behold marvellous flowers; of the essence of the stone you see the treasure of Korah.

Divine grace is eternal, and thereof a thousand keys lie hidden between the *kāf* and the ship of the *nūn*.

59

Love is nothing but felicity and lovingkindness, it is nothing but gladness and right guidance.

Bū Ḥanīfa did not teach love, Shāfi'ī had no tradition concerning it.

"Licit" and "illicit" operate till death; there is no terminus to the science of lovers.

Lovers are drowned in sugar-water; Egypt has nothing to complain about sugar.

5   How should the drunkard's soul not utter thanks for a wine to which there is no boundary and limit?

Whomsoever you have seen sorrowful and scowling is not a lover, and belongs not to that province;

Otherwise, every bud is a veil of a garden, jealousy and envy have no contagion.

The beginner in this path of Love is he who is not apprised of beginning.

Become naughted from selfhood, because there is no sin worse than being.

10   Do not be a shepherd, be a flock; shepherdry is nothing but a bar to providential care.

God is sufficient for many a servant's ill, but the servant has not this knowledge and sufficiency.

He says, "This is problematic and allegorical"; this is clear, this is not allegory.

A blind man struck his foot against a pitcher; he said, "The doorkeeper is not careful.

What are pitchers and glasses doing on the footpath? The road is not clear of these pots.

15   Remove the pitchers from the path; the doorkeeper is not attending to his job."

The doorkeeper answered, "Blind man, no pitcher is on the path, the fact is that you have no knowledge of the path.

You have left the path and are going to the pitcher; that is plain error."

Master, your drunkenness in the way of religion is the only sign from beginning to end.

You are a sign, and a seeker after a sign; there is no better sign than the seeker after a sign.

20   You are astray from the path, otherwise in the path of striving no striver goes without his wages.

Just as *an atom's weight he shall see it,* an atom's weight of slipping goes not unpunished;

An atom of good is not without a reward—open your eyes, if you are not blind.

Every herb is a token of water; what is there that is not tributary to that?

Enough, this water has many tokens; the thirsty man requires no counselling.

60

The bird of my heart has again begun to flutter, the parrot of my soul has begun to chew sugar.

My mad and drunken camel has begun to rend the chain of reason.

A gulp of that incautious wine has begun to flow over my head and eyes.

The lion of the gaze, despite the dog of the Companions of the Cave, has begun to drink my blood again.

5 The water is flowing again in this river; by the riverbank the grass has begun to shoot.

The dawn breeze is blowing again in the garden, it has begun to blow over rose and rosebed.

Love sold me for a single fault; Love's heart burned, and has begun to buy back.

He drove me away; compassion came to him and called; Love has begun to look kindly upon me.

My enemy has seen that I am with the Friend; he has begun to gnaw his hand of envy.

10 My heart has escaped from the trickery of fortune, it has begun to creep into Love's bosom.

The tale-bearer brow making hints has begun to curve over that eye.

When Love called my heart towards Him, my heart began to flee from all creation.

Creatures are sticks; the blind man flings away the stick when he begins to see.

Creatures are like milk; the infant turns from milk when it has begun to digest viands.

15   The spirit is like a falcon taking wing, for it has begun to hear the drum of the king.

Enough, for the veil of speech has begun to spin a curtain around you.

61

The hour is late, the hour is late, the sun has gone down into the well, the sun of the soul of lovers has entered the seclusion of God.

A day is hidden in night, a Turk is amongst Hindus; night, launch your assaults, for that Turk is in the tent.

If you catch a glimpse of this brightness, you will set sleep afire; for by night-faring and servitude Venus became the companion of the moon.

We are fleeing by night and running apace, and the Zangis are on our track, for we carried off the gold, and the watchman became aware.

5   We have learned nightfaring and consumed a hundred watchmen; our cheeks are lit up like candles because that pawn of ours has become king.

Happy indeed is that smiling one who has pressed cheek against that cheek! Great and glorious is that heart which has departed unto that Sweetheart!

Who is there on the path of the heart who has not a sigh in his heart? That man is truly successful who is drowned in that sigh.

When he is drowned in the sea, the sea carries him up to the surface, like Joseph of the well who emerged from the well to greatness.

They say, "Man's origin is the dust, and he returns to the dust." How should he become dust who is the dust of this doorway?

10   The crops appear all of one kind until the harvest-time arrives; one half of it has become fine grain, the other half is chaff.

62

Fair ones, fair ones, a fair one has gone mad; his bowl has fallen from our roof, he has gone to the madhouse.

He circled about the pool like men athirst seeking and searching; suddenly like a dry crust he became a sop in our pool.

Learned man, stop up your ears against this; do not listen to this incantation, for he has become a legend through our charm.

The ears do not escape from this ring which has robbed minds of their reason; having laid his head on the millstone, he vanished like a grain into the measure.

5   Regard it not as a sport, regard it not as a sport; here choose gambling away life; heads in plenty through love of his curls have become turned upside down like a comb.

Be not puffed up by your reason; many a well-trusted master who was a pillar of the world has become more lamenting than the Moaning Pillar.

I, who have cut away from life, roselike have rent my robe, thence have become such that my reason has become a stranger to my soul.

Those drops of individual reason have become vanquished in the Sea of Reason; the atoms of these fragmentary souls have become annihilated in the Beloved.

I will keep silent, I will perform the command and hide this candle—a candle in whose light the sun and the moon are moths.

63

Who is that, who is that who makes the breast sorrowful, then when you make complaint before Him, He turns your bitter sweet?

First He appears as a deaf adder, lastly He is a treasure of pearls. Sweet King, who in a moment transforms that bitterness to goodness!

Let it be a demon, He makes it into a houri, let it be a funeral, He makes it into a marriage-feast; and He makes knowing and world-beholding one blind from his mother's womb.

He makes the dark bright, He makes the thorn into a rosebud; He draws the thorn out of your palm, and fashions you a pillow of roses.

5   For the sake of Abraham His friend He causes the fire to flame, and converts Nimrod's furnace into blossoms and eglantine.

He who gives light to the stars and succour to the helpless, He benefits His servant, and too applauds His servant.

He causes all the sins of the sinners to scatter like December leaves; into the ears of those who speak Him ill He recites forgiveness of sin.

He says, "Say, O Faithful One, pardon the sin of one who slipped"; when a servant enters upon prayer, He secretly says Amen.

It is His amen which gives a man joy in his prayer; like a fig, He is inwardly and outwardly alike sweet and pleasant.

10   It is rapture which in good and evil gives strength to hand and foot, for this rapture mates the strength of a Rustam to the body of a poor wretch.

With rapture the poor wretch is a Rustam, without rapture Rustam is one full of grief; but for rapture, how would the Friend of the Soul stablish the soul?

I sent forth my heart timely (for it knows swiftly to travel the way), to carry the description of Shams-i Dīn to the Tabriz of fidelity.

64

Advice from anyone is never of profit to lovers; love is not
the kind of torrent that anyone can dam up.

No man of intellect will ever know the head's ecstasy of the
drunkard; no man of reason will ever know the heart's rapture
of the reason-lost.

Kings would become indifferent to kingship if they caught a
whiff of those wines which lovers drink in the heart's assembly.

Khusrau bids farewell to his kingdom for the sake of Shīrīn;
Farhād too for her sake strikes the axe against the mountain.

5   Majnūn flees from the circle of men of intellect for love of
Lailā; Vāmiq laughed at the mustachios of every puffed-up man.

Frozen is the life that has passed without that sweet spirit;
rotten is the kernel that is oblivious of this almond-cake.

If yonder heaven were not spinning bewildered and in love
like us, it would grow weary of its revolving, and say, "It is
enough for me; how long, how long?"

The world is like a reed pipe, and He blows in its every hole;
truly its every lament derives from those two sugarsweet lips.

Behold how, when He blows into every clod, every heart, He
bestows a need, He bestows a passion which raises lamentation
of anguish.

10   If you tear the heart away from God, to whom will you then
commit it? Tell me this. Soulless is the person who has been
able to tear his heart away from God for a single moment.

I will make enough; go you nimbly, by night climb on to this
roof; raise a fair clamour in the city, my soul, with a loud voice!

65

The springtide of lovers has come, that this dust bowl may
become a garden; the proclamation of heaven has come, that
the bird of the soul may rise in flight.

The sea becomes full of pearls, the salt marsh becomes sweet as Kauthar, the stone becomes a ruby from the mine, the body becomes wholly soul.

If the eyes and souls of lovers are raining a flood like a cloud, yet the heart within the body's cloud is flashing like lightning.

Do you know why the lovers' eyes have become like a cloud in Love? Because that moon generally is concealed in clouds.

5   Happy and laughing hour, when those clouds have begun to weep! Lord, what a blessed state, when those lightnings are laughing!

Of those hundreds of thousands of drops, not one drop falls upon the earth; for if it should fall upon the earth, the whole world would be laid in ruin.

Though the whole world be laid in ruin, yet every desolation through love becomes fellow-mariner with Noah, and so is intimate with the Flood.

Did the flood abate, the heavens would not go round; through that wave beyond direction these six directions keep in motion.

You who remain fast under these six directions, at once sorrow and do not sorrow, for those seeds beneath the ground will one day become a plantation of date-trees.

10   One day that root will raise its head from the dust, it will become a fresh green branch; what if two or three branches should wither, the rest of the tree will be pregnant with life;

And when that dry branch is set afire, the fire will be joyous like the soul; if that is not this, it will become this; if this is not that, it will become that.

Something has closed my mouth, as if to say, "What, drunk and on the edge of the roof? Whatever it may be that bewilders you, that thing is bewildered at Him."

66

My Beloved leaves me not so much as to scratch my own head; it is the body of my Beloved that presses me in its breast.

Now He draws me in His train like a string of camels, anon the King places me in front like the commander of His troops.

Anon He sucks me like a seal-ring, to plant His seal through me; anon He makes me into a ring and fastens me on His door.

He takes blood and makes a sperm, He takes sperm and fashions a creature; He slays the creature and fashions Reason, He makes manifest the resurrection.

5   Now He drives me away with a reed like a dove from the house, anon with a hundred entreaties He calls me to His presence.

Now He carries me like a ship on a voyage over the sea, anon He halts me and ties me to His own anchor.

Now He makes me water for the sake of the seeker after purity, anon He makes me a thorn in the path of His luckless ones.

The eternal eight paradises did not become the prospect of that King; how happy is this heart of mine, which He makes His prospect!

Not by the attestation of faith did I become a believer in that Beauty of the Soul; only then did I become a believer in It when I became an unbeliever in myself.

10   Whoever joined His ranks became secure from destruction by Him; I saw the sword in His hand, I burned that shield of mine.

I was like-pinioned with Gabriel, I had six hundred wings; now that I have reached Him, what shall I do with my wings?

Many days and nights I was guardian of the pearl of my soul; now in the current of the ocean of pearls I am indifferent to my own pearl.

How long will you essay to describe Him? For He comes not within description; make enough, that I may ride over my commotion.

67

The Friend is toggling me like a camel; in what train is He dragging His drunken camel?

He wounded my soul and body, He broke my glass, He bound my neck—to what task is He drawing me?

His net is carrying me like a fish to the shore; His snare is drawing my heart towards the Master of the chase.

He who makes the train of clouds, like camels under the sky, to water the plain, is drawing me over mountain and cavern.

5   The thunder beats its drum; particle and whole have become alive; the scent of spring is wafting in the twig's heart and the marrow of the rose.

He who makes the recesses of the seed to be the cause of the fruit, He is dragging the secret of the tree's heart up to the gallows.

The grace of springtide breaks the pain of the garden's crop-sickness, even though the cruelty of winter is still drawing towards crop-sickness.

68

My heart, be seated near that person who has experience of the heart, go under that tree which bears fresh blossoms.

Go not in every direction as do idlers in this druggists' market; sit in the shop of someone who has sugar in his shop.

If you have no balance, then every one waylays you; one man adorns a counterfeit coin, and you imagine that he has gold;

Cheatingly he sets you by the door, saying, "I am coming"—do not sit expectant at the door, for that house has two doors.

5   Do not bring your cup to every pot that seethes, and do not sit there, for every seething pot has within it something else.

Not every reed holds sugar; not every under has an over; not every eye has sight; not every sea holds pearls.

Lament, singing nightingale, because the drunkard's lament has some effect, some effect even on rocks and stones.

Put aside your head if you have no room, for if the thread is not contained in the eye of the needle that is because it has a head.

This wakeful heart is a lantern; hold it under your skirt; pass away from this wind and air, for the air puts it into commotion.

10 When you have passed away from the wind you have become a dweller in a fountain, you have become companion to a confederate who pours cooling water on the heart.

When you have water on your heart, you are like a green tree which constantly yields new fruit, and journeys within the Heart.

69

A fair idol that all the night teaches tricks to Venus and the moon, his two eyes by witchery sew up the two eyes of heaven.

Look out for your hearts, Moslems, for I at all events am so commingled with Him that no heart is commingled with me.

First I was born of His love, finally I gave my heart to Him; when fruit is born of a branch, from that branch it hangs.

I am fleeing from my own shadow, for the light is hidden from the shadow; where shall he rest at last who flees from his shadow?

5 The tip of His tress is saying, "Ha, quick, to the rope-trick!" The cheek of His candle is saying, "Where is the moth, that it may burn?"

For the sake of that rope-trick be brave, and become a hoop; fling yourself into the fire, when His candle is kindled.

When you have seen the joy of burning you will no more endure without the flame; even if the water of life came to you, it would not stir you from the flame.

70

My heart is like an oyster shell, the Beloved's phantom is the pearl; now I am no more contained, for this house is filled with Him.

Night split the lip of my soul with the sweetness of His talk; I am surprised at him who says, "Truth is bitter."

Mortals' food comes from without, but the lover's food is from within; he regurgitates and chews, for the lover is like a camel.

Be swift-faring like a peri, denude yourself of your body; nakedness is not allowed to him who has the mange.

5   Ṣalāḥ al-Dīn has come to the chase; all the lions are his quarry; that man is his servant who is free from the two worlds.

71

Once again the drunkards' head from drunkenness has come into prostration; has perchance that minstrel of the souls struck up music from the veil?

The reckless gamblers of head and soul once more are rioting; being has departed into annihilation, and annihilation has come into being.

Once more the world is full of the sound of Seraphiel's trumpet; the trustee of the unseen has become visible, for goods and chattels have come to the soul.

See how the earthy particles have received fresh life; all their earthiness has turned to purity, all their loss become gain.

5   That world is without colour; yet out of the crucible of the sight, like light, this red and blue have issued from the colour-mixing soul.

The body's portion of this is colour, the soul's portion is delight; for the cauldron's portion from the kitchen fire is smoke.

Consume, O heart, for so long as you are raw, the scent of the Heart will not come from you; when did you ever know anyone to produce the scent of incense without fire?

The scent is always with the incense, it never departed or returned thither; one man says, "It came late," another says, "It came early."

The Emperor has not fled from the ranks, only the helmet and armour are a veil; the veil over his moonlike face is a helmet against the blows of mortals.

72

The month of December has departed, and January too; come, for the spring has come, the earth is green and joyous, the time of the tulips has come.

See how the trees stagger and shake their hands as if drunk! The zephyr has recited a spell, so that the rosebower cannot rest.

The nenuphar said to the jasmine, "See how twisted together I am!" The blossoms said to the meadow, "The grace of the Omnipotent has descended."

The violet genuflected when the hyacinth bowed humbly, when the narcissus gave a wink, saying, "A time for taking note has come."

5   What did the tossing willow say, that it became light-headed with drunkenness? What did that fair-statured cypress behold, that it departed and returned firm of foot?

The painters have taken the brush, with whose hands my soul is intoxicated, for their lovely imageries have lent beauty to the grove.

Thousands of sweet-feathered birds seated on their pulpits are praising and reciting lauds, that the time of divulging has come.

When the soul's bird says "Yā Hū!" the ringdove replies "Where, where?" The former says, "Since you have not caught the scent, your portion is waiting."

The roses are bidden to show their hearts; it is not seemly to hide the heart, when the unveiling of the friend of the cave has come.

10 The rose said to the nightingale, "Look at the green lily—though it has a hundred tongues, it is steadfast and keeps its secret."

The nightingale replied, "Go forth, be busy disclosing my secret, for this love which I possess is reckless like you."

The plane-tree lowered its face to the vine—"Prostrate one, stand up!" The vine answered, "This prostrating of mine is not voluntary.

I am pregnant with that draught which smites at the drunkards; my inward is as fire, your outward is mere plane."

The saffron came forth gay, the mark of lovers on its cheek; the rose pitied it and said, "Ah, this poor creature, how abject it is!"

15 This encounter reached the ears of the laughing-faced, ruby apple, which said to the rose, "It knows not that the Beloved is longsuffering."

When the apple advanced this claim, that "I think well of the Lord," to put it to the proof stones rained from every side.

Someone stoned him; if he was a true lover, he laughs; why should not Shīrīn laugh when pelted by Khusrau?

The throwing of clods by the fair ones is meant for calling the lover; the cruelty of lovers to one another is not a sign of aversion.

If Zulaikhā that moment tore Joseph's shirt and collar, know that it was in sport and play that she unveiled his secret.

20 The apple absorbs the blow and comes not down, saying, "I am happy hanging here, for this honour of being hung on high has come upon me, like Manṣūr.

I am Manṣūr hanging from the branch of the gallows of the All-Merciful; such kissing and embracing has come upon me far from the lips of the vile ones."

Ho, kissing is done with; hide your heart like a turnover; within the breast utter secretly the words innumerable.

73

Today your beauty has another lineament, today your delectable lip has another sweetmeat;

Today your ruby rose has sprung from another twig, today your cypress-stature has another loftiness.

Today that moon of yours indeed is not contained in the sky, and that wheel-like die of yours has another expanse;

Today I know not from which side the commotion has arisen, I only know that through it the world has another riot.

5   That lion-overthrowing deer—it is evident in its eyes that outside the two worlds it has another desert.

This mad heart departed; both heart and madness became lost, for it has another madness loftier than this madness.

If he has no foot, the lover will fly on eternal wings, and if he has no head, the lover has other heads.

The sea of the two eyes sought him and became empty; it was not aware that another sea contains that pearl.

In love I turned the two worlds upside down; why did you seek him here? For he holds another place.

10   My heart's today is love, my heart's tomorrow the Beloved; my heart's today holds in its heart another tomorrow.

If King Ṣalāḥ al-Dīn is hidden, it is no wonder, for out of the jealousy of God every moment he has another master of the harem.

74

Morn-arising friends, who is there that discovers the dawn, who discovers us dancing in confusion like atoms?

Who has the luck to come to the brink of a river to drink water from that river, and to discover the reflection of the moon?

Who is there that like Jacob from the shirt of Joseph seeks the scent of his son, and instead discovers the light of his eyes?

Or athirst like the bedouin casts a bucket into the well, and in the bucket discovers a beauty like an ass-load of sugar?

5 Or like Moses seeking fire, who seeks out a bush, comes to gather the fire, and discovers a hundred dawns and sunrises?

Jesus leaps into the house to escape from the foe; suddenly from the house he discovers a passage to heaven.

Or like a Soloman he splits a fish, and in the belly of that fish he discovers a ring of gold.

Sword in hand, 'Umar comes intending to slay the Prophet; he falls into God's snare, and discovers a kindly regard from fortune.

Or like Adham's son he drives towards a deer to make the deer his prey, and instead discovers another prey.

10 Or like a thirsty oyster shell he comes with gaping mouth to take a drop of water into himself, and discovers a pearl within himself.

Or a man foraging who turns towards desolations, and suddenly in a desolation he discovers news of a treasure.

Traveller, have done with legends, so that intimate alike and stranger may discover without your exposition the light of *Did We not open.*

Whoever strides sincerely towards Shams al-Dīn, though his foot may grow weary, he will discover two wings from Love.

75

Friend, is sugar sweeter or He who makes the sugar? Friend, is the moon fairer or He who makes the moon?

Forgo sugars, forgo moons; He knows something other, He makes something other.

In the sea are marvels besides pearls, but none like the Monarch who makes the sea and the pearls.

Besides the water is another water springing from a marvellous waterwheel; without flaw and unsleeping It provides sustenance to the heart.

Without knowledge it is not possible to fashion an image of a bath; how shall be that Knowledge which makes intellect and awareness?

Without knowledge you cannot extract oil from fat; consider then that Knowledge which makes sight from fat.

Souls are distraught, without eating and slumber, on account of the marvellous feast which He makes at the time of dawn.

Happy dawn, when that despair of every moon makes His two hands a belt around my waist!

Yonder sky laughs at the mustachios of that deluded one; that laughingstock makes himself an ass in the train of two or three asses.

10 That ass flings himself into gold as if into barley; he is heedless of the King who makes gems of stones.

I have made enough, enough, I have quit exhalation; the rest that Darling will speak, who makes of the ear an eye.

76

That wandering slave has returned, returned; he has come before You burning and melting like a candle.

Smile upon him, O Soul, like anemone and sugar-candy; do not shut the door, O Soul, for he comes in need.

And even if You close the door, he will submit to Your decree; the servant is all servile need, the king is full of pride and disdain.

Every molten candle has become the brightness of the eye, for he who has suffered melting has become privy to the secret.

5 If I make a difference between envenomed water from His hand and wine, in the path of the Spirit my spirit has come, by Allah, but insincerely.

How should any animal drink His water of life? How should the eye which is closed behold His face?

I have abandoned travel, I have come to dwell with the Friend, I have become secure from death because that long life has come.

My heart, since you are in this stream why then do you still seek for water? How long will you say, "Come to the Feast"? The time of prayer has come.

77

Why must I dance in the glow of His sun? So that when the mote dances, He may remember me.

Every atom has become pregnant of the glow of His face, every atom of that delight gives birth to a hundred atoms.

Behold, in the mortar, how the body out of love for one fleet of spirit beats and bruises itself to become an atom.

If you are pearl and coral, only become grain-fine here, because in this presence only a mote is becoming.

5   Behold the pearl of the soul in the oyster shell of the body, how it bites its fingers at the hand of affliction.

When the spirit takes flight from you, this imprisoned essence returns to its origin like a mote—you may call to it, but it will not come.

And though its load be very firm and it digs in blood, though for a whole life it goes in blood, not one hair of it will be defiled.

Its only dwelling place is in the well of Babylon; until the soul becomes a magician, it reposes not in any place.

Tabriz! If Shams al-Dīn shines forth from your zodiac, even the cloud will become like the moon, even the moon will wax in brightness.

78

Every moment the Soul is decaying and growing before you, and how should any man plead with you for the sake of a single soul?

Wherever you set your foot a head springs from the earth; for one head's sake how should anyone wash his hands of you?

On the day when the soul takes flight in joy at your scent, the soul knows, the soul knows, what scent wafts from the Beloved.

Once your crop-sickness diminishes from the brain, the head raises a hundred laments, every hair is groaning.

5   I have emptied house, that I may be filled with your furniture; I am waning, that your love may wax and increase.

My soul in the train of Shams al-Ḥaqq-i Tabrīzī is scudding like a ship without feet over the sea.

79

Do not despair, my soul, for hope has manifested itself; the hope of every soul has arrived from the unseen.

Do not despair, though Mary has gone from your hands, for that light which drew Jesus to heaven has come.

Do not despair, my soul, in the darkness of this prison, for that king who redeemed Joseph from prison has come.

Jacob has come forth from the veil of occlusion, Joseph who rent Zulaikhā's veil has come.

5   You who all through night to dawn have been crying "O Lord," mercy has heard that "O Lord" and has come.

O pain which has grown old, rejoice, for the cure has come; O fastened lock, open, for the key has come.

You who have abstained fasting from the Table on high, break your fast with joy, for the first day of the feast has come.

Keep silence, keep silence, for by virtue of the command "Be!" that silence of bewilderment has augmented beyond all speech.

80

Die now, die now, in this Love die; when you have died in this Love, you will all receive new life.

Die now, die now, and do not fear this death, for you will come forth from this earth and seize the heavens.

Die now, die now, and break away from this carnal soul, for this carnal soul is as a chain and you are as prisoners.

Take an axe to dig through the prison; when you have broken the prison you will all be kings and princes.

5 Die now, die now before the beauteous King; when you have died before the King, you will all be kings and renowned.

Die now, die now, and come forth from this cloud; when you come forth from this cloud, you will all be radiant full moons.

Be silent, be silent; silence is the sign of death; it is because of life that you are fleeing from the silent one.

81

The weary ones have all gone; close the door of the house; laugh all in union at aweary reason.

Come forth to the Ascension, since you are of the Prophet's family; kiss the cheek of the moon, since you are on a high roof.

Since he split the moon, why are you clouds? Since he is sprightly and neat, why are you good-for-nothing?

Weary ones, why did you depart? For not like true men on this path did you like Farhād and Shaddād in a moment cleave through the mountain.

5 Since you are not moon-faced, turn not away from the moon-faced; since you are not in anguish, do not bandage your own heads.

Like that it did happen and like this; so it comes not right; do not know how you are, do not know how many you are!

When you beheld that fountain, why did you not become water? When you saw that Self, why did you approve your own selves?

Since you are in the mine of sugarcane, why are you sour of face? Since you are in the Water of Life, why are you dry and withered?

Do not contend so, do not flee from felicity; what possibility of flight is there, seeing that you are in the toils of the lasso?

10 You are caught in the lasso from which there is no security; do not writhe, do not writhe, do not scrape against the shuttle.

Like self-sacrificing moths rub against this candle; why are you dedicated to the companion? Why are you attached to the chain?

Burn at this candle, light up your heart and soul, put on a new body when you have flung away this old one.

Why are you afraid of the fox? You are of lion stock. Why are you lame asses, since you are of the loins of the swift horse?

The Friend Himself is coming, the door of felicity is opening, for that friend is the key; you are all locks.

15 Be silent, for speech has swallowed you down; the purchaser is like a parrot, and you are all sugar-candy.

82

Since your image dwelt within the house of our breasts, wherever we sit has become like highest paradise.

Those thoughts and imaginings that were as Gog and Magog—each one has become like a houri's cheek and a doll of China.

That image on account of which men and women all weep, if it was once an evil companion, has now become an excellent companion.

Above all a garden has grown, below all is a treasure—what manner of thing are you, that through you the world has become so?

5 From that day when we beheld him we augment daily; the thorn that sought him out has become a veritable rosebower.

Every unripe grape has become a ripe grape from the sun and has become full of sugar, and that black stone too through the sun has become a precious ruby.

Many an earth there is that by God's preference has become a heaven, many a left hand through the palm of divine favour has become a right hand.

If once he was darkness to the heart, now he has become the heart's window; if once he was a footpad of the faith, now he has become the leader of religion.

If it was the well of calamity that was Joseph's prison, on account of his coming forth it became the firm cord.

10   Every particle like the army of God is subject to God's command; to the servant of God it has proved security, to the infidel it has become as an ambush.

Silence! For your speech is as the Nile—to the Copts like blood, to the Israelites a pure well.

Silence! For your speech is a ripe fig, only not every bird of the air is suitable for figs.

83

At the dawn hour a moon appeared in the sky, came down from the sky and gazed upon me.

Like a hawk which seizes a bird at the time of hunting, that moon snatched me up and ran over the sky.

When I gazed at myself I saw myself no more, because in that moon my body through grace became like the soul.

When I voyaged in soul I saw naught but the moon, so that the secret of the eternal revelation was all disclosed.

5   The nine spheres of heaven were all absorbed in that moon, the ship of my being was entirely hidden in the sea.

That sea surged, and Reason arose again and cast abroad a voice; thus it happened and so it befell.

That sea foamed, and at every foam-fleck something took form and something was bodied forth.

Every foam-fleck of body which received a sign from that sea melted forthwith and became spirit in that sea.

Without the royal fortune of Shams al-Dīn of Tabriz one could neither behold the moon nor become the sea.

84

Birds, who are now parted from your cage, show your faces
again and declare where you are.

Your ship has stopped on this water, wrecked; like fishes, for
one instant rise from this water.

Is it that the mould has broken and rejoined that Friend? Or
has the trap slipped out of hand, and you are parted from the
prey?

Are you today fuel to that fire of yourselves? Or has the fire
in you died, and are you the light of God?

5   Has that wind become a pestilence and congealed you? Or
has it become the breeze of the zephyr, wherever you enter?

There is an answer from your souls in every word that pro-
ceeds, even though you may not open your mouths to answer.

How many pearls you have broken in the mortar of the days!
That is surmeh {collyrium} to the eyes; pound on, pound on!

You who have been born when you arrived at death, this is a
second birth—be born, be born!

Whether you are born Hindu or Turk a second time will
become clear on the day when you remove the veil.

10   And if it be that you have been worthy of Shams al-Ḥaqq of
Tabriz, by Allah, you are the high chamberlains of the day of
retribution.

85

Though the whole world be full of thorns, the heart of the
lover is wholly a rosebower;

And though heaven's wheel be idle and ineffective, the world
of lovers is fully employed.

Let all other men be sorrowful, yet the lover's soul will be
gay and happy and sprightly.

Give to the lover every place where a candle is extinguished, for he is endowed with a hundred thousand lights.

5   Even if the lover is alone, he is not alone, for his is companioned by the hidden Beloved.

The wine of lovers bubbles up from the breast; love's companion is in the inmost secrets.

Love is not content with a hundred promises, for the cunning of the heart-enchanters is manifold.

And if you should see a lover sick, is not the fair one at the sick one's head?

Be a rider of love, and fear not the way, for love's steed is swift of pace;

10   With a single bound it brings you to the abode, even though the road be not even.

The soul of the lover knows nothing of fodder-eating, for the souls of lovers are vintners of fine wine.

In Shams al-Dīn-i Tabrīzī you will discover a heart which is at once intoxicated and very sober.

86

Rajab has gone out and Shaʿbān has entered; the soul has quit the body, and the Beloved has entered.

The breath of ignorance and the breath of heedlessness have gone forth; the breath of love and the breath of forgiveness have entered.

The heart is sprouting roses and eglantine and basil, since from the cloud of generosity rain has arrived.

The mouths of all the sorrowful ones are laughing because of this candy which has entered the teeth.

5   Man is wearing gold brocade like the sun, since that gold-scattering moon-faced one has entered.

Clap hands and speak, minstrel of love, for that ringleader of trouble has entered stamping feet.

If yesterday has gone, may today remain forever, and if ʿUmar has departed, ʿUthmān has entered.

All the past life is returning, since this eternal prosperity has entered.

If you are drunk and asleep in the ship of Noah, why should you worry if the Flood has arrived?

10   The earth of Tabriz has become lit up like the sky, since Shams al-Dīn has entered that maidan {= arena, square}.

87

We have departed—may the remainder long remain! Inescapably every man who has been born must depart.

Heaven's bowl has never seen any dish that did not in the end fall from the roof.

Do not run about so, for in this earth the pupil has become even as the master.

Lovely one, put not on airs, for in this grave many a Shīrīn has become naughted, the same as Farhād.

5   After all, what constancy is there in an edifice whose columns are but fragments of wind?

If we were evil, we carried away evil; if we were good, then may you remember!

Though you may be the unique one of your time, today you will be departing as one by one.

If you do not wish to remain alone, make children of obedience to God and good actions.

That thread of unseen light is immortal, because it is the pith of the spirit of the Pegs;

10   That essence of love, which is the quintessence—that remains to all eternity.

If these shifting sands are unstable, another kind of foundation is laid down.

I am like Noah's ark in this dry land, for that flood is the sealing of the promised time.

Noah made his house an ark, because he saw from the unseen the wave overtowering.

We have fallen asleep amongst the silent ones, because we have passed all bounds in clamour and lamentation.

88

That Joseph handsome of cheek has come, that Jesus of the age has come;

That banner of a hundred thousand victories has come fluttering over the cavalcade of spring.

You whose business it is to bring the dead to life, arise, for the day of work has come.

The lion which seizes lions a-hunting has come into the meadowland raging drunk.

5 Yesterday and the day before have departed; seize the cash, for that coin of fair assay has come.

This city today is like paradise; it is saying, "The Prince has come."

Beat the drum, for it is the day of festival; be joyous, for the Friend has come.

A moon has lifted its head out of the unseen, in comparison with which this moon has become as dust;

Because of the beauty of those souls' repose, the whole world has become restless.

10 Take heed, spread open the skirt of love, for sprinkling has come from the ninth heaven.

O exile bird with cut pinions, in the place of two wings four have come.

Ho, heart bound in breast, open, for that lost one has come into your bosom.

Foot, come and stamp foot, for that illustrious cupbearer has come.

Speak not of the old man, for he has become young, and speak not of yesteryear, for the Friend has come.

15 You said, "What excuse shall I utter to the king?" The king himself has come making excuses.

You said, "Whither shall I escape out of his hand?" His hand has come bringing all succour.

You saw a fire, and light has come; you saw blood, and red wine has come.

That one who was fleeing from his own fortune, having fled, has come back shamefaced.

Be silent, and count not his graces; an innumerable grace it is that has come.

89

We have become drunk and our heart has departed, it has fled from us—whither has it gone?

When it saw that the chain of reason was broken, immediately my heart took to flight.

It will not have gone to any other place, it has departed to the seclusion of God.

Seek it not in the house, for it is of the air; it is a bird of the air, and has gone into the air.

5   It is the white falcon of the Emperor; it has taken flight, and departed to the Emperor.

90

We are foes to ourselves, and friends to him who slays us; we are drowned in the sea, and the waves of the sea are slaying us.

For this reason, laughing and gay, we are yielding up sweet life, because that king is slaying us with honey and sugar and sweetmeat.

We make ourselves out fat for the sacrifice of the feast, because that butcher of lovers slays the very fine and handsome.

That Iblis without light begs for a respite from Him; He gave him respite, because He is slaying him after tomorrow.

5   Like Ishmael, cheerfully lay your neck before the knife; do not steal your throat away from Him, if He is slaying, until He slays.

    Azrael has no power or way to overcome lovers; love itself and passion slays the lovers of love.

    The slain ones shout, "Would that my people knew"; secretly the Beloved bestows a hundred lives, and openly slays.

    Put forth a head out of the earth of the body, and then see that He is either drawing you to heaven, or slaying you.

    The spirit of breath He takes away, the comfort spiritual He bestows; He releases the falcon of the soul, and slays the owl of sorrow.

10   That idea the Christian carries abroad, the Moslem has not that idea, that He is slaying this Messiah upon the cross.

    Every true lover is like Manṣūr, they slay themselves; show any beside the lover who deliberately slays himself!

    Death daily makes a hundred requisitions on mankind; the lover of God without requisition slays himself.

    I make this enough, else I will myself utter the secret of the lovers' {death}, though the unbeliever slays himself of anger and fury.

    Shams-i Tabrīzī has climbed over the horizon like the sun; unceremoniously he is extinguishing the candles of the stars.

91

    Behold, those birds which lay golden eggs every morning saddle the swift colt of the skies.

    When they gallop, the seventh heaven is their arena; when they sleep, they {make their pillow} the sun and the moon.

    They are fishes, in the soul of each one of which is a Jonah; they are rosebushes which beautify and order well the skies.

    Hell-tasters, heaven-givers, on the day of resurrection they are the rulers, they know neither any blessing nor utter any imprecation.

They set the mountains dancing of subtlety in the air, and convert the seas in sweetness to be like sweet sugar.

They make bodies souls, and souls everlasting; they make stones into ruby mines, and unbelief into faith.

They are more manifest than all, and more hidden than all; if you wish to behold them, they make themselves visible before your eyes.

If you wish to behold clearly, make surmeh {collyrium} of the dust of their feet; for they cause him who was blind from his mother's womb to see the way.

If you are a thorn, be sharp of point as a thorn in the quest, that they may convert your whole thorn into the likeness of roses and eglantine.

10 If there were scope for speech, I would utter things that may be spoken, so that the spirits and the angels would applaud out of heaven.

92

Last night our elephant remembered India again, in frenzy he was rending the veil of night till dawn.

Last night the flagons of the sakis were all overbrimming— O may our life be like last night till the day of resurrection!

The wines were bubbling and the reasons were senseless on account of him; may part and whole, thorn and rose be happy because of his lovely face!

The cup-on-cup clamour of the drunkards mounted to heaven; in our hands was the wine, and in our heads the wind.

5 Thousands of uproars fell upon the skies because of these, there hundreds of thousands of Kai-Qubāds were fallen prostrate.

The day of triumph and good fortune was contained in our night; of the brethren of purity night suddenly gave birth to such a day.

The sea broke into waves; heaven received a token of this night, and in pride set that token on its head and face.

Whatever ways humanity had closed in darkness, the light of divinity in compassion was opening up.

How should the sensible forms on account of that passion remain in place? How should he remain in place who attains this desire?

10 Begin life anew, Moslems! For the Beloved has converted non-entity into being, and dispensed justice to the lovers.

Our Beloved henceforward holds the fallen to be pardonable, because wherever He is the saki no one remains on the right course.

The surging of the sea of grace, Moslems, has wrecked the pomp of personal effort and the programme of belief.

That grace is King Ṣalāḥ al-Dīn, for he is a Joseph whom the Lord of Egypt himself must purchase at a great price.

93

I have come to lay my face in the dust of the Beloved's feet, I have come to beg pardon for a moment for my actions.

I have come to take up anew the service of His rosebower, I have come to bring fire and set my thorns alight.

I have come to get purification from the dust of all that has passed, to reckon my good deeds as evil as performed in the cause of my Beloved;

I have come with eyes weeping, that my eyes may behold paradise—fountains consisting of the love of that blandisher of mine.

5 Rise, disencumbered passion, take up love anew; I have died and become void of my old faith and unbelief;

For without your straining-cloth it is impossible to become unsullied in existence, without You it is impossible ever to escape from one's sorrows and griefs.

Outwardly I have fallen silent; but You know that inwardly I have bloodstained speech in my blood-consuming heart.

In this state of silence examine well my face, that You may see on my cheeks a myriad traces of yourself.

I have shortened this ode; the rest of it is in my heart; I will utter it, if You intoxicate me with your vintner eye.

10   O silent from speaking, O you sundered from your mate, how did you become thus distraught from your clever reason?

Silent one, how are you faring with these fiery thoughts? Thoughts are arriving with their huge-panoplied army.

When people are alone, they are silent; one speaks with men, no one speaks the secret of his heart to door and wall.

Perchance you find no men to talk with, that you have fallen silent? Perchance you see no man to be intimate with your words?

Are you haply of the pure world? Do not you mix with material things, with dogs of natural being who are defiled with their own carrion?

94

The dead would rend his shroud and rise from the tomb, if that dead man had tidings of my Idol.

What will dead and living do when he discovers something of Him? For if the mountain beheld Him, it would leap and advance.

I will not flee from blame, for the blame comes from you; from your bitterness all the taste of sugar comes to the soul.

Devour whatever has come to you, leave it not to store up, for you are on the banks of a running stream—when you have drunk, more will come.

5   Behold His fair handiwork, listen to His inspiration to the hearts; become entirely light of vision—all rapture comes from vision.

Do not despair, saying, "My life is gone, and the Friend has not come"; He comes betimes and out of season, He comes not only at dawn.

Be watchful and wakeful in season and out of season, for suddenly our King enters the eyes like 'Uzaizī antimony.

When He enters this eye, this eye becomes like the sea; when He gazes on the sea, out of all its waters pearls come;

Not such a dead pearl that knows not its own essence, pearls will come all speaking, all seeking, altogether alive.

10   What do you know, what do you know what kind of mind and soul you are? It is God who knows and sees the virtue that belongs to men.

Become accustomed to speak without lips, like a balance, for lips and teeth do not remain when one passes from the world.

95

Say, do not despair because the Beloved drives you away; if He drives you away today, will He not call you back tomorrow?

If He shuts the door on you, do not go away; be patient there, for after patience He will seat you in the place of honour.

And if He bars against you all ways and passages, He will show you a secret way, which no man knows.

Is it not the case that when the butcher cuts off the head of a sheep with his knife, he does not abandon what he has slain, but first slays, and then draws?

5   When no more breath remains to the sheep, he fills it with his own breath; you will see whither God's breath will bring you!

I spoke this as a parable; else, His generosity slays no man, rather it rescues him from slaying.

He gives all the kingdom of Solomon to a single ant; He bestows both worlds, and does not startle a single heart.

My heart has travelled round the world and found none like Him; whom does He resemble? Whom does He resemble?

Ah, silence! For without speech He gives to all of this wine to taste, He gives to taste, He gives to taste, He gives to taste.

96

Ho, lovers, labour so that, when body and soul remain no more, your hearts may fly to heaven, not remain heavy like the body.

Wash your hearts and souls in the water of wisdom clean of dust, ho, that the two eyes of regret may not remain turned towards the earth.

Is it not the case with everything in the world, that love is its vital soul? Apart from love, everything you see remains not eternally.

Your nonexistence (before birth) is as the east, your death is as the west, oriented to another heaven that resembles not this visible heaven.

5 The way to heaven is within; shake the wings of love—when love's wings have become strong, there is no need to trouble about a ladder.

Consider not the world that exists without, for the true world is within the eye; when you have shut your eyes on the world, the world will not remain.

Your heart is like a roof, and your senses are waterspouts; drink water from the roof, for the waterspout remains not for ever.

Recite entirely this ode from the tablet of the heart; regard not the tongue, for lips and tongue do not remain.

Man's body is a bow, breath and speech are as its arrows; once the arrows and quiver have gone, no more work remains for the bow.

97

All slept, and yet sleep did not transport me, heart-forlorn as I am; all night my eyes counted the stars in the sky.

Sleep had so departed from my eyes as if never to return;

my sleep had quaffed the poison of separation from you, and expired.

How would it be if you concocted a remedy out of encounter for one wounded, who has committed his heart and eyes to your hands?

No, it is not right to close the door of beneficence once and for all; if you will not give pure wine, less than one mouthful of dregs will you not give?

5 God has placed all manners of delight in a single chamber; no man without you ever found the right way into that chamber.

If I have become dust in the path of love, regard me not as insignificant; how should he who beats on the door of union with you be insignificant?

Fill my sleeve with unseen pearls—a sleeve which has wiped many a tear from these eyes.

Whenever the policeman of love has constrained anyone on a dark night, your moon has compassionately pressed him in its silvery bosom.

If the wandering heart returns of your grace, it is the story of the night, the disk of the moon, the camel, and the Kurd.

10 Were not these inanimates originally of water? The world is a cold place; it came and congealed one by one.

Our blood in our body is the water of life, and sweet; when it comes forth from its place, see how it is all the same!

Do not congeal the water of speech, and bring it not from that fountain, so that it is silk on that side and striped cloth on this.

98

Have you heard that sugar has become cheap in the town? Have you heard that winter has vanished and summer is here?

Have you heard that basil and carnation in the garden are laughing surreptitiously because affairs have become easy?

Have you heard that the nightingale has returned from his travels, joined in the concert and become the master of all the birds?

Have you heard that now in the garden the branches of the trees have heard glad news of the rose, and shake their hands?

5   Have you heard that the soul has become drunk from the cup of spring, and gone off gay and dancing into the Sultan's sanctuary?

Have you heard that the anemone's cheeks are suffused with blood? Have you heard that the rose has become head chamberlain of the divan?

Have you heard about the thievishness of mad December, how the just officer of spring has come, and he has disappeared?

These idols have obtained laissez-passer from the divan, so that the earth has become green and arrayed in full splendour.

If the beauties of the garden last year wrought wonders, each one this year has emerged in beauty a hundredfold as great.

10   Rose-cheeked ones have come forth whirling out of non-existence, such that the stars in heaven are but scatter before their feet.

The deposed narcissus has become the inspector of the kingdom; the infant bud like Jesus has become understanding and chanting.

The feast of these creatures of joy has once more taken on ornament; once more the breeze of the zephyr bestows wine on the garden.

There were images hidden behind the veil of the heart; the orchards have become mirrors to the secret of their hearts.

Whatever you behold, seek from the heart, do not seek from the mirror; the mirror may receive an image, but it cannot become alive.

15   All the dead ones of the garden have come to life at the summons of God; their unbelief by God's mercy has all been turned to faith.

They are continuing in their shrouds, and are all stirring, for that which is alive cannot become pledged for ever to prison;

He said, "Make this enough, for I will expound this better than this." I shut my mouth, for He had come and become surety.

The King's lips will likewise describe all completely, if the summary has departed from you into the bosom of concealment.

99

This fledgling pigeon essayed the air and flew off when he heard a whistle and a call from the unseen.

When that Desire of all the world sent a messenger saying, "Come to Me," how should not the disciple's soul take flight?

How should it not fly upwards on discovering such pinions, how should it not rend the body's robe on the arrival of such a missive?

What a moon it is that draws all these souls! What a way is that secret way by which it drew!

5 Divine compassion sent a letter saying, "Come back hither, for in this narrow cage your soul has fluttered much.

But in the house without doors you are like a bird without wings; so the fowl of the air does when it has fallen low.

Restlessness opens to it the door of compassion at last; beat your wings against door and roof—this is the key.

Until you call on Me, you do not know the way of returning; for by Our calling the way becomes manifest to the reason."

Whatever mounts up, if it be old it becomes new; whatever new descends here, through time it becomes threadbare.

10 Ho, strut proudly into the unseen, do not look back, in God's protection, for there all is profit and increase.

Ha, silent one, depart to the Saki of Being, who gave you His pure wine in this sullied cup.

100

Lord, is this sweet scent coming from the meadow of the soul, or is it a breeze wafting from beyond the world?

Lord, from what homeland does this water of life bubble up? Lord, from what place comes this light of the attributes?

Amazing! Does this clamour arise from the troop of the angels? Amazing! Does this laughter come from the houris of paradise?

What concert is it, that the soul spins round dancing? What whistle is it, that the heart is coming flapping wings?

5   What a marriage feast it is! What a wedding! Heaven is like a curtain; the moon with this plate of gold for a sign is coming.

What a hunt! For the arrow of fate is flying; if it is not so, why comes the sound of the bow?

Good news, good news, lovers all! Clap your hands, for he who once escaped from your hands is coming clapping.

From the fortress of the skies the cry of "safe quarter" is arising, and from the sea such a wave of fear is coming.

The eye of prosperity is intoxicated with your approaching; this is a proof that is obvious to the eye.

10   Escape from this world of dearth, where lances strike for the sake of two or three loaves.

What is fairer than life? Yet if life should go, have no fear; why do you grieve about its departing, seeing that better than it is coming?

Every man is amazed at something; my amazement is, how it is that when He enters the midst, He is not contained in the midst.

Let me have done. Though it is a cipher, I will not explain it; what are you trying to explain? The soul of explanation is coming.

IOI

Amazing keeper of the hot baths! When he comes forth from seclusion, every painted figure of the baths falls into prostration!

The figures, frozen, unconscious, dead—from the reflection of his eyes their eyes open large as narcissi.

Through his ears their ears become familiar with fables, through his eyes their eyes become receptive of vistas.

You behold every single bath-figure drunk and dancing, like a boon companion who from time to time plunges in red wine.

5   The courtyard of the baths is full of their clamour and shouting; the riotous clamour marks the first day of resurrection.

The figures call one another unto themselves; one figure from that corner there comes laughing to another figure.

But no form discovers the bath-keeper himself, for all that form is running hither and thither in search of him.

All are distracted, he behind and before them, unrecognized, the king of the souls comes at the head of the army.

The rosebed of every mind is filled with roses from his cheeks; the skirt of every beggar is filled with gold from his hand.

10   Hold your basket before him, that he may fill it of himself, so that the basket of your poverty may become the despair of Sanjar.

Judge and plaintiff alike flee from less and more, when that moon for one moment enters drunk into the assembly.

The wine becomes the tavern, the dead become riotous drunk, the wood becomes the Moaning Pillar when he enters the pulpit.

He denies them his presence, and their forms freeze, their eyes vanish, their ears become deaf.

When he appears again their eyes open, the garden becomes full of birds, the orchard is verdant.

15   Go to the rosebed and the garden, behold the friends and the chatter; in the wake of this expression the soul comes to that pass.

How can one tell what was manifested, friend? How can the pen indite that, for all that it enters the inkholder?

102

Little by little the drunkards congregate, little by little the wine-worshippers arrive.

The heart-cherishers coquettishly come along the way, the rosy-cheeked ones are arriving from the garden.

Little by little from the world of being and not-being the not-beings have departed and the beings are arriving.

All with skirts full of gold as a mine are arriving for the sake of the destitute.

5 The lean and sick from the pasturage of love are arriving fat and hale.

The souls of the pure ones like the rays of the sun are arriving from such a height to the lowly ones.

Blessed is that garden, where, for the sake of the Mary's, new fruits are arriving even in winter.

Their origin is grace, and their return is grace; even from the garden to the garden they are coming.

103

Laughter tells of your lovingkindness, tears complain of your wrath;

These two mutually contrary messages relate in this world about a single Beloved.

Lovingkindness beguiles a heedless man in such a way that he is not anxious about wrath, and commits sin;

The other man wrath endows with hopelessness, so that he keeps complete despair.

5 Love, like a pitying intercessor, comes to the protection of both these lost souls.

We give thanks for this love, O God, which performs infinite
lovingkindnesses;

Whatever shortcomings in our gratitude we may be guilty of,
love suffices to make amends for it.

Is this love Kauthar, or the Water of Life? It makes life with-
out bound and term;

Between the sinner and God, like the Messenger, it runs
much to and fro and busies itself greatly.

10   Make an end of verse on verse; do not recite this; love itself
will interpret the verse.

104

The lovers visible and the Beloved invisible—who ever saw
such a love in all the world?

Not one lip having attained the form of the Beloved, hun-
dreds of thousands of souls have expired.

Two bowshots' distance shot an arrow from the heights, so
that it tore through the shields of the skies.

Not having drawn the skirt of the Beloved of the Unseen,
the hearts of thousands have suffered tribulation and
beating;

5   Not having bitten the lip of Him whose lip is sweet, how
many have bitten the back of the hand in banishment!

Not having grazed on the sugar-cane of His lip, the heart has
grazed on His thousands of blandishments.

Not one rose having blossomed from His rosegarden, hun-
dreds of thousands of thorns have pricked in the breast.

Though the soul has experienced nothing but cruelty
from Him, it has fled away from mortal fidelities in hope of
Him;

It has preferred that pain over generosities, and has chosen
that cruelty above all fidelities.

10   His thorn has triumphed over all roses, His lock is more de-
lightful than a hundred keys.

His tyranny has carried off the ball from the turn of good fortune; candies have blossomed from the poison of His wrath.

His rejection is better than the reception of others; ruby and pearl are desirous of His stone.

These worldly happinesses are nothing; seek that happiness which Bū Sa'īd possesses.

These augmentations of this world are less; seek that augmentation which Bā Yazīd possesses.

15 That augmentation is your six-fingered hand; its value is less, though apparently it is augmenting.

Seek that radiance which Sanā'ī expounded, that Unique One whose uniqueness 'Aṭṭār revealed.

Fat and sweet food appear pure and good; one night they passed with you, and became filth.

Eat the fat and sweet of the food of love, that your wings may sprout and you may know how to fly.

After all, Abraham as a child in the cave sucked from the fingertips of a lion.

20 Dismiss that; that foetus in the womb sucked the water of life from blood.

The tall stature which heaven made upright in the end became bowed like the crooked heaven;

The tall stature which Love raised up, its stature transcended the glorious Throne.

Nay, be silent; He who knows all secrets is present; He said, *We are nearer than the jugular vein.*

105

Our death is an eternal wedding-feast; what is the secret of this? *He is God, One.*

The sun became dispersed through the windows; the windows became shut, and the numbers departed.

Those numbers which existed in the grapes are naughted in the juice which flows from the grapes.

Whosoever is living by the light of God, the death of this spirit is replenishment to him.

5   Speak not evil, speak not good regarding those who have passed away from good and evil.

Fix your eye on God, and speak not of what you have not seen, that He may implant another eye in your eye.

That eye is the eye of the eye, nothing unseen or secret escapes from it.

When its gaze is by the Light of God, to such a light what can be hidden?

Though all lights are the Light of God, call not all of those the eternal Light.

10   Eternal light is that which is the Light of God, transient light is the attribute of flesh and body.

The light in this mortal eye is a fire, save for that eye which God anoints with surmeh {collyrium}.

His fire became light for the sake of Abraham; the eye of reason became in quality like the eye of an ass.

O God, the bird of the eye which has seen Your bounty flies in Your air.

The Pole, he who is the sky of the skies, is on the lookout in search of You;

15   Either grant him vision to see You, or do not dismiss him on account of this fault.

Make tearful the eye of your soul every moment, guard it against the snare of human stature and cheek.

Eye asleep and yourself wakeful—such a sleep is perfection and rectitude;

But the eye asleep that finds no interpretation (of dreams)—expel it from sleep, despite envy.

Else it will labour and be boiling in the fire of love of the One, even to the grave.

106

Everywhere the scent of God is coming—see how the people
are coming uncontrollably;
From him for whom all souls are athirst, to the thirsty the cry
of the water carrier is coming.
They are milk drinkers of divine generosity, and are on the
watch to see from whence the mother is coming.
They are in separation, and all are waiting to see whence
union and encounter are coming.
5   From Moslems, Jews, and Christians alike every dawn the
sound of prayer is coming;
Blessed is that intelligence into whose heart's ear from
heaven the sound of "Come hither" is coming.
Keep your ear clean of scum, for a voice is coming from
heaven;
The defiled ear hears not that sound—only the deserving
gets his deserts.
Defile not your eye with human cheek and mole, for that
Emperor of eternal life is coming;
10   And if it has become defiled, wash it with tears, for the cure
comes from those tears.
A caravan of sugar has arrived from Egypt; the sound of foot-
fall and bells is coming.
Ha, be silent, for to complete the ode our speaking King is
coming.

107

Again the sun of felicity has mounted to heaven, again the
desire of the souls has arrived from the way of the soul.
Again by the good pleasure of Riḍwān the gates of paradise
have been opened, every spirit is plunged up to its neck in the
pool of Kauthar.

Again that King, who is the altar to whom kings turn, has entered, again that Moon surpassing the moon has entered.

These distraught by mad passion have all mounted their steeds, for that King, the unique cavalier, has entered the heart of the army.

5 The particles of dark earth are all bewildered and amazed, having heard from placelessness the cry, "Arise, the resurrection has come!"

The inexpressible proclamation has come, not from within and not from without, not left, not right, not behind, not from before.

You say, "What direction is that?" That direction where there is questing. You say, "Whither shall I turn my face?" Thither this head has come;

Thither whence this ripeness came upon the fruits, thither whence the attributes of gems came upon the stones;

Thither where the dry fish came to life before Khiḍar, thither whence Moses' hand became as a radiant moon.

10 This burning in our hearts has become bright as a candle, this decree has come upon our heads like a crown of pride.

The soul has not leave to utter this exposition, else every infidel would have escaped from unbelief.

The unbeliever in hardship turns his face thither; when he experiences pain on this side, he believes in that side.

Continue in pain, that pain may show you the road thither; that place who sees? The man who is constrained by pain.

That most mighty Emperor has closed the door fast; today he has put on human apparel and entered by the door.

108

The sea can always dispense with the fish, for in comparison with the sea the fish is contemptible.

You will not find fish, my soul, like the sea of the ocean; in the sea of God's ocean there are many fish.

The sea is like a nurse, the fish like a sucking child; the wretched infant is always weeping for milk.

Yet for all this indifference, if the sea should compassionately incline towards a fish, great will be the grace;

5 And that fish which knows that the sea is seeking him—his foot in pride rises above the ether.

That fish which—the sea does no task without the fish's opinion is its counsellor—

You might say that so highly favoured a fish is an emperor, and that infinite sea is his minister.

If anyone should dare to call him a fish, every drop in his wrath would be as an arrow.

How long will you speak in riddles? Your riddles bring bewilderment; expound a little more clearly, that the heart may perceive.

10 Worshipful Shams-i Dīn is both Lord and Master, for by him the earth of Tabriz is all musk and ambergris.

Should the thorns of the world behold his graces, in softness and delicacy they would become like silk.

May I never have a soul, if my soul after tasting his wine and being drunk with his beauty is self-aware.

109

There was no grace left which that fair idol did not perform; what fault is it of ours, if he acted not generously towards you?

You are upbraiding because that beauty was cruel; whoever saw a lovely one in both worlds who acted not cruelly?

His love is sugar enough, even if he gave not sugar; his beauty is all fidelity, even if he was not faithful.

Show me a house that is not filled with lamps of him; show me a portico which his cheek has not filled with brightness.

5 This eye and that lamp are two lights, each one on its own; when the two met, none made parting between them.

When the spirit became lost in contemplation, it said this: "None has contemplated the beauty of God but God."

Each one of these similitudes is at once an exposition and an error; only out of jealousy God named His Face, *By the Forenoon*.

The sun of the face of Shams al-Dīn, Pride of Tabriz, never shone on aught transient but it made it eternal.

110

The fire the day before yesterday whispered secretly to the smoke, "The aloes-wood cannot rest without me, and with me it is happy.

It knows well my worth, and expresses thanks to me, for the aloes-wood has perceived that in its passing away there is profit.

The aloes-wood was knotted and tied from head to foot; in the release of nonexistence these knots were resolved.

Hail and welcome to you, my flame-eating friend, my passer-away and martyr and pride of all witnesses."

5   See how heaven and earth are pawns of existence; flee into nonexistence from the blindness of the one and the blueness of the other.

Every soul which flees away from poverty and nonexistence is misfortune fleeing away from prosperity and good fortune.

Without expunging, no one profits from the tablet of nonexistence; make peace between me and expunging, O loving One!

Until yonder dark earth passed away from itself, it did not begin to augment or escape from inertia.

So long as sperm was sperm and did not become obliterated from seminal fluid, it attained not the cypress' stature nor the cheeks' beauty.

10   When bread and broth ferment in the intestines, they then become reason and soul, the despair of the envious.

So long as black rock did not pass away from itself, it did not become gold and silver, neither found its way into coins.

First comes lowliness and bondage, then afterwards there is
kingship; in the ritual prayer men first stand, and then sit.

For a lifetime you have made trial of your own being; once it
is also necessary to experience not-being.

The pomp and pride of poverty and passing-away is no
empty boast; whenever smoke appears, it is not without a fire.

15   If our minds and desires belong not to love, how did love
wantonly rob us of heart and turban?

Love entered, and draws us along by the ear every morning
to the school of *those who fulfil their covenants.*

Love sets flowing the water of penitence from the eye of
the believer, to wash his breast clean of anger and stubborn
denial.

You are fallen asleep and the water of Khiḍar splashes beside
you; leap up from slumber and seize the goblet of immortality.

Let love tell you the rest of it secretly from me; be one with
the Companions of the Cave, alike *sleeping* and *waking.*

III

The sweetheart appeared asleep. I called from the garden,
"Quick, I have stolen a peach!" The sweetheart in fact was not
asleep;

He laughed and said, "The fox then with cunning—how did
it so easily steal the quarry from the lion's hands?"

Who milks a cloud? Who succeeds in reaching there, unless
perchance the cloud of itself shows generosity?

How can the nonexistent contrive to bring into existence? It
is God's bounty that bestows existence on the nonexistent.

5   Sit as if nonexistent; for in ritual prayer one only gives the
greeting when seated.

It is through humility that water avails against fire, for fire
stands up whereas water is prostrate.

When the lip is silent, the heart has a hundred tongues; be
silent—how long, how long do you desire to make trial of Him?

112

Dawn has arrived and drawn his polished blade, and from heaven camphor-white morn has broken forth.

The Sufi of the skies has rent his blue robe and shawl deliberately even to the navel.

After being routed, the Rumi of day having found the strength has dragged the Zangi of night from the royal throne.

From that direction whence the Turk of joy and the Hindu of grief arrived there is everlasting going and coming, and the way is not to be seen.

5   O Lord, whither has the army of the Abyssinian king fled? Whence so suddenly has the army of the Caesar of Rum arrived?

Who can catch the scent of this invisible road wrapped in enigma? He who has drunk or tasted of the wine of love preeternal.

Night is bewildered at who has blackened its face; day is bewildered at who has created it so fair.

Earth is bewildered at how one half of it became grass, and the other half grazing, and grazed upon that continually;

Half of it became eater and half for eating, half eager for purity and the other half impure.

10   Night has died and come to life again; it is life after death. O sorrow, slay me, for I am Ḥusain and you are Yazīd.

The pearl held auction, saying, "Who will buy this?" None had the price, so the pearl bought itself from itself.

Saki, today we have all become your guests; every night through you has become a Night of Power, every day a day of festival.

Give from your bowl the wine of *they shall be given to drink of pure wine,* for only new joy will cut away anxiety.

The heart-thirsty reprobates, when they drink wine to excess, when they lose themselves, then they find that key.

15   You have taken up your station beside the vat of Unity along with Noah and Lot and Karkhī and Shiblī and Bā Yazīd.

Be silent; for the spirit in joy is flapping its wings, so that that draught has coursed into the head and veins of the spirit.

113

Unbelief has put on black garments; the Light of Muhammad has arrived. The drum of immortality has been beaten; the eternal kingdom has arrived.

The face of earth is turned green; heaven has rent her robe; once again the moon is split; the incorporeal spirit has arrived.

The world is filled with sugar; happiness has bound its waist; arise, for once again that moon-cheeked one has arrived.

The heart like an astrolabe has become the token of the seven heavens; the commentary on the heart of Aḥmad has arrived in seven volumes.

5   One night shackled reason approached the sultan of love, saying, "Fettered spirit has arrived to your good favour."

The messenger of the lovers' hearts ran head-downwards like a pen; the good tidings sweet as sugar have arrived in the heart of the page.

How long will the pure spirits endure under the earth? Ho, leap forth from the tomb—God-assisted victory has arrived.

The drum of resurrection has been beaten, the trumpet of uprising is sounding; the time has come, you dead ones—the mustering renewed has arrived.

Scattered is what is in the tombs, known is what is in the breasts; the voice of the trumpet has sounded; the spirit has arrived at its goal.

10   Last night a tumult arose amongst the stars, for the most auspicious star arrived from the propitious ones.

Mercury became out of control, he broke the Tablet and the Pen; in his wake Venus leaped, drunken arrived at the Pole Star.

The moon's orb grew pale, she fled towards Leo. I said, "I trust all is well"; she said, "The unselfed saki has arrived."

Reason in the midst of that tumult desired to show itself; a child is still a child, even if it has arrived at the ABC.

Arise, for this is our turn, the King of the world is ours; since His gaze fell upon our souls, eternal life has arrived.

15   The saki without hue and bragging has poured out wine unstinted; the mountain of Qāf danced like a camel; joy extended has arrived.

The Solomon of the spirit has again cried, "Welcome to the morning cup!" The pavilion smoothed has arrived to dazzle Bilqīs.

Despite the envious ones of religion, in defiance of the accursed devil, the salve of heart and eye has arrived in the ophthalmic eye.

For the sake of the uninitiated I have clapped a lock on my mouth; minstrel, arise and cry, "Eternal delight has arrived."

114

A little fox carried off the sheep's tail; was the lion perchance asleep? The blind and blue fox does not carry off its own life from the lion.

The lion purposely gave way, otherwise who would believe this, that the lame fox stole the sheep's tail from the lion?

He says, "A wolf ate Joseph son of Jacob"; even the lion of the skies cannot loose its talons on him.

Every moment the inspiration of God is guarding our hearts; how should the envious devil snatch our felicity from us?

5   God's hand is outstretched; do not seek to cheat God's hand; whoever sows a grain in God's path reaps barleycorn by barleycorn.

Whoever humiliates you, go, commit him to God; whoever seeks to dismay you, quickly turn your face to God.

Agony and fear and suffering are God's lasso; pain brings you pulling at your ear to the portal of bounty.

"Lord, Lord!" exclaiming, face to heaven turning, tears from your eyes running over your pale cheeks like a river—

Green herbage sprung from the water over your desolate heart and soul, dawn stripping off the veil—*That is the Day of Eternity.*

10   If Pharaoh's head had ached with pain and tribulation, how would that rebel have uttered the boast of divinity?

When the moment of drowning arrived he cried, "I am the least of slaves"; unbelief became faith, and he saw, when calamity showed its face.

Withhold not suffering from your body; plunge it into the current of the Nile, so that your Pharaoh-like body may be purified of stubborn denial.

The carnal soul is prince in Egypt, it is a prisoner in the current of the Nile; be like Gabriel over it, bring smoke out of the aloes-wood.

It is a miserly aloes-wood, it will not convey scent to you nor unlock its secret until it endures fire and smoke.

15   The Pride of Tabriz, Shams-i Ḥaqq u Dīn whispered, "Love is sour-faced with you: it is not fitting to add more vinegar."

115

The month of fasting has come, the emperor's banner has arrived; withhold your hand from food, the spirit's table has arrived.

The soul has escaped from separation and bound nature's hands; the heart of error is defeated, the army of faith has arrived.

The army of *the snorting chargers* has put its hand to plunder, from the fire of *the strikers of fire* the soul is brought to lamentation.

The *Cow* was goodly, Moses son of 'Imrān appeared; through him the dead became living when it was sacrificed.

5   Fasting is as our sacrifice, it is the life of our soul; let us sacrifice all our body, since the soul has arrived as guest.

Fortitude is as a sweet cloud, wisdom rains from it, because it was in such a month of fortitude that the Koran arrived.

When the carnal soul is in need, the spirit goes into Ascension; when the gate of the prison is broken, the soul reaches the Beloved.

The heart has rent the curtain of darkness and winged up to the sky; the heart, being of the angels, has again arrived at them.

Quickly clutch the rope out of this body's well; at the top of the well of water cry, "Joseph of Canaan has arrived."

10   When Jesus escaped from the ass his prayers became accepted; wash your hands, for the Table has arrived from heaven.

Wash your hands and your mouth, neither eat nor speak; seek that speech and that morsel which has come to the silent ones.

116

Hold on the skirt of His grace, for suddenly He will flee; but do not draw Him as an arrow, for He will flee from the bow.

What images does He play at, what tricks contrive! If He is present in form, He will flee by the way of spirit.

Seek Him in the sky, and He shines from the water like the moon; enter the water, and He flees up to heaven.

Call Him from the placeless and He points you to place; seek Him in place and He flees to the placeless.

5   Is not the bird of your imagination fleet as an arrow in existence? Know that for a certainty the Absolute flees from the imaginary.

I will flee from this and that out of fear (not out of weariness) because my gracious Beauty flees from this and that.

Fleet of foot as the wind am I for love of the Rose, not the rose that for fear of the autumn wind flees from the garden.

When it sees an attempt at speaking, His name flees so that you cannot say, "So-and-so will flee."

He will flee from you so that if you draw His image, the image will fly from the tablet, the expression will flee from the heart.

117

What king is He who fashions a king out of dust, for the sake of one or two beggars makes Himself a beggar!

He acts the mendicant like the poor and wretched with His *Give God a loan,* that He may give you a kingdom and fashion a throne.

He passes by the dead and bestows life on the dead, He looks upon pain and contrives a cure for the pain.

When He congeals the wind He makes of the wind water, when He causes the water to boil He fashions out of it air.

5   Look not meanly on the world, for that the world is perishing, for afterwards He will fashion it into an eternal world.

Men marvel at the alchemy which converts copper into gold; regard the copper that every instant fashions alchemy!

If there are a thousand locks on your heart, do not fear; seek the shop of love which the Sweetheart fashions.

He who, without pen and implement, in the idol-house fashions for us a thousand beauteous forms,

Has fashioned for us a thousand Lailās and Majnūns—what form is it that God fashions for the sake of God!

10   If your heart is of iron, weep not for its hardness, for the polishing of His bounty is making it into a mirror of purity.

When you cut away from your friends and go beneath the dust, He will make of snakes and ants fair-featured companions.

Did not Moses fashion the serpent into a succour and a support? Does not He every moment fashion fidelity out of very cruelty?

Look this instant into the grave of your body, what heart-ravishing phantasms He momently fashions there!

When you cleave open your breast, then you see nothing—lest any man should prate idly, saying, "Where does He fashion them?"

15 The proverb says, "Eat the grapes and enquire not of the garden"; God fashions out of stone two hundred fountains of contentment.

Look inside the stone, and there is no trace of the water; it is from the Unseen that He fashions, not out of low and high.

Out of the unconditioned came this conditioned, for out of No He fashions a myriad sayers of Yes.

Behold two rivers of light flowing from two pieces of fat; marvel not that He fashions a stave into a serpent.

Examine these two ears; where is the amber of speech? Marvel at Him who makes of a hole amber!

20 He gives the house a soul and makes it a master; when He slays the master, He fashions of him again a house;

Though the form of the master has descended under the dust, He fashions the heart of the master into an abode of majesty.

To the eye of men who worship form, the master departed, but He is fashioning the master a cloak of a different design.

Be silent, speak less with the tongue of praise and paean, that God may fashion you into paean and praise.

118

On the day of death, when my bier is on the move, do not suppose that I have any pain at leaving this world.

Do not weep for me, say not "Alas, alas!" You will fall into the devil's snare—that would indeed be alas!

When you see my hearse, say not "Parting, parting!" That time there will be for me union and encounter.

When you commit me to the grave, say not "Farewell,
farewell!" For the grave is a veil over the reunion of paradise.

5   Having seen the going-down, look upon the coming-up;
how should setting impair the sun and the moon?

To you it appears as setting, but it is a rising; the tomb appears as a prison, but it is release for the soul.

What seed ever went down into the earth which did not
grow? Why do you doubt so regarding the human seed?

What bucket ever went down and came not out full? Why
this complaining of the well by the Joseph of the spirit?

When you have closed your mouth on this side, open it on
that, for your shout of triumph will echo in the placeless air.

119

Love took away sleep from me—and love takes away sleep,
for love purchases not the soul and mind for so much as half a
barleycorn.

Love is a black lion, thirsty and blood-drinking, it pastures
only on the blood of lovers.

It clings to you in affection, and drags you to the snare;
when you have fallen in, then it looks on from afar.

Love is a tyrannous prince, an unscrupulous police officer, it
tortures and strangles the innocent.

5   Whoso falls into Love's hands weeps like a cloud; whoso
dwells afar from Love freezes like snow.

Every instant Love shatters a thousand bowls into fragments,
every moment stitches and rends a thousand garments.

Love causes a thousand eyes to weep, and goes on laughing;
Love slays miserably a thousand souls, and counts them as one.

Though the simurgh flies happily in Mount Qāf, when it sees
Love's snare it falls, and flies no more.

No man escapes from Love's cords by deceit or madness, no
reasoning man escapes from its snare by intelligence.

10 My words are disordered because of Love, else I would have shown you the ways Love travels;

I would have shown you how Love seizes the lion, I would have shown you how Love hunts the prey.

120

Henceforward the nightingale in the garden will tell of us, it will tell of the beauty of that heart-ravishing Beloved.

When the wind falls upon the head of the willow and it begins to dance, God alone knows what things it says to the air.

The plane-tree understands a little about the meadow's burning, it lifts up two broad hands sweetly and prays.

I ask the rose, "From whom did you steal that beauty?" The rose laughs softly out of shame, but how should she tell?

5 Though the rose is drunk, it is not dissolute like me, that it should tell you the secret of the intoxicated narcissus.

When you seek secrets, go amongst the drunkards, for the tipsy head shamelessly tells the secret.

Inasmuch as wine is the daughter of the vine and the family of generosity, it has opened the purse's mouth and speaks of lavishness;

Especially the wine of the heavenly trellis from the All-generous Almighty; haply God will speak of its lavishness and generosity.

That new wine ferments from the breast of the gnostic, out of the depths of his body's vat it invites you to the feast.

10 Since the breast gives milk, it can also give wine; from the breast its flowing fountain tells a pretty tale.

When that spirit becomes more intoxicated, it stakes its cloak, lays down cap, and abandons this gown.

When the reason drinks blood-red wine recklessly, it opens its mouth and tells the mysteries of Majesty.

Be silent, for no one will believe you; bad copper swallows not what the philosopher's stone says.

Bear tidings to Tabriz, Pride of the World; perchance our
Shams-i Dīn will speak your praise.

121

Love for you makes me oblivious to my own kindred, for
love of you has rooted up the foundations of well-being;

For Love desires only ruination of one's affairs, for Love ac-
cepts counsel from no calamity.

What place is there for wealth and fair repute and respect and
pomp? What is household and safety, what family or children?

When Love's sword snatches away the lover's soul, a thou-
sand lay down their sacred lives in thanks therefor.

5   What, the desire of love for you, and then the fear of ruina-
tion? You with purse fastened, and then the love for that sugar
lip?

Draw back your head and sit in the corner of safety—the
short hand aspires not to the tall cypress.

Go! In all your life you have not caught the scent of Love;
this is not Love, this is reason self-satisfied.

What is it to exercise patience and snatch the skirt out of
temptation, seated to see what will come down from heaven for
a few days?

Love's fire arrived and consumed all that is beside Him; since
all is consumed, sit content and laugh gaily!

10   Especially the love of that One the like of whom, from Alast
till now, has never been so devoted to chastity.

If you say, "I have seen Him," for God's sake open another
eye and close these twain;

For by this glance, thousands of thousands like me and you
in both worlds have been destroyed and blinded for ever.

If to my eye other than that Beauty should come, may my
two eyes be gouged out with an axe!

The sight of all heroic men has proved powerless; how
should the slothful attain the Beauty and Majesty of the King?

15 Would that God had rent the veil of being, even as 'Alī the Lion rent the gates of Khaibar,

That the eye might have seen how for a thousand years, five times a day, the drums are beaten for him on the other side!

122

Love for you took away my rosary and gave verses and songs; I cried "No strength (save with God)" and repented oft, but my heart did not heed.

At Love's hand I became a singer of odes, hand-clapping; love for you consumed reputation and shame and all that I possessed.

Once I was chaste and self-denying and firm-footed as a mountain; what mountain is there that your wind did not carry away like chaff?

If I am a mountain, yet I hold the echo of your voice; and if I am chaff, in your fire I am reduced to smoke.

5 When I saw your being, I became nonexistent out of shame; out of the love of this nonexistence the world of soul came into being.

Wherever nonexistence comes, existence diminishes—brave nonexistence, from which, when it came, existence augmented!

Heaven is blue, earth like a blind squatter on the road; he who beholds your moon escapes from blind-and-blue.

The likeness of the soul of a great saint hidden in the body of the world is the likeness of Aḥmad the Messenger amidst the Guebres and Jews.

To praise you in reality is to praise oneself, for he who praises the sun thereby praises his own eyes.

10 Your praise is as the sea, our tongue is a ship; the soul voyages on the sea, and its end is praiseworthy.

The tender care of the sea is for me like wakeful fortune; why should I grieve, if my eye is stained with sleep?

123

At the night prayer, when the sun declines to sinking, this way of the senses is closed and the way to the Unseen is opened.

The angel of sleep then drives forward the spirits, even as the shepherd who watches over his flock.

To the placeless, towards the spiritual meadows, what cities and what gardens he there displays to them!

The spirit beholds a thousand marvellous forms and shapes, when sleep excises from it the image of the world.

5 You might say that the spirit was always a dweller there, it remembers not this world, and its weariness does not increase.

Its heart so escapes from the load and burden for which it trembled here, that no care for it gnaws at it any more.

124

A little apple, half red and half yellow, made tale of rose and saffron.

When the lover became parted from the beloved, the beloved carried off the airs of pride, the lover the pains.

These two contrary hues through a single separation have displayed {love} on the cheeks of both.

It is not appropriate for the beloved's cheeks to be yellow; for the lover to be red and fat is unseemly.

5 Since the beloved has begun to show airs, endure his airs, lover, and do not battle against them.

I am like a thorn and my master is as the rose; they are twain, in reality they are one.

He is as the sun, and I am the shadow; his is the heat of continuance, mine the cold.

Goliath went out against Toliath; David *measured well the links.*

The heart was born of the body but is the king of the body, even as man is born of woman.

10   Again within the heart there is a heart hidden, like a horseman hidden in dust;

The stirring of the dust is caused by the horseman—it is he who caused this dust to dance.

No chess is it, for you to apply your thoughts; with trust in God fling away your counter like dice.

Shams-i Tabrīz is the sun of the heart; that heat nurtured the fruits of the heart.

125

My verse resembles the bread of Egypt—night passes over it, and you cannot eat it any more.

Devour it the moment it is fresh, before the dust settles upon it.

Its place is the warm climate of the heart; in this world it dies of cold.

Like a fish it quivered for an instant on dry land, another moment and you see it is cold.

5   Even if you eat it imagining it is fresh, it is necessary to conjure up many images.

What you drink is really your own imagination; it is no old tale, my good man.

126

Take heed, for the time of men of fortitude has come, the hour of hardship and testing has come.

In such a time covenants are broken, when the knife reaches to the bone.

Covenants and oaths become very weak when the affairs of a man threaten his life.

Ha, my heart, do not make yourself weak; make your heart strong, for the time for that has come.

5   Laugh like red gold in the fire, that men may say, "The gold of the mine has come."

Eager and cheerful before the sword of doom, cry aloud, "The champion has come."

Be with God and pray to Him for help, for replenishment has come from heaven.

O God, shake the sleeve of bounty, since Your servant has come to the threshold.

Like an oyster shell we have our mouths open, for the cloud of Your pearl-scattering grace has come.

10   Many a dry thorn there is out of whose heart a rosegarden has emerged in Your protection.

I have pointed to You, because from You signless joys have come.

It is the time of compassion and sympathy, for a very heavy blow has come upon me.

Abābīl! Take heed, for the army of the Elephant without bounds has come against the Kaaba.

Reason says to me, "Be silent! Enough; for God who knows the Unseen has come."

15   I held my peace, O God; but without my will lamentation mounted up from my soul.

Thou threwest not when thou threwest is also of God—the arrow which suddenly came from this bow.

127

Someone said, "Master Sanā'ī is dead." The death of such a master is no small thing.

He was not chaff which flew on the wind, he was not water which froze in the cold;

He was not a comb that split on a hair, he was not a seed crushed by the earth.

He was a treasure of gold in this dust bowl, for he reckoned both worlds at one barleycorn.

5 The earthly mould he flung to the earth, the soul of reason he carried to the heavens.

The second soul of which men know nothing—we talk ambiguously—he committed to the Beloved.

The pure wine mingled with the wine-dregs, rose to the top of the vat and separated from the dregs.

They meet together on the journey, dear friend, native of Marghaz, of Rayy, of Rum, Kurd;

Each one returns to his own home—how should silk be compared with striped cloth?

10 Be silent, like (a letter's) points, inasmuch as the King has erased your name from the volume of speech.

128

Ah, what was there in that light-giving candle that it set fire to the heart, and snatched the heart away?

You who have set fire to my heart, I am consumed, O friend; come quickly, quickly!

The form of the heart is not a created form, for the beauty of God manifested itself from the cheek of the heart.

I have no succour save in his sugar, I have no profit save in his lip.

5 Remember him who one dawn released this heart of mine from the chain of your tress.

My soul, the first time I saw you my soul heard something from your soul.

When my heart drank water from your fountain it drowned in you, and the torrent snatched me away.

129

A sour-faced one has come—perchance is he the bitter winter cold? Pour a winecup over his head, saki, sweet as sugar.

Either give him wine from the bottle, or send him on his way now, for it is not pleasant, boy, for an efreet to be amongst rose-cheeked beauties.

Bestow the prophetic wine, so that the ass may not continue in assishness; from Jesus' wine two wings forthwith sprout on the ass.

If a sober heart enters the assembly of the drunkards, do not let him; you know that, in the state of drunkenness, good and evil befall the drunkard.

5 Watchman, sit by the door, give not admittance to our assembly save to the heart-aflame lover from whom comes the odour of a burning heart.

If you want a hand, he gives a foot; if you want a foot, he lays down his head; if you want to borrow a hoe, instead of the hoe he brings an axe.

Since I became immersed in wine I have become without shame and heart; the shield is no protection to me, I am myself as a shield before the sword.

I desire a chanter, a living water of life, to set fire to sleep and to utter this melody till dawn.

If you find one sober vein in me, pluck it out; if a man has not been a lion catcher of God, reckon him a dog in this path.

10 Some folk dissolute and drunk and gay, some folk slaves to the five and the six; these are apart and those are apart, these are other and those are other.

I have consumed beyond measure, for I have lost the treasure; bind my hand, bind my mouth—this is how to preserve the drunkard.

Take heed, convert our sting to honey, give ear to our lament; make us senseless like yourself, senseless look upon us.

130

Yesterday at dawn passing by the Beloved said to me, "You are distraught and unaware; how long will this go on?

My cheek is the envy of the rose; and have you filled your eye with heart's blood in quest of the thorn?"

I said, "Before your stature the cypress is but a sapling!" I said, "Before your cheek the heavens' candle is dark!"

I said, "Sky and earth are topsy-turvy on account of you; it is no wonder therefore, if I have no access to you."

5   He said, "I am your soul and heart; why are you distracted? Say no word, and remain weeping against my silvery bosom."

I said, "You who have robbed my heart and soul of repose, I have not the power to be still." He said at once,

"You are a drop of my sea; why do you utter still? Become drowned, and fill the soul of the oyster shell with pearls."

131

Again in sleep that root of wakefulness gave me the opium of wild commotion and set me reeling.

With a hundred devices I try to be heedless, I make myself to ignore him; that perfect moon comes, holding in his hand such a bowl.

He says to me, "Will you not say how long with those beggarly looks, like every naked unfortunate, you will go on begging at every door?

With this complaining and reviling you are the slave of dervish habit and ewer; if you are true and a man of verity, why are you in this sack?

5   Kings are put to shame by these things which are born of you; you were an angel—why must you be the plaything of the devil?"

Who knows to speak what he speaks? For the world is not his mate; the universe is blind, and being deaf, to what he discloses and conceals.

If I had the tongue to reveal the Beloved's secret, every soul which heard would burst out of this pass.

On account of that sea-bountiful Beloved my state is very difficult, for my breast is laid waste by that leaping and charging to and fro.

If I tell the believers they will all instantly become infidels, and if I tell the infidels no infidel will remain in the world.

10   When last night his phantom came in sleep, graciously it enquired of me, "How are you?" I said, "Without you, in dire straits."

If I had a hundred souls, they would all become blood shed in grieving for you, Beloved; your heart is stone, {granite,} or a mountain of marble!

132

I grant that your prince has gold by the ton; but how happens it that the gold-rich man obtains a cheek like gold?

When they heard complaining from the wretched, frenzied lover, rose and rosebower came out from the earth to behold the spectacle.

Quick, strip off your clothes at once; jump into this pool, that you may escape from your head and the pressure of your turban.

We too like you used to disapprove of this tumult; through a single wink we became thus beguiled by the beloved.

5   How long will you break your lover out of jealous rage? Let be, that this sick heart may utter two or three laments.

No, no, let it not be, for by reason of its wretched lamentation neither earth's people remains, nor the wheeling sky.

Today it were no wonder if that veiled world were not disclosed by leave of the Veiler.

Again this mad heart has broken loose from its chain, torn its collar once more out of passionate love.

Silence! For the indication from the King of Love is thus: "In fortitude seize and compress the throat of your heart and soul!"

133

In this cold and rain the Beloved is sweeter, the Beauty in the bosom, and Love in the brain.

The Beauty in the bosom, and what a beauty! Graceful and fair and supple and fresh and shining-new.

In this cold let us flee to his quarter, for none his like was ever born of mother.

In this snow let us kiss his lips, for snow and sugar refresh the heart.

5   I have no more strength, I am gone out of hand, they have carried me away and brought me again.

When his phantasm suddenly enters the heart, the heart departs out of its place; God is Most Great!

134

There is a light in the midst of the red hair, transcending eye and imagination and spirit.

Do you desire to stitch yourself to it? Arise, and rend the veil of the carnal soul.

That subtle spirit became a form with eyebrows and eyes and brown skin.

God the Inscrutable disclosed Himself to the form of the Chosen Prophet.

5   That form of his passed away in the Form, and that eye of his, like the day of resurrection.

Every time he looked upon men, a hundred doors were opened by God.

When the form of the Chosen One passed away, "God is Most Great" seized the world.

135

I have a bad habit; I am weary; pray excuse me. How shall my habit become seemly without your fair face, my beauty?

Without you I am like winter, people are tormented because of me; with you I am as a rosebower, my habit is the habit of spring.

Without you I lack reason, I am weary, everything I say is crooked, I am ashamed of reason and reason is shamefast at the light of your face.

What is the remedy for bad water? To return to the river. What is the remedy for bad habits? To see the beloved's face again.

5   I see the water of the soul imprisoned in this whirlpool of the body; I dig out the earth to make a way to the sea.

You have a potion which you give the despairing, secretly, lest the hopeful, grieving for it, should utter lamentation.

O heart, so much as you are able do not withhold your eye from the Beloved, whether He withdraws from you or draws you into His bosom.

136

Each moment I catch from my bosom the scent of the Beloved; how should I not take my self every night into my bosom?

Last night I was in Love's garden; that desire ran into my head; his sun peeped out of my eye, so that the river began to flow.

Every laughing rose that springs from the bank of that river of love had escaped from the thorn of being and eluded Dhu 'l-Faqār;

Every tree and grass was a-dancing in the meadow, but in the eye of the vulgar was bound and at rest.

5   Suddenly from one side our Cypress appeared, so that the garden was beside itself and the plane-tree clapped its hands.

Face like fire, wine like fire, love afire—all three delightful; soul because of the intermingled fires lamenting, "Whither shall I flee?"

In the world of Divine Unity there is no room for number, but number exists of necessity in the world of five and four.

You may count a myriad sweet apples in your hand; if you want to make one, squeeze them all together.

A myriad grapes went forth from the veil of skin; when skin no more remained, there remained the wine of the Prince.

10   Without counting the letters, behold what is this speech of the heart; unicolority—is it not a form derived from the root of the affair?

Shams-i Tabrīzī is seated like a king, and before him my verses are ranged like willing slaves.

137

Reason is the chain of travellers and lovers, my son; break the chain, and the way is plain and clear ahead, my son.

Reason is a chain, heart a cheat, body a delusion, soul a veil; the way is hidden from all these heavinesses, my son.

When you have risen out of reason, soul, and heart, and you have gone forth, still this certainty and this direct vision is in doubt, my son.

The man who has not departed out of self is not a man, my son; the love which is not of the soul is but a legend, my son.

5   Set up your breast as a target before the arrow of His decree; be sharp, for the arrow of His decree is already in the bow, my son.

The breast that has been wounded by the striking of the arrow of His tug, on its brow and face are a hundred marks, my son.

If you mount like Idris to the seventh heaven, the love of the Beloved is an excellent ladder indeed, my son.

On every side where a caravan takes its proud way behold love, which is the *qibla* of the caravan, my son.

His love has cast a shadow on the earth like a snare; His huntsmanlike love is in heaven, my son.

10 Enquire not of me concerning love, enquire not of any man, enquire of Love itself; Love in speaking is like a pearl-raining cloud, my son.

Love requires not the interpreter service of me and a hundred like me; concerning realities Love is its own interpreter, my son.

Love is not the business of those asleep or soft and delicate, Love is the business of the brave and of heroes, my son.

Whoso has become the servant of lovers and true ones, he is a king, an emperor, a master of fortune, my son.

Let not this world full of magic spells lure you away from Love, for this faithless world is leaping away from you, my son.

15 If the verses of this ode have become long in its joins, the tune has changed but the meaning is the same, my son.

Take heed, close your mouth and be silent henceforth like an oyster shell, for this tongue of yours is in reality the enemy of the soul, my son.

138

Tonight is a night of union for the stars and of scattering, scattering, since a bride is coming from the skies, consisting of a full moon.

Venus cannot contain herself for charming melodies, like the nightingale which becomes intoxicated with the rose in springtime.

See how the Polestar is ogling Leo; behold what dust Pisces is stirring up from the deep!

Jupiter has galloped his steed against ancient Saturn, saying, "Take back your youth and go, bring good tidings!"

5   Mars' hand, which was full of blood from the handle of his sword, has become life-giving as the sun, the exalted in works.

Since Aquarius has come full of that water of life, the dry cluster of Virgo is raining pearls from him.

The Pleiades (nut) full of goodness fears not Libra and being broken; how should Aries flee away in fright from its mother?

When from the moon the arrow of a glance struck the heart of Sagittarius, he took to night-faring in passion for her, like Scorpio.

On such a festival, go, sacrifice Taurus, else you are crooked of gait in the mud like Cancer.

10   This sky is the astrolabe, and the reality is Love; whatever we say of this, attend to the meaning.

Shams-i Tabrīz, on that dawn when you shine, the dark night is transformed to bright day by your moonlike face.

139

That beauty handed me a broom saying, "Stir up the dust from the sea!"

He then burned the broom in the fire saying, "Bring up the broom out of the fire!"

In bewilderment I made prostration before him; he said, "Without a prostrator, offer a graceful prostration!"

"Ah, how prostrate without a prostrator?" He said, "Unconditionally, without personal impulse."

5   I lowered my neck and said, "Cut off the head of a prostrator with Dhu 'l-Faqār."

The more he struck with the sword, the more my head grew, till heads a myriad sprouted from my neck;

I was a lamp, and every head of mine was as a wick; sparks flew on every side.

Candles sprang up out of my heads, east to west was filled with the train.

What are east and west in the placeless? A dark bath-stove, and a bath at work.

10   You whose temperament is cold, where is the anxiety of your heart? How long this dwelling at rest in these baths?

Go forth from the baths and enter not the stove; strip yourself, and look upon those paintings and figures,

Until you behold the ravishing figures, until you behold the hues of the tulip-bed.

When you have beheld, look towards the window, for that beauty became a beauty through the reflection of the window.

The six directions are the bath, and the window is the placeless; above the window is the beauty of the Prince.

15   Earth and water acquired colour from his reflection, soul rained on Turk and Zanzibari.

The day is gone, and my story has not grown short—O night and day put to shame by his tale!

King Shams al-Dīn-i Tabrīzī keeps me intoxicated, crop-sickness upon crop-sickness.

140

I went there intoxicated and said, "O beauty, when you have maddened me, give ear!"

He replied, "See, in my ear is a ring; become fastened to that ring like a pendant."

I quickly reached out to touch his ring; he struck me saying, "Hold back your hand from me!

You will find the way into this ring only when you become a royal pearl in purity.

5   My golden ring, and then a bead! How should Jesus go up to heaven on an ass?"

141

Joyous spring has arrived and the Beloved's message has come; we are drunk with love and intoxicated and cannot be still.

O my darling one, go forth to the garden, do not leave the beauties of the meadow in expectation.

Strangers from the Unseen have arrived in the meadow; go forth, for it is a rule that "the newcomer is visited."

Following your footsteps the rose has come into the rose-bower, to greet and meet you the thorn has become soft of cheek.

5   Cypress, give ear, for the lily in exposition of you has become all tongue by the bank of the river.

The bud was tightly knotted; your grace looses knots; the rose blossoms thanks to you, and scatters its petals over you.

You might say that it is the resurrection, that there have raised their heads from the earth those who rotted in December and January, the dead of yesteryear.

The seed which had died has now found life, the secret which earth held has now become revealed.

The bough which held fruit is glorying for joy, the root which had none is shamefast and ashamed.

10   After all, the trees of the spirit will become even so, the tree of excellent boughs and fortunate will be manifest.

The king of spring has drawn up his army and made his provisions; the jasmine has seized the shield, the green grass Dhu 'l-Faqār.

They say, "We will cut off the head of So-and-so like chives; behold that visibly enacted in the handiwork of the Creator."

Yes; when the succour of divine assistance arrives, Nimrod is brought to destruction by a gnat.

142

Do not slacken the bowstring, for I am your four-feathered arrow; do not turn your face away, for I am a man with one heart, not two-headed.

From you is the striking of the sharp sword, from the heart and soul a hundred consents; I am a man of one word like fate, I am not "if" or "perhaps"!

If you draw Dhu 'l-Faqār I am constant and firm of foot, I do not flee like the wind, I do not die like a spark.

I will surrender my soul to the sword, I will not say alas; God has made me like a shield for the blows of His sword.

5   Sun, smite with your glow the neck of the night as with a sword; whence comes the darkness of the nights? From the forge of muddy earth.

The body is a mine of endurance, the heart is a mine of gratitude, the bosom is a mine of laughter, the liver is a mine of compassion.

Make your throne, O king, on my head as a cap; tightly draw me into your breast as a garment.

Someone said, "Whence has Love form and hands?" Love is the sprouting-bed of every hand and foot in the forms.

Did not your father and mother play at love for one moment? When they were united, one like you made his appearance.

10   Do not regard Love, which without hands made your hand a hand, as being without hand or head; look in another fashion.

You who have eyes to see, the colour of all faces, the water of all rivers—know these are Shams-i Ḥaqq, the Pride of Tabriz.

143

He said, "My sugar-sweet lip is worth a treasure of pearls." "Ah, I have no pearls." He said, "You have not? Then buy!

Make a snare for me out of pearls, and if that does not succeed, then borrow. You have mistaken the house, you lover without silver and gold!

You have come to a gambling-match; bring a purse full of gold. Else, leave us and be gone, do not vex and trouble us more.

We are highwaymen, we are renders of garments; if you are one of us, come in, drink and drink deep!

5   We tear to shreds all snares, we devour all properties; we are sweeter than all others—despite all the blind and deaf."

Those who buy garments are different from those who rend them; those who rend garments pluck out the mustachios of every garment-buyer.

The Moses of the soul plucked out the mustachios of the Pharaoh of the body, so that the body becomes all soul, every hair-tip alive.

Recognize the travellers on the path of his love by their pallid cheeks; know that the pearls of love are tears, love's silk the heart's blood.

What is the worth of the gold-pale cheek? Say: the ruby of the Beloved. What is the worth of the pearl-like tear? Say: that glance.

10   We are slaves to that saki, till eternity we continue; our world is secure and content, the worldlings are passing by.

Whoever has been born has died and committed his soul to the guardian angel; the lover was born of no man, love has no father.

If you are not of this face, then sit behind like the nape; if you are not the nape, then advance like a shield.

Advance like a shield unconscious, and behold how the conscious ones are struck unconscious by the glance of the Friend's blow.

144

God has written around the cheek of the Beloved the inscription *Therefore take heed* of him, *you who have eyes.*

Since Love devours men, it is necessary for a man to make himself a morsel before man-devouring Love.

You are a sour morsel, and are very long digesting; the saint is a sweet morsel easy to digest.

Do you break the morsel you are, because that mouth is narrow; even three elephants would not devour you, save at three gulps.

5   In face of your greed the elephant itself is a morsel; you are like the abābīl birds which made the elephant their prey.

You were born of non-entity, come after a long famine; to you, fattened bird as food and serpent and snake are the same.

You have come to a hot cauldron; now you burn your mouth, now you blacken your clothes and lips and turban.

With nothing are you sated, like the belly of hell, save perchance the Almighty Creator sets His foot on you,

Even as He sets His foot on the head of hell, and hell proclaims, "Enough, I am full, lift up Your foot!"

10 God satiates the eye of the saints and the elect, for they are delivered from self and from greed for this carrion.

No greed remains in them for knowledge and science, no desire for paradise; the lion-rider does not seek for ass or camel.

Silence! Were I to count His gifts and donations, resurrection day itself would become giddy and confounded at the tally.

Come, Pride of Tabriz, true Shams al-Dīn; the sun in the spinning skies is your humble slave.

145

Look not for happiness when the Beauty's inclination is set on sorrow, for you are prey in the clutches of a lion, my dear friend.

Though the Beloved sprinkles plaster on your head, welcome that as if it was Tartary musk.

Since within you lurks a hidden enemy, there is no repelling that monster save by harshness.

The man who beats a stick on a rug, it is not aimed at the rug, but the whole purpose is to rid the rug of dust.

5   Layers of dust are within you, consisting of the veil of egoism; that dust is not got rid of at a single blow;

With each harshness and each blow, little by little that is dispersed from the cheek of the heart, now sleeping, now awake.

If you take flight in sleep, in dreams you will see the cruelty of the Beloved and the execrations of that Benefactor.

Scraping a stick is not in order to destroy the stick, it is for a good purpose in the heart of the carpenter.

For this reason every evil on God's path is good, for that He will show man pure and refined at the end of the affair.

10   Consider the hide which the tanner rubs in all manner of filth a thousand times over,

So that the inward flaw may go forth from the hide, even though the hide knows naught of little or much.

Sun and Pride of Tabriz, you possess great virtues; make haste, for you have a mighty power in the secrets.

146

If a tree could move on foot or wing, it would not suffer the pain of the saw or the blows of the axe;

And if the sun did not travel on wing and foot all the night, how would the world be illumined at morningtide?

If the salt water did not rise from the sea to the sky, whence would the garden be revived by torrent and rain?

When the drop departed from its homeland and returned, it encountered a shell and became a pearl.

5   Did not Joseph go from his father on a journey, weeping? Did he not on the journey attain felicity and kingdom and victory?

Did not Muṣṭafā go on a journey towards Yathrib, gain sovereignty, and become king of a hundred lands?

And you—if you have no foot, choose to journey into yourself; like a ruby-mine be receptive to a print from the sunbeams.

Make a journey out of self into self, my master, for by such a journey earth became a mine of gold.

Go out of sourness and bitterness towards sweetness, just as a thousand sorts of fruits have escaped out of bitterness.

10   Seek sweetness from the Sun, the Pride of Tabriz, for every fruit gains comeliness from the light of the sun.

147

Look on me, for I shall be your companion in the grave on that night when you pass across from shop and house.

You will hear my greeting in the tomb, and you will be aware that not for a moment you have been veiled from my eyes.

I am like reason and mind within your veil, alike in time of pleasure and happiness and in the hour of pain and weariness.

On the strange night, when you hear the voice familiar, you will escape from the bite of snake and leap away from the horror of ant;

5   Love's intoxication will bring to your grave, as a gift, wine and mistress and candle and meats and sweets and incense.

On the hour when we light the lamp of the intellect, what a tumult of joy shall go up from the dead in the tombs!

The dust of the graveyard will be confounded by those cries, by the din of the drum of resurrection, the pomp and panoply of the uprising—

Shrouds rent asunder, two ears stopped up in terror; what shall avail brain and ear before the blast of the trumpet?

On whatever side you gaze, you will behold my form, whether you gaze on yourself or towards that uproar and confusion.

10   Flee from squinteyedness, and make good both your eyes, for the evil eye on that day will be far from my beauty.

Beware of mistaking me in a human shape, for the spirit is very subtle, and Love is exceedingly jealous.

What room is there for form, if the felt be a hundredfold? It is the rays of the soul's mirror that pitch the flag visibly.

Beat the drum, and wind towards the minstrels of the city; it is the day of purification to the grown lads of the road of Love.

Had they sought God, instead of morsel and pence, you would not have seen one blind man seated on the edge of the moat.

15 What sort of ogling-house have you opened in our city! Mouth shut, shoot out glances, like light.

148

My bowl has broken, and no wine has remained to me, and I am crop-sick; let Shams-e Din set in order my disordered estate—

Prince of the world of vision, lamp of the world of revelation, to whom the spirits make heartfelt obeisance from afar,

That his hand may bring out of the sea of bewilderment a thousand souls and spirits drowned and utterly whelmed.

If heaven and earth were filled with the darkness of unbelief, when he shines, his rays flood all that with light.

5 That pure radiance which the angels discover from him—if it should reach the satans, they would all become houris.

And even if that light belonged not for a single day to the devil, he would veil the devil with the veils of his bountifulness.

On the day of festival, when he begins to dispense, on every side is a marriage feast, in every quarter a wedding party.

From the direction of Tabriz that sun shines—the atoms come to life as at the blast of the trumpet.

Zephyr, for God's sake and by the right of bread and salt—for every dawn I and you have been rejoiced by him—

10 When you come to the end of the frontiers of the unseen world, pass over them, and be not lazy as one sick and suffering.

On that wing which you have gotten from him fly; for a thousand years' journey will not be far from your wing.

Fly; and when your wing becomes weary, prostrate yourself for the sake of my state, weary of soul and sundered of heart;

Tell him with tears that since the time of our separation, my day has become black and my hairs camphor-white.

You are he who dips in the sea of compassion all the sinners of the world, and makes them forgiven.

15   If the seeing eye cannot penetrate to your soul, he who has no eye may truly be excused.

So contrive by entreaty as to bring the dust of his feet to the eye, for this sickness is becoming gangrenous.

And when, zephyr, you return prospering from this journey, you will stir up commotion and sparks indeed in existence and nonexistence alike.

When you bring me his eye salve, may a thousand new compassions be upon your soul for centuries beyond reckoning!

149

Minstrel of the lovers, shake the string, strike fire into believer and infidel!

Silence is not the proper course of love; unveil the face of welfare.

Until the infant in the cradle weeps, how shall the anxious mother give it milk?

Whatever is other than the phantom of the Beloved is the thorn of Love, even if it be a rosebower.

5   Minstrel, when you have reached to dilate my heart, have a care; you have set your foot in blood—

Set your foot slowly, lest a drop of the heart's blood splash out on the wall.

Minstrel, observe well the wounds of the heart; so long as they are not conscious of their pain, be at ease.

Minstrel, mention the name of the beloved who has robbed our heart of fortitude and quietude.

What have I said? Where has a heart remained still? If my heart were a mountain, it had gone out of control.

10   Speak his name, and name me less, that I may nickname you "Excellent of speech."

When I speak of how he moves, where does my heart go? Brave movement indeed!

Shams-i Tabrīz, you are the Jesus of the age; in your age there is such a sick one.

150

Who has compassion on a friend? A friend likewise. Who hears the sigh of the sick? The sick.

Where are the tears of sympathetic spring, that they may fill the thorn's skirt with roses?

Mention often the demolisher of joy; give ear to pitiless autumn.

The cave becomes paradise, when he is in it: *the second of two, when the two were in the Cave.*

5   Heaven splits in two at the sigh of a lover; the lamentation of lovers is not to be despised.

Heaven revolves for the sake of lovers; on account of love the sky spins around,

Not for the sake of baker and smith, not for the sake of carpenter and druggist.

The skies rotate about love; rise, that we may also circle around.

Consider who said, "But for thee I would not have created"; Ahmad the Chosen is the mine of love.

10   For a while let us circle about loverhood; how long shall we circle about this carrion?

Where is the eye to behold the spirits, putting their heads out from door and wall?

Door and wall tell subtleties, fire and earth and water re-
hearse a tale;

Like the balance, the yardstick and the touchstone they are
without tongue, yet arbiters of the market.

Lover, circle about like the sky, silent from speaking, and
altogether speech.

151

So drunk am I, so drunk am I today that I have leaped out of
the hoop today.

Such a thing as never enters the mind, even so am I, even so
am I today.

In spirit I departed to the heaven of Love, even though in
form I am in this low world today.

I took reason by the ear and said, "Reason, go out, for I have
escaped from you today.

5   Reason, wash your hands of me, for I am joined with the
mad lover today.

That Joseph gave into my hand an orange; as a result, I have
wounded both my hands today."

That jug full of wine has brought me to such a state that I
have broken so many jars today.

I do not know where I am, but it is a blessed station in which
I am today.

Good fortune came coquettishly to my door; out of drunk-
enness I closed the door to him today.

10   When he returned, I kept running after him, I did not sit
down for a moment today.

Since *We are nearer* has been realized, I will not worship
myself any more today.

Do not tie up that tress, Shams al-Dīn-i Tabrīz, for I am like
a fish in this net today.

152

The love of that cherisher of lovers has come to his own
house; Love has in form-conceiving a form melting all forms.

You have come to your own house; welcome, enter! Your
coming is with joy; enter by the door of the heart, run to the
vestibule of the soul.

Every mote of my being is in love with your sun; take heed,
for motes have long transaction with the sun.

See how before the window the motes gracefully suspended
beat; whoever has the sun for a *qibla* prays after this fashion.

5   In the concert of the sun these motes are like Sufis; no one
knows to what recitation, to what rhythm, to what harmony.

In every heart there is a different note and rhythm, all stamp-
ing feet outwardly, and the minstrels hidden like a secret.

Loftier than all is our inward concert, our particles dancing
therein with a hundred kinds of glory and pride.

Shams-i Tabrīzī, you are the sultan of the sultans of the soul;
no Maḥmūd like you ever came into being, nor like me any
Ayāz.

153

Night is broad and long for the sake of lovers and thieves;
ho, come, strumpet night, and do the business of both!

I steal carnelians and pearls from the sultan's treasury, I am
not mean that I should steal the draper's cloth.

Within the veil of the nights there are subtle thieves who by
cunning find a way to the roof of the house of mystery.

My ambition in night-faring and knavery is nothing less than
the king's treasury and the carnelian of that king of glory.

5   The cheek before whose onslaught night remains no more
in the world—brave lamp, which lights the sun and fashions the
moon!

All the needs of men are granted on the Night of Power, for Power attained that exaltation from a full moon like you.

You are all, and beyond all what else is there, that it should enter the imagination that anyone is your peer?

Ho, pass away from this; open wide your ears, for I am beginning a tale entirely rare and strange.

Since you have not seen Messiah, give ear to the legend; fly like a white falcon towards the falcon-drum.

10   Since you are a coin of red gold, receive the seal of the king; if you are not red gold, then why all this snipping?

In the time when you became a treasure you did not realize that, wherever a treasure is, the informer sets to work.

Bring your treasure, and play no tricks, for you will not escape by vapouring and prostration and commemoration and abstinence and prayer.

Do you steal, and then sit in the corner of the mosque saying, "I am the Junaid of the age, the Bā Yazīd of supplication"?

Give back the cloth, then get on with your abstinence; do not make feeble excuses and babble your tale.

15   Hush your pretexts, for in this station men do not purchase a single grain by dissimulation and artful trickery.

Seize the skirt of felicity of Shams-i Tabrīzī, that your perfection may be embroidered from the magic of his sleeve.

154

Sour-faced one, in my presence you spoke evil of me; the mouth of the vulture always smells of carrion.

Your filthy words became apparent in your face; vileness is ever manifest in the face and complexion of the nobody.

I have a Friend and Beloved, so go on grinding away at death and enmity; take heed, the ocean was never defiled by the mouth of any dog.

Though the Holy City has become filled with Frankish pigs, after all how has that brought the Holy Temple a bad name?

5 This is the face of the mirror; Joseph shines in it; the back, however that it is gilded, is a stranger.

If the bat thinks evil, the sun is not grieved—how is the sun impaired, if the shadow is upside down?

Jesus was a laugher, John the Baptist a frowner; the former laughed out of trust, the latter frowned from fear.

They said, "O Lord, which of these two is better in Your eyes? Which of these two is better in the well-founded path?"

God said, "He is superior who thinks better thoughts of Me; the good thoughts of the sinner leave him not defiled."

10 You are a frowner not out of fear and religious aspiration, you are pale from envy or dark red from gloating.

Neither of these gets anywhere, they are proper only to the fire; woe to him in whom envy is rooted!

Let it go from your hand; *cursed* is it; whoever is enemy of the moon has only shadows.

Know for sure, O sun, that bats are your enemies, they are a disgrace to all birds, fellow-prisoners in *brooding night*.

The sun's enemy is *docked*, that rank does not remain to him; how long shall the mote there remain if it falls into the eye?

155

Consorts of the Moon are your two Mars, which are those two eyes of yours, Darling; with that Hārūt and Mārūt of yours draw the litigious ones to Babylon.

Solomon, with that ring (for you are the sealing of all the fair ones) by force drag in chains all the divs and peris.

You have opened the treasure of beneficence for the sake of jinns and men; draw the likeness of *We have given thee* over the needy beggar.

Illumine the body with the spirit, root up envy utterly; fix the gaze on the orient skies, draw the reason into problems.

5 When the lip recites *Praise,* give it dessert and wine unli-

mited; when it recites *Nor those astray,* do you draw it into guiding proofs.

When the soul hurries towards you, give it a candle to find the way; when it seeks your sun, draw it like the moon into the "houses."

Give the crop-sick lover the wine of Kai-Kā'ūs' cup; draw before the thoughts of the man of reason hairsplitting and craft.

With the advancing of your favours draw the spirit and make it receptive; draw your acceptance and investiture towards the receptive soul.

To the prisoner of pain and regret give the message of *Do not despair;* draw him slain of love for your beauty from this slaying-place to the slayer.

10   If this body is infidel at heart, propose "testimony" to it; and if this spirit is fruitless, what matters that? Draw it to the fruit.

Quicken it, and if you cannot, make Messiah your deputy; grant it union, or if you grant it not, draw it by your grace to the Lord of grace.

Earthy one, the earth trembled when it saw that holiness and purity; recite *When it is shaken,* draw the vision into trembling.

Make an end of it, ho, at once, for you are the King of State and Word; whoever proffers speech, do you draw a line over speech and speaker.

156

The fair one whom I am seeking with all my soul I do not see amongst those present here.

Where has he gone? He is not amongst those present; I do not see any sign of him in this assembly.

I am casting my gaze in every direction and every place; I do not see any trace of his rosebower.

Moslems, where has he gone, that illustrious one whom I used to behold in the midst like a candle?

5 Speak his name; for whoever has spoken his name, his bones will not crumble in the tomb.

Blessed is the man who has kissed his hand; at the time of death his mouth has become sweet.

Shall I give thanks for his countenance, or his character? For the world beholds none his like.

If earth does not find his form, what matters it, seeing that his heaven revolves in this love?

Speak the nicknames of Shams al-Dīn-i Tabrīz; do not keep him concealed from the ears of the yearners.

157

Last night I went into the midst of the assembly of my king; I saw my soul in a beaker in the hand of the saki.

I said to him, "O soul of the soul of the sakis, for God's sake fill me a measure, and do not break your pledge."

Smiling sweetly he said, "Noble sir, I do you service; I respect you by the right and respect of my faith."

He brought a cup and kissed it and placed it in my hand, full of wine shining like his own shining cheeks.

5 I prostrated before him and drew the bowl to me; the wine lighted a fire in me from its own brazier.

When the saki had poured continuously and dispensed for me many glasses after that wise, that wine like red gold transported me to its own quarry.

I saw my garden fresh and gay with the rose of his cheek; I saw my bread well baked with his hyacinthine brow.

Let every man find his own fortune and portion in a tavern; who am I? I have found true sympathy to belong to me.

I saw Bū Lahab there biting hard his hand, Bū Huraira putting his hand in his own wallet;

10 Bū Lahab was like the back (and no back sees the face), Bū Huraira turning his face to his own moon and seventh heaven;

Bū Lahab plunged in thought, seeking proof and demonstration, Bū Huraira his own proof and his own demonstration.

Not every jar is suitable for wine; beware, stop up the jar, that the saki may produce another jar from his own cellar.

I make this enough, that the Prince of the Assembly may tell you the tale of his own myriad secret assemblies.

158

I am you, you are I, O friend; do not depart from your own breast; do not deem yourself other, do not drive yourself from your own door.

Do not mislead head and foot through your endless temptation, that as one bewildered I should stamp the foot of cruelty on my own head.

The one who like a shadow is never apart from your form, is I; do not, beloved, draw your dagger against your shadow.

O tree, in every direction of which there are thousands of shadows, cherish the shadows and do not cut them off from their source.

5   Hide all the shadows and naught them in the light; disclose the countenance of the sun of your radiant cheek.

The heart's kingdom has become disordered through your two-heartedness; mount the throne, do not step down from your own pulpit.

"Reason is the crown"—so ʿAlī spoke in a similitude; bestow on the throne a new jewel out of your own essence.

159

My drunkenness of today is not like yesterday's drunkenness; do you not believe me? Take a glass, and drink!

I am drowned in wine; the waters have carried away my reason. Intellect said, "Farewell, I will not become sober again."

Reason and intellect have departed in madness out of the world, like a pot overbrimming when it boils beyond measure.

This mad, intoxicated heart burst its bonds and escaped; do not argue with the drunkards—say nothing; depart; keep silent.

5   At dawn the watchman said to me from the ladder, "Last night I heard an uproar proceeding from the seventh heaven.

Saturn said to Venus, 'Strike your plectrum more gently. Leo, seize Taurus by the horns and milk him.'

See how as a result of terror the milk in Taurus' nipples has turned to blood! Behold how the Leo of the skies out of fear has become like a mouse!

Leo, charge fiercely; how long will you flee like a cur? Make display, O moon-faced one; how long will you veil your face?

Open your eyes to the six directions, behold the glittering of the light; open your ears to heaven, you whose eyes have become ears.

10   Hear the greeting from the Soul, that you may escape from speech; gaze upon the Form-fashioner, that you may escape from the forms."

I said to him, "Master, go, say, let what will be be; I am pure and newly free, slave to the dregs-seller."

Fear and hope for you are assigned to the reason; wild creatures are the game for your grain and snare.

Since the dregs of his anguish have taken me into protection, speak not to me of these things; that task is yours—do you labour!

160

When union with the Beloved showed itself to Manṣūr, it was right that the gallows should bring him to the heart's Origin.

I snatched a cap's length from his robe; his cap's length consumed my reason and head and foot.

I broke off a thorn from the top of the wall of his garden; what itching and questing is in my heart from that thorn of his!

Since one morning through his wine this heart became a lion-taker, it is only meet that it should be smitten by the monster of separation from him.

5 Though heaven's colt appeared refractory and untamed, it was tethered and headstalled by the hand of His love.

Though reason is high-ranking and very learned, its gown and turban have been pawned for the cup of love.

Many a heart came seeking refuge from His love; dragging it along He dragged it to Him, and gave it no quarter.

One cold day a fur coat was in a river; I said to a naked man, "Jump in and seek, and bring it out!"

It was not a fur coat, it was a bear in the river; it had fallen in, and the current was carrying it along.

10 The man entered eagerly and reached the skin of the bear; that eagerness made him prisoner in the bear's arms.

I said to him, "Let go the fur coat, come back! How long and far you have remained through toiling and battling with it!"

He said, "Go; the coat has so seized me that I have no hope of escape from its powerful clutches.

Every moment it immerses me a thousand times; there is no escape from its lover-squeezing claws."

Silence, of stories enough; just give a hint; what need has the reason for long volumes?

161

They say, "The king of love is not faithful." Lies! They say, "Your night will never have a dawn." Lies!

They say, "Why do you slay yourself for love's sake? There is no survival after the body's death." Lies!

They say, "Your tears shed in love are vain; once the eyes are closed, there will be no encounter." Lies!

They say, "When we have gone outside the cycle of time, beyond this soul of ours will not travel." Lies!

5   Those persons who have not escaped from fancy say, "The
stories of the prophets were all mere fancies." Lies!
    Those persons who have not gone on the right way say,
"The servant has no way to come to God." Lies!
    They say, "He who knows all secrets tells not the servant the
secrets and mysteries of the Unseen without intermediary!" Lies!
    They say, "They open not to the servant the heart's secret,
and He does not graciously carry the servant up to heaven."
Lies!
    They say, "That one who has earth in his composition will
never be familiar with the heavenly host." Lies!
10 They say, "The pure soul will never fly on the wings of love
out of this earthly nest to the free air." Lies!
    They say, "That sun of God will never bring retribution for
the several atoms' weight of evil and good of men." Lies!
    Keep silent from speaking; and if anyone says to you,
"Speech has no other expression but letters and sounds"—Lies!

162

    We two or three gay reprobates have gathered together
on this side like camels, face to face, muzzles plunged in the
provender.
    From left and right every camel is coming, raging with de-
sire, lips thrust out like camels, bringing up foam.
    Do not worry; not every camel finds the way to this sheep-
cote, for they are in the lowlands and we are on top of the
mountain.
    How shall any attain the mountaintop by stretching up his
neck? Even though they bark like dogs, we will not worry about
their barking.
5   If the world becomes all sea, enter the ark of Noah; how
should Noah's ark be overwhelmed and destroyed?
    We are a mine of emeralds, a bane to the eye of the snake; he
who is bitten by sorrow, his portion is "Woe is me!"

All the world is full of grief in quest of rank and money; we are happy and glad and revered, drunk with joy in this protection.

The gnostics have become drunk; minstrel of gnosis, come, quickly utter a quatrain, come forward, take the tambourine.

Cast wind into the forest, blow on the head of cypress and willow, that willow and plane-tree rank by rank may toss their heads.

10   When the willow is dry and bald, it has neither leaves nor fruit; how should it move its head to the breath and wind of *Do not fear?*

The remedy for the dry and succourless is the blast divine, for He is engaged on action one by one, He is not weak and contemptible.

The dry palm-tree gave fruit to a Mary by the fiat of God; the dead found life anew from the breath divine.

If the fool wags his chin, do not lose the path of Love; choose the trade of Love, count as folly all other trades.

When you complete one ode, recite the praises of Shams-i Dīn and recall Tabriz, despite the villainous adversary.

163

I have no need of wine, I am indifferent to lees and pure liquor; I thirst for my own blood, the time of battle has come.

Draw the sharp sword, shed the blood of the envious until the head without the body circumambulates about its own body.

Make a mountain of skulls, make a sea of our blood, that earth and sand may drink blood in great gulps.

You who are aware of my heart, go, do not stop up my mouth, else my heart will split, the blood will leap out of the rent.

5   Do not listen to the tumult, show no special favour; rulership and authority are not so hand-woven.

I will enter the heart of the fire, I will become a morsel for the fire; foretelling what, have they cut the navel of the sulphur-like soul?

Fire is our child, it thirsts and is in bondage to us; we two are becoming one so that no difference may prevail.

Why does it crackle and smoke? Because two-colouredness is still there; when it becomes fuel, it no longer crackles boastfully.

Or if it leaps half-ablaze, it now becomes a coal, heart-athirst and black-faced, seeking union and marriage.

10 The fire says, "Go, you are black and I am white." The fuel says, "You are burnt, I am preserved."

This side of it no face, that side of it no face, making seclusion in blackness between the two friends;

Like an exiled Moslem, no way for him to come to people nor to emperor, left on one side like the fringe of a garment.

Rather, he is like the 'Anqā which was greater than all the birds, but having no way to the sky, remained upon that mountain of Qāf.

What am I to say to you? For you are fixed in your grief for bread, your back curved like a *lām,* your heart constricted like a *kāf.*

15 Ho, trouble-seeker, dash that pitcher against a rock, that I may not draw river-water, that I may not suck it up.

I will abandon water-carrying, I will drown myself in the sea, far from warfare and conflict, unaware of any description,

Like pure spirits under the earth, their bodies like a bride with earth on them for a coverlet.

164

Look at that false prince with his little horse and little saddle, knavish and scoundrelly, his head bound in cloth of gold;

Since he disbelieves in death, he says, "Where, where is doom?" Death comes to him from all six directions and says, "Here am I!"

Doom says to him, "Donkey, where now is all that galloping about? Those moustaches, that arrogant nose, that pride, that wrath?

Where is the beautiful idol, where happiness? To whom have you given your coverlet? A brick is now your pillow, your mattress the earth."

5 Bid farewell to eating and sleeping; go seek the true religion, that you may be a prince of eternity without your little laws and customs.

Do not unsoul this soul; do not convert this bread to dung, O you who have flung the pearl into the bottom of the dung.

Know that we are attached to dung for the pearl's sake, O soul; be broken, and seek the pearl, proud and conceited one.

When you see a man of God, act like a man and offer him service; when you experience anguish and affliction, do not furrow your brow.

This is my lampoon, O body, and that prince of mine is also I; how long will you go on speaking of little *sīns* and *shīns*?

10 Shams al-Ḥaqq-i Tabrīzī, you are yourself the water of life; what shall discover that water, save the tearful eye?

165

What, loverhood and then concern for name and shame? That should not be; Love's village is stone on stone!

If you become lame from everything, depart far away; what, a far and stony way, and a lame man?

If death is a man, let him come before me that I may draw him fondly and tightly into my bosom;

I will carry off from him a soul without hue and scent, he will seize from me a cloak of many colours.

5 Impose on your soul the cruelty and tyranny of the Beloved; or if you will not, then welcome to war and war!

If you do not desire the scraping of His polishing, then be like a mirror full of rust.

Lay your hand on your eye and say, "With all my eye!" Open your eye; do not gaze distraught and stupefied.

166

I cried out at midnight, "Who is in this house of the heart?" He said, "It is I, by whose countenance the sun and the moon are put to shame."

He said, "Why is this house of the heart full of all sorts of images?" I said, "These are the reflections of You, whose face is the envy of Chigil."

He said, "What is this other image, full of the heart's blood?" I said, "This is the image of me, heart wounded and feet in the mire."

I bound the neck of my soul and brought it before Him as a token: "It is a sinner of love; do not acquit your sinner."

5 He gave me the end of a thread, a thread full of mischief and craft; he said, "Pull, that I may pull, pull and at the same time do not break."

From that tent of the soul the form of my Turk flashed out fairer than before; I reached my hand towards him; He struck my hand, saying, "Let go!"

I said, "You have turned harsh, like So-and-so." He said, "Know that I am harsh for a good purpose, not harsh out of rancour and spite.

Whoever enters in saying, 'It is I,' I strike him on the brow, for this is the sanctuary of Love, animal, it is not a sheep-cote."

Salāḥ-i Dil u Dīn is truly the image of that Turk; rub your eyes, and behold the image of the heart, the image of the heart.

167

Why does the soul not take wing, when from the presence of Glory the address of grace like sugar comes to the soul saying, "Come up"?

How should a fish not leap nimbly from the dry land into the water, when the sound of waves reaches its ear from the limpid sea?

Why should the falcon not fly from the quarry towards the king, when it hears from drum and drumstick the tidings *Return*?

Why should not every Sufi begin to dance like a mote in the sun of immortality, that it may deliver him from decay?

5   Such grace and beauty and loveliness and life-bestowing—can any man dispense with Him? What misery and error!

Fly, fly, O bird, to your origin, for you have escaped from the cage and your feathers and wings are outspread.

Journey away from the brackish water towards the water of life; return to the high table of the soul from the porter's lodge.

Off, off! For we too, O soul, are arriving from this world of separation to that world of union.

How long like children in this earthly world shall we fill our skirts with dust and stones and crocks?

10   Let us leave go of earth and fly heavenwards, let us flee from childhood to the banquet of men.

Look not to see how the earthly mould has put you in a sack; split the sack and lift your head out of the sack.

Take from the air this book in your right hand; you are not a child, not to know your right from your left.

God said to Reason's messenger, "Lift up your foot!", to the hand of Death, "Beat the ear of concupiscence!"

A call came to the spirit, "Speed away into the Unseen; take the gain and the treasure, and lament the pain no more."

15   Do you call aloud, and proclaim that you are King; yours is the grace of the answer, and yours is the knowledge of the question.

168

This time I am wholly involved in loverhood, this time I am wholly cut off from well-being.

I have plucked out my heart from myself, I am living with something else, I have burned up from root and stock reason and heart and thought.

O men, O men, manhood comes from me no more; the madman even does not meditate what I have meditated in my heart.

The unlucky madman has fled from my turbulence; I am commingled with death, I have flown into not-being.

5   Today my reason has become wholly disgusted with me; it desires to terrify me, thinking that I have no eyes.

Why indeed should I be afraid of it? I have put on a grimace for its sake. How should I be confused? But I am purposely so confounded.

I am quit of the bowl of the stars and the blood of the skies; I have licked many a bowl for the benefit of the beggarly-faced people.

For a good purpose I have remained in the prison of this world; what have I to do with prison? Whose property have I stolen?

In the body's prison I am drowned in blood, and of the tears of every stubborn one's eyes I have rubbed in the dust my bloodstained skirt.

10   Like an infant in the womb my nurture is of blood; ordinary men are born once, I have been born many times.

Examine me as much as you will, you will not recognize me, for I have become a hundred different manners from what you have seen me to be.

Enter my eye and behold me with my own sight, for I have chosen a dwelling place beyond all sight.

You are drunk, drunk and happy, I am drunk and happy,

without a head; you are a lover with laughing lips, I am laughing without any mouth.

A strange bird am I, who of my own desire, without snare or catcher, have crept into the cage;

For the cage in the company of friends is sweeter than orchard and garden; to please the Josephs I have reposed in the well.

Do not bewail his blow, do not claim sickness; I have given a hundred sweet lives to purchase this calamity.

Like a silkworm at the cost of suffering you enter into satin and silk; give ear to a silkworm that has withered in the very garment.

You have withered in the tomb of the body; go before my Israfil saying, "For my sake blow on the trumpet, for I am weary of the tomb of the body."

No, no, like the well-tried falcon hood your eyes from yourself; I have put on brocade like a fine peacock.

Bow your head to the physician saying, "Give me the antidote, for in this pleasant net I have swallowed many poisons."

Before the confectioner of the soul you will become sweet and sweet of soul, for from the confection of the soul I have waxed great as a sugarcane.

He will make your essence confection better than by giving a hundred confections; I have not heard the delight of the soul's confection save from his lips.

Be silent, for in speaking the confection falls out of the mouth; without speech a man catches a scent such as I have snuffed.

Every unripe grape is lamenting, "O Shams-i Tabrīzī, come, for on account of unripeness and lack of savour I groan within myself."

169

Yesterday my darling placed a golden crown on my head; however many blows you may strike, it will not fall from my head.

The cap-stitching king of eternity from his brows on my brows sets the nightcap of love, so of course it remains for ever.

And even if my head does not remain with the cap, I will become all head like the moon; for my pearl will appear brighter without casket and shell.

Here is my head, and there a heavy mace; strike, to make proof; and if this bone breaks, I am more full of marrow than intellect and soul.

5   That nut lacking pith which has chosen the husk—how shall it have perceived the relish of the almond-essence of my Prophet?

A sweetmeat full of his nuts, his sugar, and almonds sweetens my throat and lip, gives light to my eyes.

When you discover the pith, my son, and have learned to disregard the husk, when you have entered the quarter of Jesus, you will not any more say, "Where is my ass?"

My soul, how long will you complain? Give up one ass from the herd; behold the stoutness of the rider, not my lean draught-horse.

Know that the stoutness of the lover derives from the stoutness of his Beloved, for the pride of lovers arises from "I am God Most Great."

10   O sighing pains, do not say "Ah, ah," say "Allah"; speak not of the well, speak of the throne, O Joseph my soul-nourisher.

170

I was dead, I became alive; I was weeping, I became laughing; the power of love came, and I became everlasting power.

My eye is satiated, my soul is bold, I have the heart of a lion, I have become shining Venus.

He said, "You are not mad, you are not appropriate to this house"; I went and became mad, I became bound in shackles.

He said, "You are not intoxicated; go, for you belong not to this party"; I went and became intoxicated, I became overflowing with joy.

5   He said, "You are not slain, you are not drenched in joy"; before his life-giving face I became slain and cast down.

He said, "You are a clever little man, drunk with fancy and doubt"; I became a fool, I became straightened, I became plucked up out of all.

He said, "You have become a candle, the *qibla* of this assembly"; I am not of assembly, I am not candle, I have become scattered smoke.

He said, "You are shaikh and headman, you are leader and guide"; I am not a shaikh, I am not a leader, I have become slave to your command.

He said, "You have pinions and wings, I will not give you wings and pinions"; in desire for his pinions and wings I became wingless and impotent.

10   New fortune said to me, "Go not on the way, do not become pained, for out of grace and generosity I am now coming to you."

Old love said to me, "Do not move from my breast"; I said, "Yes, I will not, I am at rest and remain."

You are the fountain of the sun, I am the shadow of the willow; when You strike my head, I become low and melting.

My heart felt the glow of the soul, my heart opened and split, my heart wove a new satin, I became enemy of this ragged one.

The form of the soul at dawn swaggered insolently; I was a slave and an ass-driver, I became king and lord.

15   Your paper gives thanks for your limitless sugar, for it came into my embrace, and I dwelt with it.

My darkling earth gives thanks for my bent sky and sphere, for through its gaze and circling I became light-receiving.

The sphere of heaven gives thanks for king and kingdom and angel, for through his generosity and bounty I have become bright and bountiful.

The gnostic of God gives thanks that we have outraced all; above the seven layers I have become a shining star.

I was Venus, I became the moon, I became the two hundredfold sky; I was Joseph, henceforth I have become the waxing Joseph.

20 Famous moon, I am yours, look upon me and yourself, for from the trace of your smile I have become a smiling rose-garden.

Move silently like a chessman, yourself all tongue, for through the face of the king of the world I have become happy and blissful.

171

Of these two thousand I's and we's I wonder, which one am I? Give ear to my babble, do not lay your hand on my mouth.

Since I have gone out of control, do not put glass on my path, for if you do I will stamp and break all that I find.

Because every moment my heart is confused with your fantasy, if you are joyous I am joyful, if you are sorrowing I am sorrowful.

You give bitterness and I become bitter, you give grace and I become all grace; with you it is pleasant, O my sugar-lipped, sweet-chinned idol.

5 You are the original—what person am I? A mirror in your hand; whatever you show, that I become, I am a well-proved mirror.

You are like the cypress of the meadow, I am like your shadow; since I have become the shadow of the rose, I have pitched my tent beside the rose.

If without you I break off a rose, it will become a thorn in my hand; and if I am all thorn, through you I am all rose and jasmine.

Every moment I drain a bloody beaker of the blood of my heart; every instant I break my own pitcher against the saki's door.

Every second I reach out my hand towards the skirt of an idol, that he may scratch my cheek, that he may rend my shirt.

10   The grace of Ṣalāḥ-i Dil u Dīn shone in the midst of my heart; he is the heart's candle in the world; who am I? His bowl.

172

I saw a tree and a fire. A call came, "My darling!" That fire is calling me; am I Moses son of 'Imrān?

I entered the wilderness with affliction, and tasted manna and quails; for forty years like Moses I am wandering about this desert.

Ask not about ship and sea; come, look at these marvels—how that for so many years I have been sailing a ship in this dry land.

Come, soul! You are Moses, and this bodily form is your staff; when you pick me up I become a staff, when you cast me down I am a serpent.

5   You are Jesus and I am your bird; you made a bird out of clay; just as you breathe on me, even so I fly in the zenith.

I am the pillar of that mosque against which the Prophet leaned; when he leans against another, I moan from the pain of separation.

Lord of Lords and Formless Maker of forms, what form are You drawing over me? You know; I do not know.

Now I am stone, now iron; for a while I am all fire; now I am a balance without a weight, now I am both weight and balance.

For one time I pasture here, another they pasture on me; now I am a wolf, now a sheep, now the form of a shepherd.

10   The material body came as a token; how shall the token remain for ever? Neither this remains nor that; He who is mine knows that I am that.

173

I circumambulate with the pilgrims, I circle around the Beloved; I have not the character of dogs, I do not go around carrion.

I am like a gardener; shovel laid on my neck, searching for a cluster of dates I go around the thorns—

Not the kind of dates which, when you have eaten them, turn to phlegm and make one bilious, but the kind that makes wings to grow so that I circle like Ṭaiyār.

The world is a snake, and below it is a treasure very hidden; I am on top of the treasure, and circle about it like the tail of a snake.

5   I am not grieving for a grain, though about this house I circle deep in thought like the heron.

I do not seek a house in the village, neither ox and fat herd, but I am intoxicated with the Prince and circle seeking the Prince.

I am the companion of Khiḍar and momently seek his approach, foot fast and circling, for like compasses I circle.

Do you not know that I am sick? For I am seeking Galen; do you not see that I am crop-sick? For I circle the vintner.

Do you not know that I am Simurgh? For I fly around Qāf; do you not know that I have caught the scent? For I circle about the rosebower.

10   Count me not one of these men; recognize a phantom circling; if I am not a phantom, O soul, why do I circle about the secrets?

Why do I not become still? I beat about this and that, for he has unminded me and made me drunk, therefore I circle unevenly.

You say to me, "Go not so hurriedly, for that shows disrespect"; I am ashamed of respect, therefore I circle shame.

I made bread my pretext, but I am intoxicated with the baker; it is not about gold I circle, I circle about vision.

In every image which confronts me I behold the engraver; know that it is for love of Lailā that like Majnūn I circle.

15 In this palace of self-sacrificers in which is not contained even the head, I, bewildered, am pardonable if I circle without a turban.

I am not a flame-moth burning my wings and pinions, I am a moth of the King, for I circle about the lights.

Why do you bite my lips privily saying, "Be silent, do not speak"? Is it not your doing, your craft too that I circle about speech?

Come, Shams-i Tabrīzī, like twilight although you flee; like twilight in the track of your sun I circle about these lands.

174

I am not that luckless lover, to flee from the Beloved; I do not hold that dagger in my hand to flee from battle.

I am that plank with which the carpenter has much to do, I do not shrink from the axe or flee from the nails.

I am unselfed like a plank, I think not to oppose the axe; I am fit only for the flames if I flee from the carpenter.

I am as a worthless and cold stone if I do not journey oft to rubiness; I am as a dark and narrow cave if I flee from the Companion of the Cave.

5 I do not feel the kiss of the peach if I flee from leaflessness; I do not catch the scent of Tartary musk if I flee from the Tartar.

I am distressed with myself because I am not contained; it is meet, when the head is not contained, if I flee from the turban.

Many centuries are required for this fortune to emerge; where shall I find it again, if this time I flee?

It is not that I am sick and unmanly, that I shun the fair ones; it is not that my bowels are corrupt, that I flee from the vintner.

I am not mounted on a packsaddle to remain then in the arena; I am not a farmer of this village, to flee from the Prince.

10   I say, "My heart, have done"; my heart replies, "I am in the quarry of gold, why should I flee from the lavishing of riches?"

175

When the thunder and lightning laugh, I recite paeans of praise, I am full of light as the clear sky, I am circling around the moon.

My tongue is knotted like Moses because of the Pharaohs, for jealousy lest a Pharaoh should discover my proof.

Bind my hands if you find me in the encampment of a Pharaoh, for I am the Sultan's spy.

I am not a spy, I am not a scandal, I am one of the secrets of sanctity; let me go, since I am drunk, that I may let fly a vaunt.

5   From wine wind arises, for wine stirs up wind, especially the kind of wine through which I am distraught.

If a whiff of this wine were to reach all the world's ascetics, what a desolation then will appear, what shall I say? I know not.

Why speak of the wine? For if a whiff of those drunkards' breaths were to penetrate stone and marble, they would brag, "I am the Water of Life."

My being is a bachelor's apartment, and those drunkards are gathered together therein; my heart is distraught to know whether I am one of them—amazing!—or myself I am they.

Whether I am their congener, or whether I am other than they, I do not know; all I know is this, that I am in peace and well-being.

176

I went to the physician of the soul, I said, "Look at my hand. I am heartlorn and sick at once, both lover and intoxicated.

I have a hundred ailments—would that they were all one! With all these distempers I have reached the very end."

He said, "Were you not dead?" I said, "Yes, but when your scent came to me I leaped out of the grave."

That spiritual form, that orient divine, that Joseph of Canaan on whose account I wounded my hand,

5   Gently, gently came towards me and laid a hand on my heart. He said, "Of what band are you?" I said, "Of this band."

When I brawled he gave me wine, and I drank; my pale cheek glowed and I ceased to brawl.

Then I stripped off my clothes, I raged like a drunkard, I sat in that drunkards' ring, on the right hand.

I drank a hundred jars, I roared a hundred ways, I scattered a hundred glasses, I shattered a hundred pitchers.

Those folk worshipped the golden calf; I am a mangy calf, if I do not worship Love.

10   Again the spiritual king is secretly calling me, he is drawing me up royally from these depths.

I am foot-tied to you, O soul, I am intoxicated with you, my soul, I am in your hand, my soul, whether I am arrow or thumbstall.

If I am nimble, you make me so, if I am drunk you make me so, if I am lowly you make me so, if I am in being, you make me so.

You brought me into the circling sphere when you intoxicated me with you; since now you have sealed the vat, I too have closed my mouth.

177

Not for one single moment do I let hold of you, for you are my whole concern, you are my whole affair.

I eat and enjoy your candy, I labour at your counselling; I am a heart-wounded quarry, you are my heart-devouring lion.

You might say that my soul and your soul are one; I swear by this one soul that I care not for other than you.

I am a bunch of herbs from the garden of your beauty, I am a strand of your union's robe of honour.

5   Around you this world is thorn on the top of a wall; in the hope of culling the rose of union it is a thorn that I scratch.

Since the thorn is like this, how must be your rosebower! O you whose secrets have swallowed and borne away my secrets.

My soul, in the sky the sun is the moon's companion; I know that you will not leave me in this assembly of strangers.

I went to a dervish and he said, "May God befriend you!" You might say that through his blessing a king such as you became my friend.

I beheld the whole world to be a painting on the gates of a bath; you who have taken my turban away, likewise towards you I stretch my hand.

10   Every congener bursts his chain to come to his congener; whose congener am I, who am held fast in this snare here?

Like a thief, my soul, you ever steal around me; I know what you are seeking, crafty sweetheart of mine.

My soul, you are hiding a candle under the cloak, you desire to set fire to my stook and rick.

O my rosebower and rosegarden, O cure of my sickness, O Joseph of my vision and lustre of my market,

You are circling round my heart, I am circling round your door; circling am I giddily in your hand like a compass.

15 In the gladness of your face if I tell the tale of woe, if then sorrow drinks my blood, by Allah, I deserve it.

To the beat of the tambourine of your decree all these creatures are dancing; without your melody does a single lute-string dance? I do not think so.

The voice of your tambourine is hidden, and this dance of the world is visible; hidden is that itch, wherever I scratch.

I will be silent out of jealousy, because from your sugarcane I am a cloud scattering sugar, it is only your candy that I rain.

I am in water, in earth, in fire, in air; these four are all around me, but I am not of these four.

20 Now I am Turk, now Hindu, now Rumi, now Zangi; it is of your engraving, my soul, that I believe or disbelieve.

Tabriz, my heart and soul are with Shams-i Ḥaqq here, even though in body I vex him no more.

178

I am a painter, a picture-maker, every moment I fashion an idol, then before you I melt away all the idols,

I raise up a hundred images and mingle them with spirit; when I see your image, I cast them in the fire.

You are the vintner's saki or the enemy of the sober, or the one who lays waste every house I build.

Over you the soul is poured forth, with you it is mingled; since the soul has the perfume of you, I will cherish the soul.

5 Every drop of blood that flows out of me says to your dust, "I am one in colour with your love, I am the playmate of your affection."

In the house of water and clay this heart without you is desolate; either enter the house, O soul, or I will abandon the house.

179

I am your disciple, for all that I am stupid and twisted of mouth, so that I may learn one smile from your smiling lip.

Fountain of learning, do you want me for a pupil? What device shall I invent to stitch myself to you?

At least I may descry through the crack of the door the lightning of your cheek; from that fire of the portico I will kindle a hundred candles.

One instant you rob me of my load on the way, saying, "I am the tithe-collector"; one instant you go before me, meaning, "I am the guide."

5   Now you drive me to sin, now towards repentance; twist my head and my tail, for I am a compressed *hamza*.

In sin and in penitence, like a fish on the pan, this side and that side I am burning on the pan.

On your pan I am turning this way and that; in the darkness of night, with you I am brighter than day.

Enough, I am all diversified in craft and thought; for one instant like turquoise, for one instant like Pīrūz.

180

Once again, once again I have escaped from my chains, I have burst out of these bonds and this trap which seizes the infirm.

Heaven, the bent old man full of wizardry and deceit— by virtue of your youthful fortune I have escaped from this old man.

Night and day I ran, I broke away from night and day; ask of this sphere how like an arrow I sped.

Why should I fear sorrow? For I am the comrade of death. Why should I fear the general? For I have escaped from the prince.

Reason bore me down with anxiety for forty years; sixty-two has made me quarry, and I have escaped from devising.

All creatures have been made deaf or blind by predestination; I have escaped from the attack and retreat of predestination, and from predestination.

Outwardly skin, inwardly stone, the fruit is a prisoner; like a fig, I have escaped from that skin and that stone.

Delay causes mischief, and haste is of the devil; my heart has escaped from haste, and I have escaped from delay.

In the first place blood was the food, in the end blood became milk; when the teeth of reason sprouted, I escaped from that milk;

I ran after bread, a loaf or two, by imposture; God gave me a food, so that I escaped from imposture.

Be silent, be silent, speak no more in detail; I will speak of the interpretation, I have escaped from the stench of garlic.

181

Like a mirror my soul displays secrets; I am able not to speak, but I am unable not to know.

I have become a fugitive from the body, fearful as to the spirit; I swear I know not—I belong neither to this nor to that.

Seeker, to catch a scent is the condition of dying; look not upon me as living, for I am not so.

Look not on my crookedness, but behold this straight word; my talk is an arrow, and I am as a bow.

This gourdlike head on top of me, and this dervish habit of my body—whom am I like, whom am I like in this market of the world?

Then this gourd on my head, full of liquor—I keep it upside down, yet I let not a drop trickle from it.

And even if I do let trickle, do you behold the power of God, that in exchange for that drop I gather pearls from the sea.

My eyes like a cloud gather pearls from that sea; this cloud of my spirit rises to the heaven of fidelity.

I rain in the presence of Shams al-Ḥaqq-i Tabrīz, that lilies may grow in the form of my tongue.

182

Saki, my spirit is moving in the track of love, but because of your weariness my tongue is tied.

Like an arrow I am flying towards your joyous company; beloved, do not break my bow with cruelties.

Like a tent I remain standing before you on one foot; beloved, bring me into your tabernacle and seat me there.

Ho, lay that flagon's lip on my dry lip, then hear the veritable magic from my mouth;

5   Hear the story of Babylon and the tale of Vā'il, for by way of meditation I travel the world.

Excuse me if my turbulence goes beyond bounds, since love grants me security not for a single moment.

When you are weary, I am weary of your weariness; when you wash your hands of me, I bite my fingers.

On the night when you dispense light like the moon until daybreak, in your wake I am running like a star;

On the day when you put up your head from the east like the sun, like the sun I am altogether spirit.

10   But on the day when like the spirit you are hidden from my eyes, like the heart of a bird I am fluttering with anxiety.

On the day when your light shines through my window, in my apartment I dance for joy like a mote.

Rational soul, be silent and depart into hiding like the thought, so that he who thinks of causes only may not find my track.

183

I am the slave who set the master free, I am the one who taught the teacher.

I am that soul which was born of the world yesterday, and yet erected the ancient world.

I am the wax whose claim is this, that it was I who made steel steel.

I have painted with surmeh many a sightless one, I have taught many a one without intelligence.

5   I am the black cloud in the night of grief who gladdened the day of festival.

I am the amazing earth who out of the fire of love filled with air the brain of the sky.

In joy that king slept not last night, because I the slave remembered him.

It is not to blame, since you intoxicated me, if I am scandalous and wrought injustice.

Silence, for the mirror is rusting over; when I blew upon it, it protested against me.

184

I made a journey, I ran to every city, no man I saw with your grace and beauty.

I returned from banishment and exile, once more I attained this felicity.

Since I became far from the garden of your countenance, I saw no rose, I plucked not one fruit.

Since by bad luck I fell far from you, I have endured trouble from every unlucky one.

5   What shall I say? I was utterly dead without you; God has created me anew once more.

Amazing! Would you say that I have beheld your face? Would you say that I have heard your voice?

Suffer me to kiss your hand and foot; give festively, for today is festival.

Joseph of Egypt, I have brought you as a present such a bright mirror.

185

How close your soul is to my soul! For whatever thing you are thinking, I know.

I have a token even closer than this; come close, and behold my token.

In dervish guise you come into the midst; do not jest and say, "I am in the midst."

I am like the column amidst your house; I am like a water-spout hanging down from your roof.

5   I am a sharer of your secrets on the day of mustering and resurrection, I am not a passing host like worldly friends.

In your banquet I go round like the wine, in time of your battle I go before you like a lance.

If like lightning I make a trade of dying, like the lightning of your beauty I am without a tongue.

Always I am joyful; it makes no difference whether I yield my soul, or seize a soul.

If I give you my soul, it will be good trade, for in exchange for a soul you will give me a hundred worlds.

10   In this house thousands and more are dead; there you are seated saying, "Behold my household!"

A handful of dust says, "I was once a tress"; another says, "I am a bone."

You become bewildered; then suddenly Love comes saying, {"Come to me, for I am the one eternally alive.

Embrace my smooth breast to your breast, so that I may} deliver you this very instant from yourself."

Silence, Khusrau, speak no more of Shīrīn; my mouth is burning with sweetness.

186

Out of all the world I choose you alone; do you deem it right for me to sit sorrowful?

My heart is like a pen in your hand; through you it is, whether I am glad or grieve.

What shall I be other than what you wish? What shall I see except what you show?

Now you cause thorns to grow from me, now roses; now I smell roses, now I pluck thorns.

5 Since you keep me so, I am so—since you wish me so, I am so.

In that vat where you dispense dye to the heart, what should I be? What my love and hate?

You were the first, and you will be the last; do you make my last better than my first.

When you are hidden, I am of the infidels; when you appear, I am of the faithful.

What do I possess other than the thing you have given? What are you searching for in my pocket and sleeve?

187

Come, for today we are the quarry of the King, we have no need for self and the world.

Come, for today like Moses son of 'Imrān {with manliness} we will lift up dust from the sea.

All night we were fallen like a staff; now that day has come we are restless as serpents.

Having circumambulated round our own breast, we bring out of the soul's pocket the White Hand.

5 By that power whereby a serpent became a staff, every night we are like a staff, daily a serpent;

For arrogant Pharaoh we are serpents, for Moses we are staves and obedient.

By zeal we shed the blood of Nimrods; do not regard the fact that we are slender as gnats.

We will exceed over lions and elephants, though in the hand of that Lion we are helpless.

Though like camels we are crooked of nature, like camels we travel smoothly towards the Kaaba.

10 We will not attach our hearts to a two-days' fortune, for we are successful in everlasting fortune.

Like sun and moon we are near and far, like love and the heart we are hidden and patent.

For the sake of blood-lapping, blood-devouring Love we are as blood in the platter of Love's dogs.

As fish in the time of silence we are silent, in the time of speech we are the dustless moon.

188

I was intent on seeking a stratagem, that that moon-faced one might set his face on mine.

I said, "I have one word in my mind; come forward, that I may speak it in your ear.

Last night, dear soul, I saw a dream, and I desire to seek from you its interpretation.

I have none intimate with this dream but you; do you listen, my king whose habit is to conceal."

5 He moved his head and laughed—that head which knows me hair by hair—

As if to say, "You are hatching a trick to play on me, for I am the mirror of every hue and scent."

I am as a plaything in his hands, for I am the picture drawn by his gold-stitching needle.

Not lifeless shall be the image which he has made; I am his least image, I am therefore in ecstasy.

189

I departed, ridding the world of the trouble of my presence, I escaped from anguish with my life;

I bade farewell to my companions, I transported my soul to the signless world.

I went forth from this house of six doors, gaily I carried my baggage to placelessness.

When I beheld the master of the hunt of the Unseen I flew like an arrow, carrying my bow;

5 When the polo-stick of death approached me, I carried off from the midst the ball of felicity.

A marvellous moon shone through my window; I went to the roof, carrying a ladder.

The roof of heaven which is the assembly-place of souls, was fairer than I had ever imagined.

Since my rose-branch had become withered, I carried it back again to the garden and rosebower.

As there was no purchaser for my coin, I carried it quickly to the source of the source of the mine;

10 From these counterfeiters I carried also as a present a filing of the soul to the goldsmith.

In the Unseen the boundless world I saw; to that bound I transported my tent.

Do not weep for me, for I am happy because of this journey, inasmuch as I have travelled the road to the realm of paradise.

Write this saying upon my tomb, that I have come safely out of trial and tribulation.

Sleep sweetly, body, in this earth, for I have carried your message up to heaven.

15 Bind up my chin, for I have carried all lamentations to the Creator of lamentation.

Speak no more the grief of your heart, for I have carried your heart to the presence of Him who knows all secrets.

190

We are dancing like motes, we obey the command of your sun.

Every dawn out of Love's east like the sun we rise.

We thresh about in dry and wet, we become not dry, nor turn wet.

We have heard brasses making much lament, "O light, shine, that we may become gold."

5   For the sake of their need and anguish we rise to the spheres and the stars.

We come as amber for a necklace from the silver-bosomed Beloved.

We have beaten our dervish frock, to emerge from that to a gown of Shushtar.

We are the drainers of pure wine on the path of poverty, we are intoxicated with the red wine.

If they impose on us the world's poison, we come as sugar out of our inward parts.

10   On the day when brave men flee, we come as Sanjar in the thick of the battle;

We make wine of the foeman's blood, then we drain it and come like daggers.

We are the ring of drunken lovers, every day we come as a ring on the door.

He wrote the sign-manual of security for us; how should we come to the rattle of mere death?

In the supernal kingdom and placelessness we come on the steed of the green sphere.

15   We went into hiding from the world of the flesh, we come more manifest in the world of Love.

In the body the soul has become pure; we become bodiless and come yet purer.

Shams-i Tabrīz is the soul of the soul; we come shoulder to shoulder in the house of eternity.

191

Last night I vowed anew, I swore an oath by your life,
That I would never remove my eyes from your face; if You smite with the sword, I will not turn from You.

I will not seek the cure from any other, because my pain is of separation from You.

If You should cast me into the fire, I am no true man if I utter a sigh.

5   I rose from your path like dust; now I return to the dust of your path.

192

If I do not express in speech your elegance, I have your love within my breast.

If I smell a rose without your love, forthwith burn me like a thorn.

If I am silent as a fish, yet I am restless as the waves and the sea.

You who have set a seal on my lips, draw my toggle towards You.

5   What is your design? What should I know? I only know that I am in this train.

I chew the cud of grief for you like a camel, like a raging camel I bring up foam.

Though I keep hidden and do not speak, in the presence of Love I am manifest.

I am like a seed under the soil, I am waiting upon the signal of spring,

That without my own breath I may breathe sweetly, that without my own head I may scratch a head.

193

On the day when you pass over my grave, bring to mind this terror and confusion of mine;

Fill full of light that bottom of the tomb, O eye and lamp of my light,

That in the tomb this patient body of mine may prostrate to you in gratitude.

Harvest of roses, pass me not in haste, make me happy a moment with that perfume;

5   And when you pass by, do not suppose that I am far from your window and portico.

If the stones of the tomb have blocked my way, I am unwearying on the path of fantasy.

Though I should have a hundred winding-sheets of satin, I am naked without the vestment of your form.

I will emerge into the hall of your palace, in breaking a hole in the wall perchance I am like an ant.

I am your ant, you are Solomon; not for one moment leave me without your presence.

10   I have fallen silent; do you speak the rest, for I am shunning henceforth my own speaking and listening.

Shams-i Tabrīz, do you invite me, since your invitation is my blast of the trumpet.

194

We are living by the light of Majesty, we are strangers and exceeding familiar.

The carnal soul is like a wolf, but in our secret heart we are superior to Joseph of Egypt.

The moon repents of his conceit when we display to him out face;

The feathers and pinions of the sun consume when we open our feathers and pinions.

5   This form of man is a veil; we are the *qibla* of all prostrations.

Regard that breath, do not see the Adam in us, that we may transport your soul with grace.

Iblis looked with a separate regard, he supposed that we are apart from God.

Shams-i Tabrīz himself is the pretext; it is we who are in the beauty of grace, we.

For the sake of a veil say to men, "He is the noble king and we are beggars."

10   What have we to do with kingship and beggary? We are happy because we are worthy of the king.

We are effaced in the beauty of Shams-i Tabrīz; in that effacement neither he is, nor are we.

195

O world of water and clay, since I knew you I have known a myriad tribulations and pains.

You are the pasturage of asses, not the abode of Jesus; why have I known this pasturage of asses?

You first spread the table, then gave me sweet water; you bound me hand and foot, so that I knew hand and foot.

Why should you not bind hand and foot, seeing God called you a cradle?

5   Like a tree I lift up my hands from the earth in desire for that One from whom I knew desire.

"O cluster, how is it that in childhood you become like a perfect old man?" Answer came, "I escaped from youthful passion when I knew the zephyr."

The branch goes upwards because it came from above; I hasten towards my origin, because I know my origin.

How long shall I speak of "below" and "above"? Placelessness is my origin, I am not of place, for I know whence place comes.

No, be silent, depart into nonexistence, become naught in nonexistence; behold, how I know things from no-things!

196

Since my sun and star arose higher than form, I am happier to go from realities into realities.

I have become lost in realities—so it is sweeter; I will not return towards form, I will not look upon the two worlds.

I am melting in meanings till I become of one colour with Him, for meaning is as water and I am as sugar.

No man's heart wearies of the life of his own soul; naturally in view of this reality I will not recall form.

5   I stroll from garden to garden with the spiritual ones, graceful as a red rose and fresh as a nenuphar am I.

I am as a wave to the body's boat, I break it plank by plank; I smash myself when I am anchor to myself.

And if out of hardness of heart I am slack in my affairs, swiftly out of the sea surge my flames of fire.

I am laughing happily as gold amidst his fire, because if I emerge from the fire I congeal as gold.

From an incantation like a snake I have put down my head on his line—brother, what will fall on my head from his line?

10   I was weary of form, I came towards attributes; each attribute said, "Enter here, for I am the green sea."

Shams-i Tabrīz, I have a realm like Alexander; consequently out of grace I am army-leader towards the armies of meaning.

197

Give me that last night's wine, for I am intoxicated by your potion; Ḥātim of the world, give into my hand a huge cup.

Saki of true men, turn not your face from me for one moment; do not break my heart, else I shall break cup and glass.

A cup was in my hand, I flung it down and broke it; I wounded the soles of a hundred naked feet with that glass.

You are a glass-worshipper because your liquor is from glass; my wine is not of must, so why should I worship glass?

5   Drink, my heart, the spiritual wine, and sleep secure and free of care; for I have beheaded anguish, I have escaped from sorrow and anguish.

My heart has gone up, my body has gone down; where am I, the helpless one? I am neither above nor below.

What a fine hanging apple am I, who cannot endure without your stone! How should I endure without *balā* if I am drunk with *alast*?

Ask of me, what a treasure this love is and what it holds; ask concerning me also of him, that he may say who I am.

Why do you hang about the riverbank? Leap from the river, if you are a true man; leap from the river and seek for me, for I have leaped from the river.

10   If you remain, we remain, and if you go, we depart; when you ate I ate, when you sat I sat.

I am that drunken drummer who went drunk into the arena, I tied my drum like a flag to the top of my lance.

What a happy and unselfed king you are! Ho, silent as a fish— since I have escaped from being, why do you draw me back to being?

198

I am that lover of your love who have no occupation but this, for I have nothing but disapproval for him who is not a lover.

I seek no heart but yours, I hurry only towards you; I do not smell the roses of every garden, I have no heed for every thorn.

In you I have put my faith, my heart has become Mussulman; my heart said to you, "Darling, I have no beloved like you."

Since you are my eye and tongue, I do not see two, I do not recite two, I acknowledge none but the one darling that is you.

5   Since I drink of your honey, why should I sell vinegar? Why should I labour for my daily bread? It is not the case that I do not possess an ample allowance.

I eat to my fill at this table of the Sultan's sugarcakes, not as a guest of Satan; I have no appetite for lunch.

I will not grieve, I will not grieve, I will not boast of asceticism; if you think I have not abundant gold, behold my gold-pale cheeks.

The Khusrau of the heart grieves only for Shīrīn; with what heart should I grieve? After all, I have not a grieved heart.

I would explain for all, both fearful and secure alike; but I have not the heart to speak of inward words.

10   You who are unbranded by madness, tell me now, how are you? For I have no further traces of how and after what manner.

Since from Tabriz has come the moon of Shams al-Ḥaqq u Dīn to me, I have no care for the moon of the dormitory of the commander.

199

If I am hand-clapping, I belong not to the clappers; I am neither of this nor of that, I am of that mighty city.

I am not for fluting and gambling, I am not for wine and

liquor, I am neither leaven nor crop-sickness, I am neither like this nor like that.

If I am drunk and dissolute, I am not drunk with wine like you; I am not of earth nor of water, I am not of the people of time.

The mind of the son of Adam—what knowledge has it of this utterance? For I am hidden by two hundred veils from the world entire.

5   Hear not these words as from me, nor from this clear thought, for I neither receive nor seize this outward and inward.

Though your face is beautiful, the cage of your soul is of wood; run away from me or you will burn, for my tongue is a flame.

I am not of scent nor colour, I am not of fame nor shame; beware of my poplar arrow, for God is my bow.

I seize not raw wine, nor borrow from anyone, I seize neither breath nor snare, O my youthful fortune.

I am as the rosebower of paradise, I am the joy-garden of the world, for my spirit is flowing through the spirits of all men.

10   The sugarbed of your phantom brings rose-sugar to me; in the garden of realities I scatter the rose of a hundred petals.

When I enter the rose-showering garden of union with you, make me sit down, for I am a target for your brand.

Love, what a mate you are, how strange, how marvellous! When you seized my mouth, my expression went inwards.

When my soul reaches Tabriz, to come to Shams al-Ḥaqq u Dīn, I will bring to an end all the secrets of speech.

200

There is a passion in my head that I have no inclination for mankind, this passion makes me so that I am unaware of myself.

The king of love bestows every moment two thousand kingdoms; I desire nothing from him save his beauty.

The girdle and cap of his love are enough for me in both worlds; what matter if my cap falls? What care if I have no girdle?

One morning his love transported my wounded heart to a place where I transcended day and night, and have no knowledge of dawn.

5   A journey befell my soul to the kingdom of realities, such that the sky and the moon say, "I have no such journey."

Through separation if my soul scatters pearls from my eyes, think not that I have not a heart full of pearls from him.

What sugar-seller have I to sell sugar to me! Never on any day he said, "Go, for I have no sugar."

I would have shown a token of his beauty, but the two worlds would be confounded; I have no inclination for such clamour and riot.

Tabriz, I have sworn that after Shams-i Dīn comes I will in gratitude lay down this head, for I have nothing but a head.

201

The ravings which my enemy uttered I heard within my heart; the secret thoughts he harbored against me I also perceived.

His dog bit my foot, he showed me much injustice; I do not bite him like a dog, I have bitten my own lip.

Since I have penetrated into the secrets of individuals like men of God, why should I take glory in having penetrated his secret?

I reproach myself that through my doubtings it so happened that purposely I drew a scorpion towards my own foot.

5   Like Iblis who saw nothing of Adam except his fire, by God I was invisible to this insignificant Iblis.

Convey to my friends why I am afflicted in mind; when the snake bit my thigh I started away from the black rope.

The blessed silent ones, their lips and eyes closed—by a way unknown to any man, I ran into their thoughts;

Since there is a secret and perfect way from heart to heart, I gathered gold and silver from the treasuries of hearts.

Into the thought that was like a brazen stove I flung the dead dog; out of the thought that was like a rose bower I plucked roses and jasmine.

10 If I have hinted at the evil and good of my friends, I have spun that like a weaver as the choicest veil.

When my heart rushed suddenly to a heart mighty and aware, out of awe for his heart I fluttered like the heart.

As you are happy with your own state, how did you fall in with me? Attend to your own business, for I am neither shaikh nor disciple.

As far as you are concerned, brother, I am neither copper nor red gold; drive me from your door, for I am neither lock nor key.

Take it as if I had not ever spoken these words; if you had been in my mind, by God I would not have quarreled.

202

I closed my eyes to creation when I beheld his beauty, I became intoxicated with his beauty and bestowed my soul.

For the sake of Solomon's seal I became wax in all my body, and in order to become illumined I rubbed my wax.

I saw his opinion and cast away my own twisted opinion; I became his reed pipe and likewise lamented on his lip.

He was in my hand, and blindly I groped for him with my hand; I was in his hand, and yet I inquired of those who were misinformed.

5 I must have been either a simpleton or drunk or mad that fearfully I was stealing from my own gold.

Like a thief I crept through a crack in the wall into my own vine, like a thief I gathered jasmine from my own garden.

Enough, do not twist my secret upon your fingertips, for I have twisted off out of your twisted fist.

Shams-i Tabrīz, from whom comes the light of moon and stars—though I am grieving with sorrow for him, I am like the crescent of the festival.

203

Reason says, "I will beguile him with the tongue"; Love says, "Be silent. I will beguile him with the soul."

The soul says to the heart, "Go, do not laugh at me and yourself. What is there that is not his, that I may beguile him thereby?"

He is not sorrowful and anxious and seeking oblivion that I may beguile him with wine and a heavy measure.

The arrow of his glance needs not a bow that I should beguile the shaft of his gaze with a bow.

5   He is not prisoner of the world, fettered to this world of earth, that I should beguile him with gold and the kingdom of the world.

He is an angel, though in form he is a man; he is not lustful that I should beguile him with women.

Angels start away from the house wherein this form is, so how should I beguile him with such a form and likeness?

He does not take a flock of horses, since he flies on wings; his food is light, so how should I beguile him with bread?

He is not a merchant and trafficker in the market of the world that I should beguile him with enchantment of gain and loss.

10   He is not veiled that I should make myself out sick and utter sighs, to beguile him with lamentation.

I will bind my head and bow my head, for I have got out of hand; I will not beguile his compassion with sickness or fluttering.

Hair by hair he sees my crookedness and feigning; what's hidden from him that I should beguile him with anything hidden.

He is not a seeker of fame, a prince addicted to poets, that I should beguile him with verses and lyrics and flowing poetry.

The glory of the unseen form is too great for me to beguile it with blessing or Paradise.

15 Shams-i Tabrīz, who is his chosen and beloved—perchance I will beguile him with this same pole of the age.

204

My mother was fortune, my father generosity and bounty; I am joy, son of joy, son of joy, son of joy.

Behold, the Marquis of Glee has attained felicity; this city and plain are filled with soldiers and drums and flags.

If I encounter a wolf, he becomes a moonfaced Joseph; if I go down into a well, it converts into a Garden of Eram.

He whose heart is as iron and stone out of miserliness is now changed before me into a Ḥātem of the age in generosity and bounty.

5 Dust becomes gold and pure silver in my hand; how then should the temptation of gold and silver waylay me?

I have an idol such that, were his sweet scent scattered abroad, even an idol of stone would receive life through joy.

Sorrow has died for joy in him of "may God bind your consolation"; how should not such a sword strike the neck of sorrow?

By tyranny he seizes the soul of whom he desires; justices are all slaves of such injustice and tyranny.

What is that mole on that face? Should it manifest itself, out of desire for it forthwith maternal aunt would be estranged from paternal [uncle].

10 I said, "If I am done and send my story, will you finish it and expound it?" He answered, "Yes."

205

When I am asleep and crumbling in the tomb, should you come to visit me, I will come forth with speed.

You are for me the blast of the trumpet and the resurrection, so what shall I do? Dead or living, wherever you are, there am I.

Without your lip I am a frozen and silent reed; what melodies I play the moment you breathe on my reed!

Your wretched reed has become accustomed to your sugar lip; remember wretched me, for I am seeking you.

5   When I do not find the moon of your countenance, I bind up my head [veil myself in mourning]; when I do not find your sweet lip, I gnaw my own hand.

206

The time has come for us to become madmen in your chain, to burst our bonds and become estranged from all;

To yield up our souls, no more to bear the disgrace of such a soul, to set fire to our house, and run like fire to the tavern.

Until we ferment, we shall not escape from this vat of the world—how then shall we become intimate with the lip of that flagon and bowl?

Listen to true words from a madman: do not suppose that we become true men until we die.

5   It is necessary that we should become more inverted than the tip of a comb in the top of the twisted tress of felicity;

Spread our wings and pinions like a tree in the orchard, if like a seed we are to be scattered on this road of annihilation.

Though we are of stone, we shall become like wax for your seal; though we be candles, we shall become a moth in the track of your light.

Though we are kings, we shall travel straight as rooks for your sake, that we may become blessed through your queen on this chessboard.

In the face of the mirror of love we must not breathe a word of ourselves; we must become intimate with your treasure when we are changed to waste.

10 Like the tale of the heart we must be without head or ending, that we may become dwellers in the heart of lovers like a tale.

If he acts the seeker, we shall attain to being sought; if he acts the key, we shall become all the wards of the lock.

If Muṣṭafā does not make his way and couch in our hearts, it is meet that we should lament and become like the Wailing Column.

No, be silent; for one must observe silence towards the watchman when we go towards the pavilion by night.

207

Last night my soul cried, "O exalted sphere of heaven, you hang indeed inverted, with flames in your belly.

"Without sin and crime, eternally revolving, upon your body in its complaining is the deep indigo of mourning,

"Now happy, now unhappy, like Abraham in the fire; at once king and beggar like Ibrāhīm-i Adham.

"In form you are terrifying, yet your state is full of anguish: you turn round like a millstone and writhe like a snake."

5 Heaven the blessed replied, "How should I not fear that one who makes the Paradise of the world as Hell?

"In his hand earth is as wax, he makes it Zangi and Rumi, he makes it falcon and owl, he makes it sugar and poison.

"He is hidden, friend, and has set us forth thus patent so that he may become concealed.

"How should the ocean of the world be concealed under straws? The straws have been set adancing, the waves tumbling up and down;

"Your body is like the land floating on the waters of the soul; your soul is veiled in the body alike in wedding feast or sorrow.

10 "In the veil you are a new bride, hot-tempered and obstinate; he is railing sweetly at the good and the bad of the world.

"Through him the earth is a green meadow, the heavens are unresting; on every side through him a fortunate one pardoned and preserved.

"Reason a seeker of certainty through him, patience a seeker of help through him, love seeing the unseen through him, earth taking the form of Adam through him.

"Air seeking and searching, water hand-washing, we Messiah-like speaking, earth Mary-like silent.

"Behold the sea with its billows circling round the earthy ship; behold Kaabas and Meccas at the bottom of this well of Zamzam!"

15 The king says, "Be silent, do not cast yourself into the well, for you do not know how to make a bucket and a rope out of my withered stumps."

208

Every day I bear a burden, and I bear this calamity for a purpose:

I bear the discomfort of cold and December's snow in hope of spring.

Before the fattener-up of all who are lean, I drag this so emaciated body;

Though they expel me from two hundred cities, I bear it for the sake of the love of a prince;

5 Though my shop and house be laid waste, I bear it in fidelity to a tulip bed.

God's love is a very strong fortress; I carry my soul's baggage inside a fortress.

I bear the arrogance of every stonehearted stranger for the sake of a friend, of one long-suffering;

For the sake of his ruby I dig out mountain and mine; for the sake of that rose-laden one I endure a thorn.

For the sake of those two intoxicating eyes of his, like the intoxicated I endure crop sickness;

10   For the sake of a quarry not to be contained in a snare, I spread out the snare and decoy of the hunter.

He said, "Will you bear this sorrow till the Resurrection?" Yes, Friend, I bear it, I bear it.

My breast is the Cave and Shams-i Tabrīzī is the Companion of the Cave. I bear ridicule for the sake of the Companion of the Cave.

209

If I weep, if I come with excuses, my beloved puts cotton wool in his ears.

Every cruelty which he commits becomes him, every cruelty which he commits I endure.

If he accounts me nonexistent, I account his tyranny generosity.

The cure of the ache of my heart is the ache for him; how shall I not surrender my heart to his ache?

5   Only then are glory and respect mine, when his glorious love renders me contemptible.

Only then does the vine of my body become wine, when the wine-presser stamps on me and spurns me underfoot.

I yield my soul like grapes under the trampling, that my secret heart may make merry,

Though the grapes weep only blood, for I am vexed with this cruelty and tyranny.

He who pounds upon me puts cotton wool in his ears say-
ing, "I do not press unwittingly.

10   "If you disbelieve, you are excusable, but I am the Abu'l
Ḥikam [the expert] in this affair.

"When you burst under the labor of my feet, then you will
render much thanks to me."

210

I have got out of my own control, I have fallen into uncon-
sciousness; in my utter unconsciousness how joyful I am with
myself!

The darling sewed up my eyes so that I might not see other
than him, so that suddenly I opened my eyes on his face.

My soul fought with me saying, "Do not pain me"; I said,
"Take your divorce." She said, "Grant it"; I granted it.

When my mother saw on my cheek the brand of your love
she cut my umbilical cord on that, the moment I was born.

5   If I travel to heaven and read the Tablet of the Unseen, O
you who are my soul's salvation, without you how I am ruined!

When you cast aside the veil the dead became alive; the light
of your face reminded me of the Covenant of Alast.

When I became lost, O soul, through love of the king of the
peris, hidden from self and creatures, I am as if peri-born myself.

I said to the Tabriz of Shams-i Dīn, "O body, what are you?"
Body said, "Earth"; Soul said, "I am distraught like the wind."

211

Without you, Darling, in both worlds I have seen no joy;
many wonders I have seen, a wonder like you I have not seen.

They said, "The blaze of fire will be the infidel's portion";
none have I seen exempted of your fire save Bū Lahab.

I have oft laid the ear of my soul at the window of the heart;
I have heard much discourse, but I have seen no lips.

Suddenly you scattered compassion on your servant; I saw
no cause for that save your infinite tenderness.

5   Chosen saki, apple of my eyes, the like of you never appeared
in Persia, in Arabia I never saw.

Be lavish with that wine whose juice never came to festive
gathering and that glass the equal of which I saw not in Aleppo.

Pour wine in such abundance that I set out a foot from my-
self, for in selfhood and existence I have seen only weariness.

You who are sun and moon, you who are honey and sugar,
you who are mother and father, no lineage have I seen but you.

O infinite love, O divine manifestation, you are both stay and
refuge; an epithet equal to you I have not heard.

10   We are iron filings and your love is the magnet; you are the
source of all questing, in your quest none I have seen.

Be silent, brother, dismiss learning and culture; till you re-
cited culture, no culture in you I saw.

Shams-i Ḥaqq-i Tabrīz, source of the source of souls, with-
out the Baṣra of your being, no date have I ever known.

212

Lord, what a Beloved is mine! I have a sweet quarry; I pos-
sess in my breast a hundred meadows from his reed.

When in anger the messenger comes and repairs towards me,
he says, "Whither are you fleeing? I have business with you."

Last night I asked the new moon concerning my Moon. The
moon said, "I am running in his wake, my foot is in his dust."

When the sun arose I said, "How yellow of face you are!"
The sun said, "Out of shame for his countenance I have a face
of gold."

5   "Water, you are prostrate, you are running on your head
and face." Water said, "Because of his incantation I move like a
snake."

"Noble fire, why do you writhe so?" Fire said, "Because of the lightning of his face my heart is restless."

"Wind-messenger of the world, why are you light of heart?" Wind said, "My heart would burn if the choice were mine."

"Earth, what are you meditating, silent and watchful?" Earth said, "Within me I have a garden and spring."

Pass over these elements, God is our succorer; my head is aching, in my hand I hold wine.

10   If you have barred sleep to us, the way of intoxication is open. Since I have one to assist, he offers wine in both hands.

Be silent, that without this tongue the heart may speak; when I hear the speech of the heart, I feel ashamed of this speech.

213

Weary not of us, for we are very beautiful; it is out of very jealousy and proper pride that we entered the veil.

On the day when we cast off the body's veil from the soul, you will see that we are the envy and the despair of the moon and the Polestars.

Wash your face and become clean for beholding us, else remain afar, for we are beloveds of ourselves.

We are not that beauty who tomorrow will become a crone; till eternity we are young and heart-comforting and fair of stature.

5   If that veil has become worn out, the beauty has not grown old; the life of the Veil is transient, and we are boundless life.

When Iblīs saw the veil of Adam, he refused; Adam called to him, "You are the rejected one, not I."

The rest of the angels fell down prostrate, saying as they bowed themselves, "We have encountered a beauty:

"Beneath the veil is an idol who by his qualities robbed us of reason, and we, prostrate, fell."

If our reason does not know the forms of the foul old men from those of the beauties, we are apostates from love.

10   What place is there for a beauty? For he is the Lion of God. Like a child we prattled, for we are children of the alphabet.

Children are beguiled with nuts and raisins, else, how are we meet for nuts and sesame-grains?

When an old woman is hidden in helmet and chainmail, she says, "I am the illustrious Rustam of the battle ranks."

By her boast all know that she is a woman; how should we make a mistake, seeing that we are in the light of Aḥmad?

"The believer is discriminating"—so said the Prophet; now close your mouth, for we are guided rightly without speech.

15   Hear the rest from Shams the Pride of Tabriz for we did not take the end of the story from that king.

214

Rise, lovers, that we may go towards heaven; we have seen this world, so let us go to that world.

No, no, for though these two gardens are beautiful and fair, let us pass beyond these two, and go to that Gardener.

Let us go prostrating to the sea like a torrent, then let us go foaming upon the face of the sea.

Let us journey from this street of mourning to the wedding feast, let us go from this saffron face to the face of the Judas tree blossom.

5   Trembling like a leaf and twig from fear of falling, our hearts are throbbing; let us go to the Abode of Security.

There is no escape from pain, since we are in exile, and there is no escape from dust, seeing that we are going to a dustbowl.

Like parrots green of wing and with fine pinions, let us become sugar-gatherers and go to the sugar-bed.

These forms are signs of the signless fashioner; hidden from the evil eye, come, let us go to the signless.

It is a road full of tribulation, but love is the guide, giving us instruction how we should go thereon;

10   Though the shadow of the king's grace surely protects, yet it is better that on that road we go with the caravan.

We are like rain falling on a leaky roof; let us spring from the leak and go by that waterspout.

We are crooked as a bow, for the string is in our own throats; when we become straight, then we will go like an arrow from the bow.

We cower like mice in the house because of the cats; if we are lion's whelps, let us go to that Lion.

Let us make our soul a mirror in passion for a Joseph; let us go before Joseph's beauty with a present.

15   Let us be silent, that the giver of speech may say this; even as he shall say, so let us go.

215

Did I not say to you, "Go not there, for I am your friend; in this mirage of annihilation I am the fountain of life?"

Even though in anger you depart a hundred thousand years from me, in the end you will come to me, for I am your goal.

Did I not say to you, "Be not content with worldly forms, for I am the fashioner of the tabernacle of your contentment?"

Did I not say to you, "I am the sea and you are a single fish; go not to dry land, for I am your crystal sea?"

5   Did I not say to you, "Go not like birds to the snare; come, for I am the power of flight and your wings and feet?"

Did I not say to you, "They will waylay you and make you cold, for I am the fire and warmth and heat of your desire?"

Did I not say to you, "They will implant in you ugly qualities so that you will forget that I am the source of purity to you?"

Did I not say to you, "Do not say from what direction the servant's affairs come into order?" I am the Creator without directions.

If you are the lamp of the heart, know where the road is to the house; and if you are godlike of attribute, know that I am your Master.

216

Bring wine, for I am suffering crop sickness {hang-over} from the vintner; God has seized me, and I am thus held fast.

By love's soul, bring me a cup of wine that is the envy of the sun, for I care nothing for aught but love.

Bring that which if I were to call it "soul" would be a shame, for the reason that I am pained in the head because of the soul.

Bring that whose name is not contained in this mouth, through which the fissures of my speech split asunder.

5   Bring that which, when it is not present, I am stupid and ignorant, but when I am with it, I am the king of the subtle and crafty ones.

Bring that which, the moment it is void of my head, I become black and dark, you might say I am of the infidels.

Bring that which delivers out of this "bring" and "do not bring"; bring quickly, and repel me not, saying, "Whence shall I bring it?"

Bring, and deliver the roof of the heavens through the long night from my abundant smoke and lamentations.

Bring that which after my death, even out of my dust, will restore me to speech and thanksgiving even as Najjār.

10   Bring me wine, for I am guardian of wine like a goblet, for whatever has gone into my stomach I deliver back completely.

Najjār said, "After my death would that my people might be open-eyed to the ecstasy within me.

"They would not regard my bones and blood; in spirit I am a mighty king, even though in body I am vile.

"What a ladder I, the Carpenter, have chiseled! My going has reached the roof of the seventh heaven.

"I journeyed like the Messiah, my ass remained below; I do not grieve for my ass, nor am I asslike of ears.

15 "Do not like Iblīs see in Adam only water and clay; see that behind the clay are my hundred thousand rose bowers."

Shams-i Tabrīzī rose up from this flesh saying, "I am the sun. Bring up my head from this mire.

"Err not, when I enter the mire once more, for I am at rest, and am ashamed of this veil.

"Every morning I will rise up, despite the blind; for the sake of the blind I will not cease to rise and set."

217

What hidden sweetness there is in this emptiness of the belly! Man is surely like a lute, no more and no less;

For if, for instance, the belly of the lute becomes full, no lament high or low will arise from that full lute.

If your brain and belly are on fire through fasting, because of the fire every moment a lament will arise from your breast.

Every moment you will burn a thousand veils by that fire; you will mount a hundred steps with zeal and endeavor.

5 Become empty of belly, and weep entreatingly like the reed pipe; become empty of belly, and tell secrets with the reed pen.

If your belly is full at the time of concourse, it will bring Satan in place of your reason, an idol in place of the Kaaba.

When you keep the fast, good habits gather together before you like slaves and servants and retinue.

Keep the fast, for that is Solomon's ring; give not the ring to the *dīv*, destroy not your kingdom.

Even if your kingdom has gone from your hand and your army has fled, your army will rise up, pennants flying above them.

10 The table arrived from heaven to the tents of the fast, by the intervention of the prayers of Jesus, son of Mary.

In the fast, be expectant of the table of bounty, for the table of bounty is better than the broth of cabbages.

218

I have a fire for you in my mouth, but I have a hundred seals on my tongue.

The flames which I have in my heart would make one mouthful of both worlds.

Though the entire world should pass away, without the world I possess the kingdom of a hundred worlds.

Caravans which are loaded with sugar I have in motion for the Egypt of nonexistence.

5 The drunkenness of love makes me unaware whether I have profit or loss therefrom.

The body's eye was scattering pearls because of love, till now I have a pearl-scattering soul.

I am not housebound, for like Jesus I have a home in the fourth heaven.

Thanks be to Him who gives soul to the body; if the soul should depart, yet I have the soul of the soul.

Seek from me that which Shams-i Tabrīzī has bestowed, for I have the same.

219

By the God who was in pre-eternity living and knowing and omnipotent, everlasting,

His light lit the candles of love so that a hundred thousand secrets became known.

By one decree of Him the world was filled—lover and loved, ruler and ruled.

In the talismans of Shams-i Tabrīzī the treasure of His marvels became concealed.

5 For from the moment that you journeyed forth, we became separated from sweetness like wax;

All the night we are burning like candles, paired to his flame and deprived of honey.

In separation from his beauty my body is a waste, and the soul in it is like an owl.

Turn those reins in this direction, twist the trunk of the elephant of joy.

Without your presence concert is not lawful; music has been stoned like Satan.

10 Without you not one ode has been uttered, until that gracious vision of yours arrived and was understood;

Then out of the joy of hearing your letter five or six odes were composed.

May our eventide through you be radiant dawn, O you in whom Syria and Armenia and Rūm glory.

220

Heart pure of breath and firm of foot, you came in order to warn the best of communities.

Only at the direction of the heart you set your head like a pen on the page of eternal love.

In joy at your air and your justice we are dancing like a pennant.

Master, whither are you going, dancing? Towards liberation and the place of the plain of nonexistence.

5 Master, say, which nonexistence in this? The ear of eternity knows the letter of eternity.

Love is a stranger, and his tongue is strange, like that Arab stranger in Persia.

Rise up, for I have brought you a tale; give ear to your servant neither more nor less;

Give ear to this strange speech; the tale is strange, and the speaker too.

From the face of that Joseph the bottom of the well became bright and happy as the Garden of Iram;

10   That prison became a palace with orchards and meadows, Paradise, and a royal hall and vestibule of sanctity.

As when you fling a clod into the water, the water that very moment parts open;

Like a night of cloud, when the sun of dawn suddenly puts up its head from the well of grief;

Like the wine which the Bedouin drank and said, "God bless its jar and praise God";

Out of the joy of this imprisonment in humiliation and loss he [Joseph] looks upon the high-exalted heaven.

15   Reason be not envious of my mouth; God has born witness and counted the blessings.

Though the tree drinks hidden water, there is clearly seen on its branches what it has concealed.

Whatever the earth has stolen from heaven, it yields up momently in the season of spring.

Whether you have stolen a bead or a jewel, whether you have hoisted a flag or a pen,

Night has departed, and lo, your day has arrived; the sleeper shall see that which he has dreamed of.

221

Stealthily as the soul, you are going in the midst of my soul; O luster of my garden, you are my gracefully moving cypress.

When you go, go not without me; soul of my soul, go not without my body, and depart not out of my sight, O my blazing torch.

I tear up the seven heavens and pass beyond the seven seas, when lovingly you gaze into my giddy soul.

Since you came into my bosom, infidelity and faith are my servitors, O you whose vision is my religion, whose face is my faith.

5   You have made me headless and footless, you have made me sleepless and foodless; enter drunken and laughing, O my Joseph of Canaan.

Through your grace I have become soul-like and have become hidden from myself, O you whose being has become hidden in my hidden being.

The rose rends its garment because of you, O you with whom the narcissus' eye is intoxicated, of whom the branches are pregnant, O you my infinite garden.

One moment you brand me, the next you draw me into the garden; you draw me before the lamp so that my eyes may be opened.

O soul before all souls, O mine before all mines, O moment before all moments, O my very own, O my very own!

10   Our resting place is not earth; though the body crumbles, it matters not. My thought is not the skies, O you, union with whom is my heaven.

The grave of mariners is the sea forevermore; in the water of life where is death, O you, my Sea, my Ocean?

O you whose scent is in my sigh, whose sigh is my fellow traveler, in the hope of my Emperor color and scent have become distraught with me.

My soul, since like a mote in the air it has become separated from all heaviness, why should it be without you, O origin of my four elements?

O my king Ṣalāḥ al-Dīn, you who know my way and see my way, you who are free of concern with my little dignity, loftier than my potentiality.

222

Lovers, lovers, it is time to migrate from the world; the drum of departure is reaching my spirit's ear from heaven.

See, the driver has arisen, the camel train is arrayed, he has begged us for quittance; caravaners, why are you asleep?

These sounds ahead and behind are the sounds of departure and the camel-bells; every moment a soul and a breath is setting off into placelessness.

From these inverted candles, from these indigo veils, there issues a wondrous people that the things unseen may become visible.

5 If heavy slumber fell upon you from this revolving sphere, alas for this light life! Beware of this heavy slumber!

Heart, depart to the Sweetheart; friend, depart to the Friend; watchman, be wakeful—a watchman should not sleep.

On every side are candles and torches, on every side noise and tumult, for tonight the pregnant world gives birth to the eternal world.

You were clay and became heart, you were ignorant and became intelligent; he who has drawn you on so far will draw you beyond [this world].

In drawing and drawing you his pains are delectable; his flames are like water, do not frown thereon.

10 His business is to dwell in the soul, his business to break penitence vows; by his abundant contrivance these motes are trembling at heart.

Laughing stock, jumping out of your hole as if to cry, "I am the lord of the land," how long will you jump? Bend your neck, or they will bend you like a bow.

You sowed the seeds of deceit, you indulged in mockery, you deemed God nonexistent; now look, you cuckold!

Ass, you were apter for straw; a cauldron, you were better black; you were better at the bottom of the well, you disgrace to house and household!

In me there is Another from whom these angers leap; if water scalds, it is through fire—realize this!

15 I have no stone in my hand; I have no quarrel with anyone; I deal harshly with none, for I am gay as a rose bower.

My anger is therefore from that source, it is from the other world; this side a world, that side a world—I am seated on the threshold.

That man sits on the threshold who is mutely eloquent; you have uttered this hint, that is enough; say no more, draw back your tongue.

223

O gardener, gardener, autumn has come, autumn has come; see on branch and leaf the mark, see the mark of heart-anguish.

O gardener, attend, give ear, hearken to the lament of the trees; on every side a hundred tongueless ones, a hundred tongueless ones bewailing.

Never without cause are eyes weeping and lips parched; no one without heart-anguish is pale of cheek, pale of cheek.

In short, the raven of grief has entered the garden and is stamping his feet, demanding in mockery and oppression, "Where is the rose bower, where is the rose bower?

5 "Where is lily and eglantine? Where cypress and tulip and jasmine? Where the green-garmented ones of the meadow? Where the Judas tree, where the Judas tree?

"Where are the nurses of the fruits? Where the gratis honey and sugar? Every breast, every breast is dry of this flowing milk.

"Where is my sweet-voiced nightingale? Where is my cooing ringdove? Where is the peacock fair as an idol? Where are the parrots, where are the parrots?"

Like Adam having eaten a grain fallen from his abode, their crown and fine robes have flown from this dazzling array, this dazzling array.

The rose bower constrained like Adam, alike lamenting and expectant, since the Lord of Bounty said to them, "Do not despair."

10 All the trees drawn up in ranks, black-robed, plunged in mourning, leafless and sad and lamenting because of that trial.

O crane and lord of the village, at last return some answer; "Have you gone into the depths or departed to heaven, to heaven?"

They replied, "Enemy raven, that water shall return to the streams, the world will become full of scent even as Paradise, even as Paradise."

O babbling raven, be patient three months more, till there arrive despite you the festival of the world, the festival of the world.

Through the voice of our Seraphiel our lantern will become bright, we shall become alive from the death of that autumn festival, that autumn festival.

15   How long this denial and doubt? Behold the mine of joy and salt; fly to heaven like a manikin without a ladder, without a ladder!

The beastlike autumn dies, you stamp upon its grave; lo, the dawn of fortune is breaking, O watchman, watchman!

O dawn, fill the world with light, drive afar these Hindus [of the night], set free the time, recite a spell, recite a spell!

O sweet-working sun, return to Aries, leave neither ice nor mud, scattering ambergris, scattering ambergris.

Fill the rose bower with laughter, bring to life those dead ones, make shining the concourse; ha, see what comes to sight.

20   The seeds are escaped from prison, we too from the corner of our houses; the garden out of hidden places has brought a hundred presents, a hundred presents.

The rose bower fills with beauties, fur coats are a drug on the market, the cycle of time, the cycle of time is giving birth and generating.

The crane is coming with his drooping wings over the palace, tall as the sky, babbling as if to say, "Yours is the kingdom, O refuge in need, O refuge in need!"

The nightingale enters playing the lute, and that dove cooing, the other birds celebrate with song, youthful fortune, youthful fortune.

I am pregnant with this resurrection; I abandon the speech of the tongue; the thoughts of my heart come not into the tongue, into the tongue.

25   Silence! Listen, father, to the news from garden and birds: flying arrowlike they have come from placelessness, from placelessness.

224

Enough now from the cry *dush*—"dismount"—I have remained far from my road; enough from the cry *qush*—"set off"—I have missed my tent.

When will you deliver me from this *qush*? When will you deliver me from this *dush*, that I may arrive at your prosperity, at my moon and threshing floor?

Though I am happy on the journey over plain and mountain and valley, in your love, O sun of splendor, timely and untimely,

Yet where is the broad highway? Where is the sight and justice of the king? Especially for me, consumed in yearning for my king.

5   How long must I ask news of you from the zephyr? How long must I seek your moon's image in the water of my well?

I have been burnt up a hundred ways like the garden, and likewise I have learned from spring—in both states I am dumbfounded at the handiwork of my God.

225

I become not satiated with you—this is my only sin; be not satiated with compassion for me, O my refuge in both worlds!

Satiated and weary of me have become his jar, and water-carrier and waterskin; every moment my water-seeking fish becomes thirstier.

Break the pitcher, tear up the waterskin, I am going towards the sea; make clear my road.

How long will the earth become mire from my teardrops? How long will the sky be darkened by the grief and smoke of my sighs?

5   How long will my heart lament, "Alas, my heart, my ruined heart?" How long will my lips wail before the phantom of my king?

Go towards the sea from which the wave of delight is coming; behold how my house and hospice are drowned in its wave.

Last night the water of life surged from the courtyard of my house; my Joseph yesterday fell like the moon into my well.

Suddenly the torrent came and swept all my harvest away; smoke mounted from my heart, my grain and chaff were consumed.

Though my harvest is gone, I will not grieve; why should I grieve? The halo of the light of my moon is more than enough for a hundred like me.

10   He entered my heart; his image was of fire. The fire rose over my head; my cap was consumed.

He said, "Concerts impair dignity and respect." You can have dignity, for His love is my luck and dignity.

I desire not intellect and wisdom; his learning is enough for me. The light of his cheek at midnight is the blaze of my dawn.

The army of sorrow is mustering; I will not grieve at his army because my horses, squadron on squadron, have seized even heaven.

After every ode my heart repents of discoursing; the summons of my God waylays my heart.

226

If any man asks you about the houris, show your face, saying, "Like this"; if any man speaks to you of the moon, get up onto the roof—"Like this."

If any seeks a peri, show him your countenance; if any mentions musk, open your tresses—"Like this."

If any says to you, "How does cloud disclose the moon?,"
loosen knot by knot the strings of your gown—"Like this."
If one asks you how the Messiah revived the dead, before
him kiss me on the lips—"Like this."
5   If any says to you, "Say, how is he who is slain of love?" ex-
hibit to him my soul—"Like this."
If any asks you compassionately about my stature, exhibit
your own brow folded double—"Like this."
The soul is separated from the body, and thereafter re-
turns again; ho, show to those who disbelieve, enter the
house—"Like this."
Whenever you hear a lover's lament, by God's right, all that
is our story—"Like this."
I am the home of every angel, I am the black and blue beaten
chest; raise your eyes and look well at heaven—"Like this."
10   To none but the zephyr have I told the secret of union with
the Beloved, so that the zephyr said in the joy of its secret
heart—"Like this."
Despite him who says, "How shall the servant attain God?"
put in the hand of every one a bright candle—"Like this."
I said, "How does the scent of Joseph travel from city to
city?" The scent of God breathed from the world of Hū—"Like
this."
I said, "How does the scent of a Joseph give back sight?"
Your breeze irradiated my eyes—"Like this."
From Tabriz haply Shams-i Dīn will be benevolent, and out
of his grace in fidelity lift up his head—"Like this."

227

Lord, would that I knew what is the desire of my Beloved;
He has barred my road of escape, robbed me of my heart and
my repose.
Lord, would that I knew whither He is dragging me, to what
purpose He is dragging my toggle in every direction.

Lord, would that I knew why He is stonyhearted, that loving King of mine, my long-suffering Darling.

Lord, would that I knew whether my sighing and my clamor, "My Lord and my defense!"—will reach my Beloved at all.

5 Lord, would that I knew where this will end; Lord, this my night of waiting is very long.

Lord, what is this ferment of mine, all this bashfulness of mine?—Seeing that you are mine, you are at once my one and my thousand.

Your love is always both silent and eloquent before the image of my eye, my sustenance and my fate!

Now I call him quarry, now I call him spring, now I nickname him wine, now my crop sickness.

He is my unbelief and faith, my light-beholding eye, that of mine and this of mine—I cannot escape from him.

10 No more patience has remained for me, nor sleep, nor tears nor water; Lord, how long will he raid all the four of mine?

Where is the house of water and clay, compared with that of soul and heart? Lord, my sole desire has become my hometown and habitation.

This heart is banished from the town, stuck in dark mire, lamenting, "O God, where is my family and retinue?"

Lord, if only I might reach my city and behold the compassion of my prince, and all that city of my friend!

Gone then my hard road, the heavy load from my back; my long-suffering Darling would come, carrying off my load.

15 My lion-catching deer would drink to the full of my milk, he whose quarry I am would have become my quarry.

Black-faced night is then not the mate and consort of my day; stonyhearted autumn follows not in the wake of my springtide.

Will you not be silent? How long will you beat this drum? Alas, my veiled lip, that you have become veil-rending!

228

Suddenly today the enemy of my penitence and patience approached me midway on the road and cherished me like a king.

Seizing a cup like any drunkard, in it a hundred blandishments and charms, he held before me the wine cup, saying, "If you are a winebibber, take."

Illumined as the face of Moses, blessed as Mount Sinai, gleaming as the White Hand, dilated with joy as the heart of ʿImrān.

Ho, come take this clean tablet from this Moses; be not arrogant like Pharaoh, contend not like Hāmān.

5   I said to him, "Moses, what is in your hand?" He said, "One time this is a staff, one time a serpent.

"From every separate atom a hundred various shapes appear; for whatever is necessary for Bū Huraira is in the bag.

"In my hand is the control of it, I change it into every form; I make poison into medicine, I make the difficult easy.

"Now I strike it on the sea and bring up dust from the sea; now I strike it on the rock and the fountain of life gushes out.

"Now I showed the limpid water of the Nile to the enemy as blood, to the common folk I showed stone and earth as pearl and coral.

10   "To the eye of the envious I am the wolf; to Jacob himself, Jospeh; to the ignorant, Bū Jahl; Muhammad, before him who knows God."

Sweet-breathed rosewater is death and asphyxiation to the black beetle; sugary syrup is fatal to the bilious.

Apparently all seekers are fellow travelers; in reality they are back to back. One has made his lodging in the lowest depths, the other in the highest heaven.

Like a child and an old man, though apparently fellow travelers, one is increasing every day, the other every moment on the decline.

What a cup of poison and candy is this! What magic and jugglery! This turn and this revolution keep you giddy.

15   The world is fixed and you see it as revolving; when a man's head is spinning, he sees the house as spinning.

Know as a station of fear that in which you are secure; know as a station of security that in which you tremble.

Since you are contrary and false you see everything contrariwise; foolish man, when you consult a woman, oppose her!

That one is a woman whose road and *qibla* is color and scent; truly woman is the evil-commanding soul in human form.

The counsel of the spiritual is like the buzzing of bees; from its lip it fills the floor of the house to the attic with its sweets.

20   Bravo the incomprehensible comprehended, bravo the familiar stranger, bravo the sourness better than sweet, bravo the unbelief better than faith!

Be silent, for the tongue has become a door keeper from measuring words; when the heart speaks without words, it occupies the high throne like a king.

Shine, Shams-i Tabrīzī, upon the Houses of the heart, for the sun of a secure seat is not like this spinning sun.

229

My world-illuminating lamp is not shining so brightly; strange—is this the fault of the eye, or the light, or the window?

Has perchance the end of the thread become lost? What has become of that past state? In that state the tip of the needle does not remain hidden.

Happy the moment when the *farrāsh* of "we spread" within this mosque pours oil from the olive of God into this lantern of the heart!

Heart, enter the crucible of fire, sit there quietly like a man, for through the influence of this fire the iron became such a mirror.

5   When Abraham entered the flames like gold coin, there grew from the face of the fire a jasminebed and roses and lilies.

If you do not bring your heart out of this tumult into this passion, what will you do with this heart? Come, sit here and tell me.

If out of unmanliness you do not enter the ring of true men, be outside like a ring on men's door and knock.

Since the prophet said "Fasting is a protection," lay hold of that, do not cast away this shield before the arrow-shooting carnal soul.

On this dry land a shield is necessary; when you reach the sea, then there will grow on your body a coat of mail like a fish to repel his shafts.

230

It is the rule with drunkards to fall upon one another, to fight and squabble and make tumult.

The lover is worse then the drunkard; the lover also belongs to that party. I will tell what love is; it is to fall into a goldmine.

What may that gold be? The lover is the king of kings; it means becoming secure from death and not caring for the golden crown.

The darvish in his cloak, and in his pocket the pearl—why should he be ashamed of begging from door to door?

5   Last night that moon came along, having flung his girdle on the road, so drunken that he was not aware that his girdle had fallen.

I said, "Leap up, my heart, place wine in the hand of the soul; for such a time has befallen, it is time to be roistering,

"To become hand in hand with the garden nightingale, to fall into sugar with the spiritual parrot."

I, heart-forlorn and heart-yielded, fallen upon your way—by Allah, I know of no other place to fall.

If I broke your bowl, I am drunk, my idol. I am drunk—leave me not from your hand to fall into danger.

10   This is a newborn rule, a newly enacted decree—to shatter glasses, and to fall upon the glassmaker!

231

Go, know that the code of lovers is opposite to all other ways, for from the Beloved lies are better than truth and beneficence.

His impossibility comes to pass, his insalubriousness is a bonus, his injustice is all rectitude. Calumny from him is justice.

His hard is soft, his synagogue is the Kaaba, the Beloved's thorn is better than roses and basil.

The moment when he is bitter is better than a sweetshop, and the moment when he becomes weary, that is kissing and embracing.

5   The moment when he says to you, "By Allah, I am indifferent to you"—that is the water of Khiḍar from the fountain of life.

The moment when he says "No," in his "No" are a thousand "Yeses"; his strangerhood is kinship according to the code of the unselfed.

His infidelity becomes all faith, his stone all coral, his miserliness all beneficence, his crime all forgiveness.

If you criticize, you say, "You have a crooked way of going on"; I have bought the way of his brow and given my life.

I am drunk with this crooked way; I have made enough, and closed my lips—rise up, bright heart, and recite the rest of it.

10   Shams al-Ḥaqq-i Tabrīzī! Dear Lord, what sugar you sprinkle! You might say that out of my mouth proceed a hundred proofs and demonstrations.

232

Become placeless in the Unity, make your place in the essence of annihilation; every head which possesses duality put on a Christian neck.

In the cage of being, before this bird of sanctity flies on the wing, make it sugar-cracking in thankfulness.

Since you were drunk in pre-eternity, seize the sword of post-eternity, like a Turk plunder the Hindu-Bay of existence.

Filter and purify the dregs of your separate being, and fill that glass of true reality with pure wine.

5 So long as you are a snake of earth, how shall you be a fish of religion? Snake, when you have become a fish, then charge into the sea.

Observe the beast, how it holds its head towards the earth; if you are a man, why then, lift your head towards the heights.

When in Adam's school you have become intimate with God, sit on the high throne of the King and teach the Names.

If you desire the kingship of *illā*, proceed first to *lā*; seize the broom from *lā* and become a sweeper of *things*.

If you intend to journey, go on the mount of meaning, and if it be so that you take up residence, let it be in the green dome of heaven.

10 Be like the sufferer from dropsy who is never satiated; however high you get, strive to rise still higher.

Every spirit that has an aim keeps his face to the door; you aim at this madness, so turn your head towards madness.

The body is not without a shadow, and the shadow cannot be bright; fly towards the window and make your flight unaccompanied.

Following Majnūn's rule, be an agent of turmoil, for this love is declaring, "Make yourself quit of reason!"

Become at once a burning fire, and become roasted and well-browned; become at once drunk and wine, seize fast without either.

15 Become at once secretive and intimate, be silent and become companion; at once become us and become ours, likewise be servant to us.

Lest the Christian should steal into your monastery, now be a lover of the girdle, now aim at the cross.

You have become learned, but only in existential learning; go without existential eyes, make your eyes see.

A moses with the character of Khiḍar, Shams al-Ḥaqq-i Tabrīzī—lay your head at his foot, seek the White Hand.

233

Come, how much is a kiss from that precious ruby? If a kiss is for a life, it is a duty to buy.

Since the kiss is pure and not proper to earth, I will become a disengaged spirit, I will emerge from this body.

The sea of purity said to me, "No aspiration is granted gratis; the pearl of price is with you—come, break the shell."

For a kiss of the rose, which confers splendor on wine, the whole world is putting out its tongue like a lily.

5 I blunder, if you be all kings, if you be like Mars and the moon, ask not for a kiss from that untamed Darling.

Enter, moon of heaven, for I have opened the window; for one night shine on my face, press your lips on mine.

Close the door of speech and open the heart's window; you will not obtain a kiss of this moon save by way of the window.

234

A call came to the soul from the sphere of the Pleiades: "Come up, do not sit below like the dregs."

No one remains so long on a journey apart from his homeland and former friends.

Well, you have heard the call, *Return* from that king and sweet emperor.

In this ruined waste owls are dwelling; what habitation have you fashioned, poor falcon?

5   What rest does he get, on whichever side he turns, who makes his mattress of thorns?

What bond is there between money-changer and counterfeiter? What relation is there between crow and falcon?

Why do you adorn with plaster a ruin which above is covered with paintings and beneath is a prison?

Why do you not adorn your soul with wisdom? For its every word is worth a hundred Chinas and Māchīns;

That wisdom which is the source of disputation is not that wisdom which causes the soul to see God.

10   Become a jewel so that willy-nilly they will plant you altogether on the golden crown.

Be done with going back like a twisted foot; be as *alif*, sit single and upright.

Since meaning is a horse and words are as a saddle, say, how long will you draw along this saddle without the horse?

Throw clods at the love of men; you too are a man, but a man of clay;

The wedding of clay creature with clay creature brings a shower of clods and stones for a dowry.

15   Look at the tombs beneath the bricks, for you cannot tell apart their heads from their foundations.

O God, bring my soul safely to the souls by that road on which the family of Yāsīn went;

Mingle our prayers with theirs, so that from us comes the prayer and from Thee the amen.

Grant that thy grace and loving kindness may be such that, as little as our good works may be, from Thee comes the "Well done."

Bring us safely from lustfulness to reasonableness, unto the zenith above from this lower abode.

235

Whither would you fly from my clutch? Who knows how to rend the net of omnipotence?

Since you have not the foot to flee from me, bend down your neck, have done with obstinacy.

Run towards sweetness like unripe grapes, if you know not how to run inwardly.

Caught in the net you are biting the rope; this rope shall not be broken by biting.

5   Do you not see how your head is in my bowstring? You are a bow, you must bend to the string.

Why do you kick up your hind legs saying, "I have escaped the load?" I have merely let you go for a moment to graze.

In fear and awe of me the sea's heart surges with billows and throbbing.

If the rocky mountain should encounter that blow, it would not be able to leap out of my chains.

Until my command says to heaven, "Enough," it must go on spinning around my earth.

10   Desire is a milk from the teats of Satan; your reason is to suck asses' milk.

Earth's mouth is dry out of despair for me, without me it cannot swallow a single mouthful.

Who is able to attack my quarry? Who is able to purchase my slave?

He whom I have seized and chosen, whom shall he choose other than me?

The soul has no security save in love; it is necessary to creep amongst lovers.

15   Lovers have security in both worlds; even so they were at the time of creation.

It behooves not the sheep to scatter away from the shepherd towards the wolves because the shepherd is cruel.

This shepherd will not shed the blood of the sheep, for he knows to rear them to eternal life.

Know that the companions of the body are the Companions of the Elephant; how can such ever reach the Kaaba?

For the Kaaba is the world's navel, the elephant is the nose; it is not possible to draw the nose to the navel.

20   Become as *ababil*, and do not flee from the elephant; the heart is like *ababil* in picking up grains.

It plucks the enemy like grains, it knows to hear the message of the Kaaba.

Through the heart you will mount to the heavens, through the heart the rose of felicity will blossom;

Through the heart you will travel to the Beloved, through the heart you will escape the body's shame.

The heart has a cauldron cooked for your sake; wait patiently until it is cooked.

25   Shams al-Dīn-i Tabrīzī is the heart of hearts; the bat is unable to see the sun.

236

See how every particle of the world is passing by, see how everyone has arrived from a journey;

See how everyone desirous of his own sustenance has bowed his head before his king.

See how, like the stars, for the sake of its glow, are all fallen helpless at the foot of the sun;

See how, like torrents in quest of water, all are tumbling headlong towards their sea.

5   See how for each from the king's kitchen a table is prepared according to his needs.

See how the sea of the world is contracted before their sea-drinking cup.

And as for those whose sustenance is the king's countenance, see how their mouths are filled with sugar of the king's beauty.

Behold with the eyes of Shams-i Tabrīzī, see another ocean filled with pearls.

237

This is love: to fly to heaven, every moment to rend a hundred veils;

At first instance, to break away from breath—first step, to renounce feet;

To disregard this world, to see only that which you yourself have seen.

I said, "Heart, congratulations on entering the circle of lovers,

"On gazing beyond the range of the eye, on running into the alley of the breasts."

Whence came this breath, O heart? Whence came this throbbing, O heart?

Bird, speak the tongue of birds: I can heed your cipher!

The heart said, "I was in the factory whilst the home of water and clay was abaking.

"I was flying from the workshop whilst the workshop was being created.

"When I could no more resist, they dragged me; how shall I tell the manner of that dragging?"

238

That enemy of soul and mind and faith has returned, shaking his sleeves—

Plunderer of a hundred thousand houses, devastator of a hundred thousand shops,

Stirrer-up of a hundred thousand tumults, amazement-focus of a hundred thousand amazed ones,

That nurse of reason and bane of reason, that friend of the soul and enemy of the soul.

5   Whither will he transport my light reason? He seeks a reason like that of Luqmān.

How does he accept my worthless soul? He seeks a soul like the sea of Oman.

He came, saying, "Bring the tribute of the village!" I said, "What village? It is a ruined village.

"Your flood has shattered cities; how shall a village stand amid the flood?"

He said, "Ruins are the abode of treasures; it is our ruin, O Muslim!

10   "Give us the ruin, or go forth; do not upbraid, do not speak at random."

The ruin is of yourself; once you have gone it thrives through the justice of the King.

Do not dissemble and say I have gone; do not hide behind the door.

Make yourself as one dead, that you may become living by the spirit of a man.

You said, "You shall not be in the midst"; that saying of yours is the essence of Koran.

15   The work you do, yourself not in the midst, that is work done by God—know this for sure.

I will recite the rest of the poem in secret; it cannot be told before the uninitiated.

Silence! For there are a hundred thousand differences between the tongue's utterance and the light of revelation.

239

Do not grieve over any joy that has gone forever, for it will return to you in another form, know that for sure.

Did not the child find joy in its nursing and in milk? When the child was weaned from milk, the joy came from wine and honey.

This joy is an unqualified thing which enters various forms, moves from box to box between water and clay;

It suddenly displays its grace in the water of the rain, again enters into the rosebed, and lifts its head from the earth.

5 Now it comes by water, now by way of bread and meat, now by way of beauty, now by way of horse and saddle.

From behind these veils suddenly one day it peeps and shatters all the idols, that which is neither that nor this.

The soul in sleep leaves the body and appears in a phantasm; the body is deposed and idle—in another form it is manifest.

You might say, "In a dream I saw myself like a cypress, my face as a bed of tulips, my body as roses and jasmine."

That phantasm of the cypress vanished, the soul returned to its house; *verily in this and that is a warning to all beings.*

10 I fear stirring up trouble, though I would have spoken what may be spoken, God speaks fairer than I—do not let go of the saddlestraps of the faith.

Fā‘ilātun fā‘ilātun fā‘ilātun fā‘ilāt, if you have not goldwheat bread, yet speak the golden words.

At last, Tabriz of the soul, look upon the stars of the heart, that you may see this mundane sun to be a reflection of Shams-e Din.

240

My king of moonfaced ones went up to his sick lovers, saying, "O pale cheeks and saffronbed of mine!

"I will water my saffronbed, I will convert the saffron to roses with my fountain of life.

"Yellow and red, thorn and rose are at my control and command; set not your head save on the line of my command, my command!

"The world's rosefaced ones have stolen beauty from my beauty; they have stolen an atom of my beauty and beneficence.

5 "In the end these moonfaced ones are becoming strawfaced; that is the state of thieves in the presence of my King."

Day has come; earthly ones, restore the stolen goods. O my soul, whence come goods for earthly man, and whence beauty?

When at night the sun has vanished, the stars make boast. Venus says, "Know it is mine"; the moon says, "No, mine."

Jupiter produces Ja'far gold from his purse; Mars says to Saturn, "See my cutting dagger!"

Mercury takes the high seat—"I am the Ṣadr al-Ṣudūr, the heavens are my kingdom, the zodiacs are my pillars!"

10 With dawn the sun draws up his army from the east saying, "Thieves, where have you gone? See, it is mine!"

Venus is terrified, the moon's neck is broken; Mercury has become dry and cold with my shining face.

The business of Mars and Saturn is ruined by our light; Jupiter is bankrupt, saying, "Alas, my purse is gone!"

When the sun had run afield, came a cry, "Ho, mannerless one, get out of my field!

"I am the sun of the sun: sun, depart! Sink into the well of the west: enter my prison.

15 "At dawn lift your head from the {grave} of the east and come to life; make the deniers of the resurrection aware of my proof.

"Every man's festival is the month [moon] to which he is a sacrifice; your festival is my month [moon], you who are a sacrifice to me!"

When Shams-i Tabrīzī shone from the House of *not-of-the-East*, the glow of his essence surpassed my bounds and potentialities.

241

The intellectual is all the time engaged in showing off; the lover is all the time becoming unselfed and distraught;

Intellectuals are running away, afraid of drowning; the whole business and trade of lovers is drowning in the sea.

Intellectuals find repose by contriving repose; lovers think it a shame to be attached to repose.

The lover will be in a circle, alone from everyone, just as oil and water, though in the same place, are separate.

5 The man who goes to the trouble of offering advice to lovers gets nothing for his pains but to be a mockery of passion.

Love has the scent of musk, it is therefore notorious; how can musk escape from such notoriety?

Love is like a tree, and lovers are the shade of that tree; though the shade fall afar, yet it must attend the tree.

For the station of intellect a child must become an old man; in the station of love you see an old man become youthful.

Shams-i Tabrīzī, whoever has chosen to be lowly in love for you, thereby rises to heights sublime as your love.

242

Saki, now that you are drunk, fling yourself on me; to recollect tomorrow is credit—smite the neck of credit.

The year is our year, and the ascendant is the ascendant of Venus and the moon; O heart, this pleasure and joy has no bounds—be at rest.

Glow and gaiety have penetrated to the heart of stone and steel; if you do not believe, strike the stone upon the steel.

Look at the host, see the happiness upon his face; sit at this table and dip your bowl in the oil.

5 Summon up nimble reason and seat it beside happiness; jovially apply your bright soul to bright wine.

The branches are drunk and dancing in the wind of spring; jasmine, be drunk, and cypress, stroke the lily.

They have cut green garments at the shop of the unseen; tailor, rise up, sit at your shop, stick in your needle.

243

What light is that in the midst of the darkness of your soul?
A royal splendor is shining in my heart—who is that?

It appears that it is the fantasy of the king's moonlike face,
that it is the succoring shelter of the day of misery.

All this splendor and beauty and grace and loveliness and
charm is the Pride of Souls, Shams-i Ḥaqq-i Dīn-i Tabrīzī.

The human soul cannot endure the clear exposition of his
qualities; all that it can endure of his qualities, my heart, is by
allusion.

5 For how should eternal qualities display themselves in mor-
tality to a mixture which itself is of the mortal world?

How far does that beauty, which God engraved of His own
hand, transcend an image created by Āzar or Mānī!

The eye that has beheld him, and then looked on another
than him, must be stoned, for it is worthless.

O heart, in loverhood abandon your good name, for the
beginning of love is notoriety and evil fame.

In the sea of his love the soul's clothes are an embarrassment;
to seek in love for name and bread is rawness, my heart.

10 Even the love of the generality of people has this specialty,
my heart; all the more especially this love which belongs to that
lofty assembly.

Zephyr, bring the earth of Tabriz as a present for my sake,
for in preciousness it compares with a jewel of the quarry.

244

Lover, open your two eyes and behold in yourself four
streams—a stream of water, a stream of wine, streams of milk
and honey.

Lover, look into yourself, do not be a laughingstock of men,
so that So-and-so says this, and So-and-so says that.

I am the slave of that all-seeing rose which is indifferent whether So-and-so calls it thorn, or So-and-so calls it jasmine.

Then open your eyes henceforward, walk not with the eyes of men, that So-and-so says you are a Guebre and So-and-so a man of true religion.

5 God of his generosity gave you the eye of vision, to whose languidness the pinion of Gabriel prostrates.

Bandage not the narcissus-eye, and take not the vulture-eye; bandage not the first eye, and look not with the squint-eye.

Lovers of form have fallen into form, like the fly which falls from honey into a vat of whey.

Rejoice, you who play at love with the eternal Almighty; with such wings, why should you sorrow over water and clay?

If you desire that Gabriel should become your slave, be gone; prostrate before Adam at once, accursed *dīv*!

10 If the blood-drinking desert had knowledge of my Kaaba, on all sides a rose bower would appear, on all sides springwater.

You who continue to regard the evil and good of people, how is it you have become content with that? May the Lord help you!

Since heaven itself had not the strength to bear God's trust, how is it that Shams-i Tabrīzī has diffused it in the earth?

245

By God, I have no inclination towards either fat or sweet, nor for the purse full of gold, neither for the golden cup.

You draw the people of earth to heaven; the moon exclaims, "What grace and generosity! What amazing power and authority!"

When your fantasy shines on me like the moon at the full, Venus and the Pleiades bite their forearms and fingers in envy.

Ha, thanks be to God that I have attained this kingdom; it was all true, what your love said to me again and again of old.

5   When he saw me on tiptoe, he signaled to me saying, "What you desire has come to pass; ho, be secure and be seated!"

All creatures in intoxication of joy bow down before him; lamb and wolf are friendly together, no envy or hatred in the heart;

They are so drunk they cannot tell the way to town from the way home; they know not "whether we are men, extraordinary, or colored clay."

Goblet in hand and distraught, I wonder what am I to do with this? Drink it or bestow it? You tell me, sweet king!

"You drink; what bestowing should there be? For your turn has come." Lo, I have drunk; lo, I have drunk, since I am specified before you.

10   "Drink this wine of the throne, whereof if you were to place one cup in the hand of a dead man, he would respond to the prompting."

246

Beautiful one, by your roguish eye, signal with your eye; for one moment repair with a glance this your ruin.

Heart and soul, martyrs to your love, in the tomb of the body—pass along by the tomb of those martyrs, pay a pilgrimage.

You are come like a Joseph, all Egypt has cut its hands; display your charm and take my heart and soul, do a deal!

Or if you have stamped your foot tyrannically and sworn a vow, then break your vow—what matter? Do expiation.

5   Say not, "What profit shall I have from this offering of yours?" You need not profit; give, and take a loss!

Convert this saffronlike cheek into the like of roses and anemones; make a rejoicing heart out of three or four drops of blood.

Since fortune is your slave, it will never rebel against you; king, be an ambassador between us and fortune.

Since sins are as a straw before the mountain of your clemency, look with disdain upon our mountain of sins.

Our body was two drops of blood that became pure and human; you also cleanse the impure quality.

10 Since souls here become the prisoner of water and clay from the world of the spirit, deliver them from the clay, Abode of War, and make a raid!

Since I have repented of words, for the sake of the disciples instead of words issue a meaningful signal and command.

This firelike breath is for the sake of making warm; make a glow other than your breath a source of heat.

You who are King Shams-i Dīn, by the shining manifestation of yourself, make lovely Tabriz the abode of vision.

247

Since you deserted me death is for me joy and ease; without you, death has become for me like honey and milk.

The waterless fish quivers on that rough sand until its feeble soul may become parted from its body.

For the living ones, the water of life has become the water of bitterness; pure sugar has become worse for them than the grave and winding-sheet.

It is no mere game, the drawing of the part to the origin, the All; how often the prophet wept for love of his homeland!

5 The child who does not know his homeland and birthplace desires a nurse; Istanbul or Yemen—they are all one to him.

The star goes to graze in the pasture of the skies; the animal worships earth, like cypress and jasmine.

Though I close my mouth to silence this lamentation, it is not possible to close one's mouth in the belly of the water.

The frog's breath is of water, not of the wind of the air; this is the custom and craft of sea creatures.

Gnostics who are hidden in that ocean of light, their breath is all of darkness-shattering light.

10   When I reached this point, my pen and tablet broke; the mountain is shattered when it becomes aware of the Lord of Grace.

248

All have eaten and fallen asleep, and the house has become empty; it is time for us to saunter forth to the garden,

To draw the skirt of the apple towards the peach, to carry a few words from the dewy rose to the jasmine.

Springtide is like the Messiah, it is all art, a spell, that the plant-martyrs may arise from their winding-sheets.

Since those fair idols opened their mouths in gratitude, the soul not attaining a kiss is drunk with the perfume of their mouths.

5   The glow on the cheeks of rose and tulip informs me that there is a lamp hidden in this place under the screen.

The leaf trembles on the twig, and my heart is trembling; the leaf trembles in the wind, my heart for the beauty of Khotan.

The hand of the zephyr has fanned the censor till it taught good manners to the children of the garden.

The breath of the Holy Spirit has encountered the trees of Mary; see how husband and wife are playing with hands together [in joy].

The cloud, seeing the lovely ones beneath the canopy, scattered over them jewels and pearls of Aden.

10   Now that the red rose in joy has rent its skirt, the time has come for the shirt to reach Jacob.

Since the Yemeni carnelian of the Beloved's lips laughed, the scent of God reaches Muhammad from Yemen.

We have spoken much at random, and our heart has not found repose save upon that scattered tress of the King of the time.

249

Wherever you set your foot, my darling, tulip and violet and jasmine spring up.

You breathe upon a piece of clay, and it becomes either a dove or a kite.

You wash your hands in a dish and from the water of your hand that basin becomes of gold.

You recite the *Fātiḥa* over a grave and a Bu'l-Futūḥ raises his head from the winding-sheet.

5   Your skirt strikes against the clutch of a thorn, and its clutch becomes a strumming lute.

Every idol you have broken, O Abraham, receives life and finds intellect from that breaking.

Since the new moon shone upon an evil-starred one, it became the greatest good fortune and he escaped from misfortune.

Every moment there springs from the court of your breast a newborn without mother or father, like Adam.

And thereafter from his side and loins children abound in the earth.

10   I wanted to speak fifty couplets on this rhyme; I closed my lips, that you might open your mouth.

250

Hear the wordless subtleties, and understand what catches not the understanding.

Inside the stonelike heart of man is a fire which burns up the veil, root and branch;

When the veil is burnt he discovers all the stories of Khiḍar and *the knowledge from us.*

Between the soul and the heart appears new and ever new forms from the ancient love.

5   When you recite *By the sun* behold the sun! Behold the mine
of gold when you recite *Lam yakon.*

251

Last night I saw Poverty in a dream, I became beside myself
from its beauty.

From the loveliness and perfection of the grace of poverty I
was dumbfounded until dawn.

I saw poverty like a mine of ruby, so that through its hue I
became clothed in silk.

I heard the clamorous rapture of lovers, I heard the cry of
"Drink now, drink!"

5   I saw a ring all drunken with poverty; I saw its ring in my
own ear.

I saw many forms in the light of poverty, I saw many a form
of the soul in its face.

From the midst of my soul a hundred surgings rose when I
beheld the surging of the sea.

Heaven uttered a hundred thousand cries; I am the slave of
such a leader.

252

Though long enough I have sat in fire up to my neck, now I
am up to my neck in the water of union with the Beloved.

I said, "I am immersed in your graces up to my neck." The
Darling was not content with me up to the neck.

He said, "Make your head a foot, descend into the depths
of love, for this affair does not come out right only up to the
neck."

I said, "My head, Beloved, is your shoe; only be content, my
two eyes, with up to my neck this time."

He said, "You are less than a thorn which was up to the neck in earth for nine months waiting for the rose."

I said, "What is the thorn? For the sake of your rosebed I have sat often in blood up to my neck like the rose."

He said, "Through love you have escaped from the world of allurement, where you were struggling impotently up to your neck.

"You escaped from the world, but not from yourself; your self-existence is a disgrace, and this disgrace is up to your neck.

"Lay not traps cunningly, give up trickery; the trickmaster remains in his own trap up to the neck.

"The trap of this world is a trap through which kings and lions have remained like dogs in the carrion up to the neck.

"There is a stranger trap than this, through which you may see the reasonless fallen up to the ankle, the prudent up to the neck."

Enough of speech, now that breath is cut off; after all, speech does not reach up to the neck from choking.

253

Go, lay your head on the pillow, let me alone; leave me ruined and night-faring and afflicted as I am.

I am wrestling with the wave of passion alone through night till day; if you will, come and have mercy; if you will, go and be cruel.

Flee from me that you too may not fall into calamity; choose the path of safety, leave the path of calamity.

We with our tears flowing have crept in the corner of grief; turn the mill a hundred times upon our tears.

A tyrant we have who has a heart like flint; he slays, and no one says to him, "Prepare to pay the blood-money."

To the king of the lovely ones faithfulness is not obligatory; pale lover, you endure, be faithful.

This is a pain of which no cure exists but to die, so how shall I say, "Cure this pain?"

Last night in a dream I saw an elder in the quarter of love: he beckoned to me with his hand, saying, "Set out towards me."

If a dragon is on the path, love is like an emerald; with the flash of this emerald repel the dragon.

10   Enough, for I am beside myself, if you would be a man of superior learning, recite the history of Bū 'Alī, and admonish Bu'l-'Alā.

254

Did you see what January said? Lay brushwood like a stack: if December brought not cold, the cold of both be on me.

Since the cold has become stubborn, lay brushwood on the fire. Do you spare brushwood? Is brushwood better, or the body?

Brushwood is the fleeting form, God's love is the fire: burn up the forms, O pure-skirted soul!

Until you burn up the form, your spirit will be frozen, like idol worshipers far from springtime and security.

5   In firelike love, be happy like silver; since you are a child of Abraham, fire is your dwelling.

By God's command, fire becomes for true men tulip and rose, clusters of basil, willow and lily.

The believer knows the spell and recites it over the fire; the heat remains in it no more, it remains shining as the moon.

Blessed be the spell through which peace befalls in a fire which can transform iron into needle.

The moth flings itself upon the kindled fire because the fire reveals itself lit in the shape of a window.

10   To Ḥamza arrow and spear appear as scattering roses; in a scatter of roses no man clothes himself in armor.

Pharaoh was dissolved in the water like whey; Moses sat on the brow of the water like oil.

Horses of spirit are the carriers of princes; dull and sluggish horses carry packs and dung.

Speech is like a hopper on the mill of meaning; the mill turns by water, not by regulating the hopper.

From that hopper, my brother, the wheat leaps from the bucket and falls in the mill and becomes well and truly ground.

15 So from that hopper of expression, out of the bucket of greed and negligence, you fall into the mill, that is in a clearly expressed way.

My soul, I am becoming hot, but not from chatter; it is from the golden Sun of the Faith, from whom Tabriz is like a mine.

255

Sit with lovers, altogether choose loverhood; be not for a moment companion with him who is not a lover.

And if it be that the Beloved has drawn the curtain of all might, go, gaze on the face of him who is not veiled;

Behold that face on whose cheeks are the marks of His face; contemplate him on whose brow shines the sun.

Inasmuch as the sun has laid his two cheeks on his cheeks, through his cheeks the moon on earth is checkmated.

5 In his tresses is the copy of *Thee we serve;* in his eyes the glance *in Thee we beg for succor.*

His body, like the body of a phantom, is without blood and veins; inside and outside it is all milk and honey.

Inasmuch as the Beautiful takes him into his embrace, he has carried away the scent of the Beloved and let go the scent of clay.

He is a morn without a dawn, an evening without henna, an essence without attributes, a life without sorrow.

How should the sun borrow light from the sky? How should the rosebush borrow perfume from the jasmine?

10 Be speechless as a fish and pure as the water of the sea that you may quickly become the trustee over the treasury of the pearl.

I will speak in your ear; do not tell anyone. Who is all that?
Shams-i Dīn, the pride of Tabriz.

256

I have heard that you are intending to journey; do not. That
you give your love to another friend and companion; do not.

You are a stranger in the world; why do you estrange your-
self? What heart-wounded victim are you aiming at? Do not.

Do not steal yourself from us, do not go to strangers. You
are stealthily glancing at the others; do not.

Moon for whom the heavens are topsy-turvy, you waste us
and turn us topsy-turvy; do not.

5   What promise do you make and what oath do you swear?
You make a shield of oaths and blandishments; do not.

Where are the pledge and compact you made to your ser-
vant? You depart from your pledge and word; do not.

You whose court is higher than being and not being, you are
transgressing the bound of being; do not.

You at whose command hell and heaven are slaves, you make
paradise like Gehenna to me; do not.

In your sugarcane plot we are secure from poison; you are
commingling that poison with the sugar; do not.

10   My soul is like a fiery furnace; is that not enough for you?
Through absence you are making my face pale as gold; do not.

When you withdraw your face, the moon is darkened with
grief; you are intending the eclipse of the moon's orb; do not.

Our lips become dry when you bring a draft: why are you
wetting my eyes with tears? Do not.

Since you cannot endure the shackling of lovers, why then
do you dazzle the eye of reason? Do not.

You do not give sweetmeats to one sick of a fever; you hurt
still more him whose sickness you are; do not.

15   My lawless eye is the thief of your beauty. Beloved, you re-
quite the thievish eye; do not.

Withdraw, comrade, for it is no time for speech. Why do you thrust yourself forward in the bewilderment of love? Do not.

257

Give yourself a kiss, silvery-bodied idol; you who are in Cathay, do not search for yourself in Khotan.

If you would draw a silvery-bodied one into your bosom, where is the like of you? You must kiss the Beloved, then caress your own mouth.

For the sake of your beauty are the robes of the houris; the beauty of every man or woman is the reflection of your lovely face.

The veil over your beauty is the tresses of your hair, else the light of you would have shone out, O sweet of chin.

5   The painter of the body came towards the idols of the thoughts; his hand and heart were broken, his mouth stood open.

This painted cage is the veil of the bird of the heart; you have not recognized the heart because of the heart-breaking cage.

The heart flung off the veil from the clay of Adam, and all of the angels prostrated themselves.

The intermediary would vanish if only for a moment love's Turk sat down before his grace, saying, "O Chelebi, who are you?"

The eye would be endowed with sight of the unseen, if the glance of Shams-i Dīn, Pride of all of Tabriz, stole a wink at you.

258

Whatever you do, know it is done by Me; whatever the body does, the Soul has done it.

You are my eyes, you are my ears; I have mentioned these two, remember the rest.

If that treasure was not in the world, then to what end would it be a ruined house?

Seek the treasure, my father; move your hand, move your hand.

5 His sweet scent has become our guide to rose and basil, to rose and basil.

Atom by atom all are purchasers; beware, do not sell your pearl cheaply.

The mouse will come out, the cat will come out, if you open the mouth of the bag.

When love is there, the soul suffers no diminution; may the shadow of the Beloved not be afar!

You will recite the rest of this, moonfaced moon, shining Venus!

259

By your own life I implore, do not withdraw from this heartless wretch; suffer me still, do not make for your house.

Do not think of pretexts, leave excuses aside; treat me not aloofly, be not haughty.

Wine is at hand, fortune our boon companion, and you the saki; give the wine, play not saki's frauds.

Cast your glance at your companions who are drunk with you, do not gaze at window and porch and threshold.

5 Pass not your time save in the lovers' circle, make not your nest save in the tavern quarter.

See, the world is a snare and desire the bait; hasten not into its snare, desire not the bait.

When you have passed out of its snare, set your foot on the sky; let naught but the sphere of the threshold be under your feet.

Heed not sunshine and moonshine; be alone, and seek only that Alone.

Rest not without Him, like a bowl tossed on the water; do not take the bowl and set it running to every kitchen.

10   Time is bright and dark, warm and cold in turns; make not your abode save at the fountainhead of time.

Praise him not, neither cover him with reproaches; offer not pastries, and do not throw forward that garlic.

But what is the use? For such are the ways of vain idols. Do not say to the brand of fire, "Do not make a flame."

Say to whatever your burn, "Burn," save with separation; that is not allowable, do not perpetuate this one tyranny either.

260

If my words were not worthy of your lips, then pick up a heavy stone and shatter my mouth.

When a child speaks nonsense, does not the loving mother prick his lips to teach him manners?

For the sake of the majesty of your lips, burn and tear and rend and dash to pieces two hundred mouths and worlds.

When a thirsty man boldly runs to the seashore, does not the wave lift up its sword to his neck?

5   I am the slave of the lily which, having seen your rose bower and been put to shame by your narcissus, its ten tongues became dumb.

But I am like a tambourine; when you strike your hand on me I cry out, "Beat my face like a mortar!"

Lay me not aside until the concert grows hot; draw your skirt aside from the impure world.

Yes, the eyes are intoxicated from the rose bower of meaning, yet the song of the bulbul is sweet in the rose bower.

If Joseph's beauty is fairer naked, yet the eyes are not opened save by his shirt.

10   Though the glitter of the sun of the soul is the origin, no man has reached that heaven without a body.

Silence! for if the corpse-washer binds my mouth, you will hear this melody from the grave after I am dead.

261

O seven seas, bestow pearls and transmute these things of brass;

O candle of drunkards and cypress of the garden, how long these tricks? At last keep faith.

Every granite rock wept for us, Beloved; cure this our pain.

You angrily turned away your face; for a moment have done with this behavior.

5   You once showed much beneficence and humanity; redouble that humanity.

Fair of course, O moon and star, be generous in the darkness of night like the moon.

Separate from us the ancient pain, the anguish of sickness, and the orphan's dust.

Though I be in paradise, in gold and silver, without you I am an orphan; cure me.

I have closed my lips and sat in sorrow; open my hand, make for encounter.

262

My darling came to me; through him my roof and door sprang to life.

I said, "Tonight you are my guest, O my provocation and disturbance."

He said, "Let me go; there is important business for me in the city, soul and head of mine."

I said, "By God, if you depart, tonight this bodily form of mine will not live."

5   "Why, will you not for one night show compassion upon my golden pale cheek?

"Will not your happy eye show compassion upon this lament and wet eye of mine?

"Let the rosebed of your cheek scatter roses over my tears sweet as Kauthar."

He said, "What can I do, seeing that Fate has poured the blood of all men into my cup?"

I am of Mars, and only blood is in my ascendant, my star.
10 No incense is accepted by God until it enters my crucible.

I said, "Since your aim is my life, only blood should be my food and dessert.

"You are cypress and rose, I am your shadow; I am slain by you, you are my Ḥaidar."

He said, "Only a rarity shall be my sacrificial offering, O servant of mine.

"Gurjīs is arriving, for every moment he is newly slain in my land.
15 "Isaac the prophet should have been sacrificed to the dust of my door.

"I am love, and if I shed your blood I will bring you to life in my resurrection.

"Beware, do not flutter in my clutch, do not shrink from my dagger;

"Make not a wry face at death that my breast may give thanks to you.

"Laugh like the rose when Death plucks you out and plunges you in my sugar.
20 "You are Isaac and I am your father; how should I shatter you, my jewel?

"Love is the father, the lover his flock; of him is born my pomp and pride."

So saying, he departed like the zephyr; the tears flowed from my eyes.

I said, "What would it be to you if you were to be kind and depart slowly, my master?

"Do not hasten: a little more slowly! Life and world and hundred-petaled [rose] of mine.
25 "No one ever saw me hurry; this is my more lazy pace.

"Yon sphere of heaven, if it tried its utmost, would never reach to where I pass."

He said, "Silence! for this gray horse of heaven goes lamely in my presence.

"Silence! for if you are not silent, this flame of mine will fall upon the thicket.

"Do not say the rest of it till another day, that my heart may not flee from my breast."

263

My saki rises without my speaking and brings that wine of abundant price.

There is no need for me to say, "Bring," he hears the voice of my heart without mouth.

His intercessor is his own grace, his boundless generosity and goodness.

The moon rises, do not say to it, "Arise"; it casts light on you, do not say, "Cast."

5   O you in time of festivity, the best joy and pleasure and in time of battle, the greatest breaker of ranks.

Excellent guide for all who have lost the way, fine rope for all imprisoned in the well;

The world is like night, and you the moon; you are like a candle, the souls a sconce.

The soul is restless like a mote; with you it becomes tranquil, O excellent tranquillity.

264

You are my life, you are my life, my life; you are my own, you are my own, my own.

You are my king, worthy of my passion; you are my candy, worthy of my teeth.

You are my light; dwell within these eyes of mine, O my eyes and fountain of life!

When the rose beheld you, it said to the lily, "My cypress tree came to my rose garden."

Say, how are you in respect to two scattered things! your hair, and my distracted state?

The rope of your hair is my shackle, the well of your chin is my prison.

Where are you going, drunk, shaking your hands? Come to me, my laughing rose!

265

A cry went up from my tavern, the heavens were split by my litany:

Finally victory has arrived, the Beloved has entered to tend me.

Lord, lord, how He is acting, my unequaled Beloved, to recompense me!

That philosophers' stone makes obedience and faith from my neglect and unbelief and sins.

After my shortcomings He bestows a palace, after my slips He bestows victuals.

He causes the heart of sea and mountain to surge from the heat of the day of my encounter.

If the thoughts of man were not a veil, they would be burnt to ashes by my thoughts.

My drum and flag, my cry and shouting would strike agitation in the army of the spirit;

The fire of my tryst at midnight would strike flames into the horizon of the sky.

266

Come nearer, my pretty idol, my sympathetic idol of like hue with me.

See how my heart has become constricted with your coquettishness, till you say to me, "O my suffering one!"

I battle with my heart as with an enemy till you say, "Bravo, my general!"

How long will you ask, "Why is this face of yours pale?" It is through grieving for you, my rose-hued idol.

5   Last night all night to Venus reached the lamenting of this lyre-shaped body of mine.

Purchase back my soul from my body, that my soul may escape my shame.

Through the grace of your ruby lips my stonelike heart has become a banker of gold.

Accord peace to my soul and to me, for all my war is on your account.

My foot becomes swifter going than the wind, if you say, "Come, my lame one!"

10   For this reason I am bound and suspended from you, that my rope [of grapes] through you may become like sugar.

You are indifferent to me, and I am miserable; oh, what shall I become if you desire me?

The Zangi of grief is at the door of happiness of Rum; ransom my Rum from my Zang.

I fear not the untimeliness and the distance of the way; through you my parasang has become half a foot.

My old age has become better than childhood, my wrinkled face has become fresh again.

15   Be silent, be bewildered as silent ones, so that he may say to you, "My silent and bewildered one!"

267

Once more our [crescent] moon has reaped a harvest, and we have paraded forth despite the foe.

Once more the sun has entered Aries, made the world to laugh like a rose garden.

The blossoms have mirthfully opened their lips, the lily has slily become a tongue.

What satins they have put on in the garden for that tailor who has no scissors or needle!

5   Every tree has set on its head a tray full of sweetmeats without syrup and oil.

We have made our bellies a drum once more, since the drummer of spring began drumming.

The surface of the water, which in winter was as iron, has become ruffled like chainmail by the wind;

Perchance the early spring is the David of time, who has fashioned a coat of armor out of that iron.

God proclaimed in nonexistence, "Ho, herbs: Those cold ones have left the dwelling.

10   "Turn your faces to the height of existence like the birds of Abraham from their nest."

That gnostic crane has returned from exile, about him the stammering birds uttering praises.

The routed ones who had become hidden have each put their head out of the window.

The greenclads have put forth their heads, ear and neck full of collars and jewels.

It is concert, and thousands of houris in the garden are stamping their feet on the tomb of January.

15   Ho, willow, awake and move your head and ears, if you have bright eyes like the narcissus.

I say to speech, "Abandon me"; speech is contentious, it is coming after me.

I do not desire, because of his hard face, to declare the talk of lovers.

The rose calls, "Ye Midianite, rejoice with us whoever was sorrowful."

The earth has become verdant with light, and God has said to the naked, "Adorn yourself."

20   The fugitives have returned to life, the *dīvān* of the resurrection is now organized.

By God's command they died, then they came to life. He
made them decay for a while, then made them fair.

God's sun is rising with bounty, the proof of His handiwork
is established.

We have dyed the plants without a dye, we measure their size
without a mold.

Paradise on paradise on paradise—dazzles one, take up your
home therein.

25   We have stirred up the souls to the heights; this one has at-
tained union, that one played the Pharaoh.

Ah, be silent and address them with silence, for silence is
more revealing of secrets.

268

Lovers, lovers, whoever sees His face, his reason becomes
distraught, his habit confounded.

He becomes a seeker of the Beloved, his shop is ruined, he
runs headlong like water in his river.

He becomes in love like Majnūn, head spinning like the sky;
whoever is sick like this, his remedy is unobtainable.

The angels prostrate before him who became God's dust, the
Turk of heaven becomes the servant of him who has become
His Hindu [slave].

5   His love places the aching heart on his hand and smells it;
how did not that rejoice which has become His.

Many a breast He has wounded, many a sleep He has barred;
that magical glance of His has bound the hand of the magicians.

Kings are all His beggars, beauties clippings of His [beauty],
lions drop their tail on the earth before His street-dogs.

Glance once at heaven, at the fortress of the spiritual ones, so
many lamps and torches on His towers and battlements.

The keeper of His fortress is Universal Reason, that king
without drum and tabor; he alone climbs that fortress who no
longer possesses his own ownness.

10   Moon, have you seen His face and stolen beauty from Him? Night, have you seen His hair? No, no, not one hair of Him.

This night wears black as a sign of mourning, like a black-robed widow whose husband has gone into the earth.

Night makes a pretense and imposture; secretly it makes merry, its eye closes no eye, its brow is set awry.

Night, I do not believe this lamenting of yours; you are running like a ball before the mallet of fate.

He who is struck by His mallet carries the ball of happiness, he runs headlong like the heart about His street.

15   Our cheeks are like saffron through love of His tulip bed, our heart is sunk like a comb in His hair.

Where is love's back? Love is all face, back and face belong to this side, His side is only face.

He is free of form, His business is all form-fashioning. O heart, you will never transcend form because you are not single with Him.

The heart of every pure man knows the voice of the heart from the voice of clay; this is the roaring of a lion in the form of His deer.

What is woven by the hand of the One becomes revealed, becomes revealed from the workmanship of the weaver and his hand and shuttle.

20   O souls His shuttle, O our *qibla* His street, heaven is the sweeper of this street, this earth its mistress.

My heart is burning with envy for Him, my eyes have become His water bags: how should He be wet with tears, while the sea is up to His knees?

This love has become my guest, struck a blow against my soul; a hundred compassions and a hundred blessings to his hand and arm!

I flung away hand and foot and had done with searching; my searching is dead before His searching.

Often I said, "O heart, be silent to this heart's passion"; my *hā* is useless when my heart hears His *hū*.

269

The glow of the light of daybreak is in your emerald vault, the goblet of the blood of twilight is your blood-measuring bowl.

Mile on mile, torrent on torrent come dancing and gliding to the shore of your sea.

With all the elevation and aspiration of the moon, the cap falls off the head of the moon when the moon raises its face to gaze upon your height.

Every morn the nightingales lament like the heart-forlorn ones to the melodies of those attaining your verdant meadow.

5   The spirits seek vision, the hearts all seek the Beloved; you in whose broad orchard four streams are let flow—one stream pure water, another honey, the third fresh milk, the fourth your ruby wine.

You never give me a chance, you are giving wine upon wine; where is the head, that I may describe the drinking-cup of your wine?

Yet who am I? Heaven itself in the round of this heavy bumper finds not a moment's peace from your love and the craving for you.

Moon of silver girdle, you have experience of love; heaven, loverhood is apparent in your features.

When love is yoked to the heart it wearies of the heart's chatter: heart, be silent! How long this striving and inquiring of yours?

10   The heart said, "I am His reed pipe, I wail {by His breath.}" I said, "Be lamenting now, the slave of whose passion is the soul."

We have opened your door; do not desert your companions; in thankfulness for an all-embracing love which has seized you from head to toe.

270

When laughter leaps forth from me, I keep laughter hidden from him; I make a sour face at him; I shout and scream at him.

If you joke and laugh at the sour ones, war arises; I have hidden my laughter, I drop tears at him.

A huge city is my body, grief on one side, I on the other; one side I have water from him, on the other fire.

With his sours I am sour, with his sugars I am sugar; he is my face, he is my back, through him I scratch the back of joy.

5   A hundred the likes of me and you have become drunk in his meadow, dancing, hand-clapping on the summit of every dome through him.

I am the parrot of candy and sugar, I eat only sugar; whatever sour is in the world, I am far and indifferent to it.

If he has given you sourness, to me he has given honey and sugar; he has made you jolting and lame, me smooth and even of pace.

Whoever travels not on this road, his path is all gully and steep; I who am on this royal road am on a level path through him.

My heart is the *Masjid-i Aqsā*, my heart is the Paradise home; all my traces through him have become houris and light.

10   To whomsoever God gives laughter, laughter leaps from his mouth; if you doubt Him, I am altogether in acknowledgement of Him.

The rose's portion is laughter, it has no weeping; what shall it do? Lilies and roses are blossoming in my conscious heart through Him.

Patience was saying, "I bear good tidings of union from Him; gratitude was saying, "I am the owner of stocks through Him."

Reason was saying, "I am abstinent and sick through Him"; Love was saying "I am a magician and cutpurse through Him."

Spirit was saying, "I am a pearl-possessing treasure through Him"; Treasure was saying, "I am at the foundation of the wall through Him."

15   Ignorance was saying, "I am without knowledge and consciousness through Him"; Knowledge was saying, "I am the chief of the bazaar through Him."

Abstinence was saying, "I understand the secrets through Him"; Poverty was saying, "I am without heart and turban through Him."

If Shams-i Ḥaqq returns to me from Tabriz, all my discourses will be expounded and revealed through Him.

271

Whatever comes of the world's affairs, how does that affect your business? If the two worlds have become an idol-temple, where is that roguish idol of yours?

Grant that the world is in famine, there is no bowl [of wine] and bread any more; O king of the manifest and hidden, where are your measure and store?

Grant that the world is all thorn, scorpion and snake; O joy and gladness of the soul, where are your rose bower and rosebed?

Grant that liberality itself is dead, that miserliness has slain all; O our heart and eye, where are your pension and robe of honor?

5   Grant that both the sun and the moon have sunk into hell; O succor of hearing and sight, where are your torch and light?

Grant that the jeweler is not after any customer, how shall you not take the leadership? Where is your pearl-raining cloud?

Grant there is no mouth, there is no speech of tongue to tell the secrets; where is the surging of your heart?

Come, leave all this, for we are drunk with union and encounter; the hour is late—come quickly, where is this house of your vintner?

Drunken sharp-glancer of mine, my fellow in heart and hand, if you are not dissolute and in dotage, where are your cloak and turban?

10   A whore has carried off your cap, another your gown; your face is pale with a moonlike beauty; where is your support and protection?

A stranger is waylaying the path to the drunkards of eternity: why do you not act the policeman? Where is your wound thrust? Where are your gallows?

Silence, word-scatterer! Interpret not to ordinary people what is fit only for the ears of the silent ones; where is your ecstasy and speech?

272

Say, how shall a part of the world depart from the world? How shall moisture escape from water, one leap from two?

No fire dies from another fire, my son; O my heart bleeding of love, wash not my blood in blood.

However much I fled, my shadow did not leave me; shadow must be in charge of me, even though I become as the thread of a hair.

Only the sun has the power to drive away shadows, the sun increases and diminishes them; seek this from the sun.

5   Though for two thousand years you are running in the back of the shadow, in the end you will see that you are behind and the shadow before.

Your sin has become your service, your pain your blessing, your candle your darkness, your bonds seeking and questing.

I would explain this, only it would break the back of your heart; when you break the glass of the heart, repairs are of no avail.

You must have both shadow and light together; listen to me, lay your head down and prostrate yourself before the tree of the fear of God.

When from the tree of His grace wings and feathers sprout for you, be silent as a dove, do not open your mouth for cooing.

10   When a frog enters water, the snake cannot reach it; the frog croaks and gives information so that the snake knows where he is.

Even though the cunning frog should hiss like a snake, the feeble frog-sound of his betrays the true voice.

If the frog were silent, the snake would be his prey: when it retires into its corner, the barleycorn and grain become a treasure.

When the golden barleycorn has become a treasure, it does not diminish in the earth; the barleycorn of the soul becomes a treasure when it attains the treasure of *Hū*.

Shall I finish these words, or shall I squeeze them again? Yours is the decree; what am I, O gracious king?

273

The rock splits open in yearning to encounter you; the soul beats wing and pinion in the joy of your air.

Fire becomes water, reason is lain waste, my eye becomes the foe of sleep on account of you.

Rending the robe of patience, reason departs out of itself; your love like a dragon devours both men and stones.

Do not bind the departer, do not turn laughter to weeping; be not cruel, for your servant has none to take your place.

5   When your water departs to the river, how shall my discourse flow well? Sometimes my breath ceases because you are so shy.

What is the food of your love? This roasted liver of mine. What is my ruined heart? The workshop of your fidelity.

The jar is fermenting; who will drink? The harp sings aloud in the description and praise of you.

Love entered by my door and laid a hand on my head, saw that I was without you, and said, "Alas for you!"

I saw a difficult stage, involved and very complex; I went, and now remain a heart slain by your hand at your feet.

274

Again I am raging. I am in such a state by your soul that every bond you bind, I break, by your soul.

I am like heaven, like the moon, like a candle by your glow; I am all reason, all love, all soul, by your soul.

My joy is of your doing, my hangover of your thorn; whatever side you turn your face, I turn mine, by your soul.

I spoke in error; it is not surprising to speak in error in this state, for this moment I cannot tell cup from wine, by your soul.

5   I am that madman in bonds who binds the *dīvs;* I, the madman, am a Solomon with the *dīvs,* by your soul.

Whatever form other than love raises up its head from my heart, forthwith I drive it out of the court of my heart, by your soul.

Come, you who have departed, for the thing that departs comes back; neither you are that, by my soul, nor I am that, by your soul.

Disbeliever, do not conceal disbelief in your soul, for I will recite the secret of your destiny, by your soul.

Out of love of Shams-i Tabrīzī, through wakefulness or night-rising, like a spinning mote I am distraught, by your soul.

275

All my six directions, Beloved, are graven with your beauty, you shine in the mirror, since it has been polished by you.

The mirror sees you according to the measure of its breadth; how shall the shapes of your perfection be contained in the mirror?

The sun asked your sun, "When shall I see you?" It replied, "I shall rise in the time of your setting."

You cannot travel freely in this direction, for like a camel your ropes, O reason, have bound your knees.

5   How is it that reason, whose splendor is not contained in the seven heavens, entered your snare and bag, O love?

This reason became one grain of the harvest of love, and all your feathers and wings became trapped by that grain.

You plunged once into the sea of the life of God, you saw eternal spirit [life], that spirit became your bane.

Of what use is this [reason's] kingship beside the sovereignty of your love? Of what use his pomp beside your pomp and majesty?

See in the world's ears now a hundred golden rings because of the grace of your answering, out of joy of your questioning.

10   Raw ones who never received refined gold from your hand are happy with your stones and shards instead of gold.

A hundred skies revolve around your earth, a hundred full moons prostrate before your crescent moon.

With you our carnal soul's dog plays foxy tricks, for the lion prostrates before your jackal.

Like day and night, footless we are journeying, O soul, since every moment from heaven arrives your "Come up!"

What shall be our darkness in the presence of your light? What our evil deeds with your beneficence?

15   By day we revolve about your tree like a shadow, by night till dawn we lament, secure from your wearying.

Yearning for your reproach, Adam came from the high seat of Paradise down to your vestibule.

The heart's sea thunders and boils with your praise, but I have closed my lips, yearning for your discourse.

276

Both aware and untimely he came as my guest; my heart said, "Who has come?" My soul said, "The moonfaced moon."

He entered the house, we all like madmen searching for that

moon gone into the midst of the street.

He was crying out from the house, "I am here"; we, heedless of this cry, go crying everywhere.

That drunken nightingale of ours is lamenting in our rose garden, like ringdoves we are flying and shouting, "Where, where?"

5   At midnight a crowd leaped out saying, "What? The thief has come?" That thief also is saying, "The thief has come"; and he is the thief.

His shout became so mingled with the shout of all others that not a bit of his shouting stands out in this uproar.

And He is with you means He is with you in this search; when you are seeking, seek Him too in the search.

He is nearer to you than you; why go outside? Become like melting snow, wash yourself of yourself.

Through love a tongue grows in the soul like a lily; keep your tongue silent, imitate the trait of the lily.

277

From these depths depart towards heaven; may your soul be happy, journey joyfully.

You have escaped from the city full of fear and trembling; happily become a resident of the Abode of Security.

If the body's image has gone, await the image-maker; if the body is utterly ruined, become all soul.

If your face has become saffron pale through death, become a dweller among tulip beds and Judas trees.

5   If the doors of repose have been barred to you, come, depart by way of the roof and the ladder.

If you are alone from friends and companions, by the help of God become a *ṣāḥib-qirān* [lord of happy circumstance].

If you have been secluded from water and bread, like bread become the food of the souls, and so become!

278

Sweetly parading you go—my soul of soul, go not without me; life of your friends, enter not the garden without me.

Sky, revolve not without me; moon, shine not without me; earth travel not without me, and time, go not without me.

With you this world is joyous, and with you that world is joyous; in this world dwell not without me, and to that world depart not without me.

Vision, know not without me, and tongue, recite not without me; glance behold not without me, and soul, go not without me.

5 The night through the moon's light sees its face white; I am night, you are my moon, go not to heaven without me.

The thorn is secure from the fire in the shelter of the rose's grace: you are the rose, I your thorn; go not into the rose garden without me.

I run in the curve of your mallet when your eye is with me; even so gaze upon me, drive not without me, go not without me.

When, joy, you are companion of the king, drink not without me; when, watchman, you go to the king's roof, go not without me.

Alas for him who goes on this road without your sign; since you, O signless one, are my sign, go not without me.

10 Alas for him who goes on this road without any knowledge; you are the knowledge of the road for me; O road-knower, go not without me.

Others call you love, I call you the king of love; O you who are higher than the imagination of this and that, go not without me.

279

Last night in sleep I dreamed—yet what sleep is there for lovers?—that I was searching inside the Kaaba for where a prayer-niche might be.

The Kaaba of the spirits, not that Kaaba which, when you reach it on a dark night, you say, "Where is candle or moon-light?"

Nay, rather its foundations are of the light of the whole world, from which the rays of your spirit take light. Only how can the soul endure it?

Its hospice is all light, its carpeting is knowledge and reason, its Sufis all bewildered, where is the clatter of the shoes?

5   Fortunate one, the crown and throne you hold hidden in you are beyond the imagination of Kai-Qubād and Sanjar and Suhrāb.

Bird of heart, fly amidst the garden of its beauty, for there is a secure abode; where is snare or beating-stick?

There is a gift in the midst of your body's loans; search in the middle of the soul for the gift of Giver.

In describing from afar the discourse of time became prolix; now that I have reached my tent-tope, where now is prolixity?

Since you quitted the clay, you forthright entered the garden of the heart; so from that side is there naught but concert and pure wine?

10   Since you left the salt marsh of the body for the garden of the soul, is there naught but rose and basil, tulip and fountains of water?

Since you have seen thousands of beauties that were not of body, why do you say, "Where is the beauty of the Opener of Doors?"

Faqīh, for God's sake, learn the science of love, for after death, where are "lawful," "unlawful" and "obligatory?"

When in time of pain and affliction you quickly find His
door, you say once more, "Where is He? Where is the door of
His palace?"

Wait till the wave of union with Him snatches you away and
you become unseen, then you may say, "Where is the world of
causation?"

15   If the script of Ibn Bawwāb has become your fancy in callig-
raphy, read the letter of His love, and it will show you where
the Doorkeeper is.

Beware, say not of every man that he is God's deputy; come
to the court of the *qāzi,* then see where the deputies are.

Until you box your ears, you will see only men's affairs; when
you rub your eyes, you will say, "Where is his light?"

In the tavern of reality, before the dissolute drunkards, in
such a pure wine you will not see where lees and straw are and
secondary causes.

In the mortal reckoning your life has been wasted without
reckoning; behold the purity of the Beloved; where is the simili-
tude of the reckoners?

20   When the wine makes you brave and you plunge into the
sea of the heart, you will strike up this melody: "Where is the
bottom of this sea?"

280

Happy the moment when we, you and I, sit in the palace,
with two forms and two figures but with one soul, you and I.

The beauty of the garden and the birdsong will confer upon
us the water of life at that time when we enter the garden, you
and I.

The stars of heaven will come to gaze on us; we shall show
them the moon itself, you and I.

You and I, unselfed, will be collected together in ecstasy,
joyful, and indifferent to idle fable, you and I.

5   The parrots of heaven will all be sugar-cracking in the place where we laugh in suchwise, you and I.

This is still more amazing, that you and I here in one corner in this very moment are in Iraq and Khorasan, you and I.

In one form upon this earth, and in another form in eternal paradise and the land of sugar, you and I.

281

You who have made the lovers' whole baggage a wager, do not shed the blood of these lovers, and do not depart.

See the traces of blood at the top of the road, hear the bloody cry coming from all sides.

I said to this heart, "See his mallet; if you are a ball, run into this mallet."

The heart said, "In the curve of his mallet I have become old and new a hundred thousand times."

5   How should the ball of the heart hide from the mallet? For in this desert there is neither well nor ditch.

The cat of the soul is the sneeze of the lion of eternity; the lion trembles when the cat mews.

This is the gold of the mine of Shams-i Tabrīz; search it grain by grain, it is all pure.

282

Sit with your comrades, do not go to sleep; do not go to the bottom of the sea like a fish.

Be surging all night like the sea; no, do not go scattered like a torrent.

Is not the water of life in darkness? Seek in darkness, and do not hurry away.

The nightfarers of heaven are full of light; you too, go not away from the company of your companions.

5   Is not the wakeful candle in a golden dish? Go not into earth like quicksilver.

The moon shows its face to the night-travelers; be watchful, on the night of moonshine do not go.

283

I went to the master's street and said, "Where is the master?" They said, "The master is a lover and is drunk and wandering from street to street."

I said, "I have a duty, at least you give me a clue; after all, I am the master's friend, not an enemy."

They said, "The master has fallen in love with that gardener; seek him in the garden or beside the stream."

Drunkards and lovers go after their beloved; if a man has fallen in love, go and wash your hands from him.

5   The fish that has known water remains not on land; how should a lover stay in the sphere of color and scent?

The frozen snow that has seen the face of yon sun is devoured by the sun, though it be heap on heap.

Especially he who is in love with our king, a king peerless, faithful, sweet-tempered.

Any copper which that infinite, immeasurable, incomparable alchemy touches becomes gold at the word *Return*.

Sleep away from the world, and flee from the six directions; how long will you foolishly wander and roam hither and thither?

10   Eventually in the end they will bring you of your own choice, go with glory and honor before the king.

Had there not been a meddler in the midst, Jesus would have revealed the mystery line by line.

I have closed the road of the mouth and opened the secret way; I have escaped by one cup of wine from the frenzy of speech.

284

I am not satiated, not satiated with your laughing lips; a thousand blessings on your lips and teeth!

Has any man ever wearied, my son, of his soul? You are my soul since my soul and yours are one and the same.

I am thirsty and suffering from dropsy, my death and life are from water; pass around the cup, for I am the slave of your turning around.

You make dispensation, go offer me to yourself that my head may raise itself up from your shirt.

5 Though my two hands are wounded, my hand belongs to you; of what use are my hands without your breath and incantation?

Your love said, "Sir, come into my private chamber, that no thief may make designs on your inner chamber."

I said, "Blessed one, I have become a ring on this door so that no thought of me may trouble your doorkeeper."

He said, "You are both standing at the door and in my bosom, exterior and interior—both homelands are yours.

Silence, and recite no more; sufficient should be this hospitality and table. For all eternity Rum and Turk shall eat of your table.

285

The light of my heart is your lovely face, my wings and pinions your gentleness;

Festival and 'arafa are your laughter, my musk and rose are your sweet scent.

My sign is the disc of your moon, my place of shade your lovely hair.

My prostration-place is the dust of your door, my leaping-place your delightful street.

5   My heart goes not to others, since it has gone in your sweet direction.

Even if my heart goes to others, your sweet "person" will draw it back.

My intoxication is of your being, my plunging-place your sweet river.

I have become like gold from your silvery bosom, I have become single through your sweet fold.

I lay my head; and how should not your sweet ball lay down its head before your mallet?

10   I will be silent, silent, since my clamoring is shattered by your sweet cry.

286

Come, beat the drum of fidelity, for your hour has come; give wine red as the Judas flowers, for your Judas tree has blossomed.

Let us press new wine from the sweet grapes of your garden, let us scatter fruits from your lusty young tree.

Drive not soul and reason from the table of your bounty; what do two or three flies consume to diminish the plenty of your table?

The desire of all the desirous is but one grain of your harvest; the two worlds are but two small townships in your world.

5   If all day the sun strikes the sword of light, it becomes less than a mote before your terrible lance.

Since the soul of heaven kisses the earth before you, on what wing shall earth fly towards your heaven?

It sits with broken wings, gazing towards you, for in that same moment there arrives to it the succor of your present.

No night nor dawntide has passed in the world, in which my breath has not been set afire by the threat of your watchman.

Did you not make a promise to me? Did you not swear an oath, that at the time of my going up your ladder should arrive?

10   When you gaze on your servant with that narcissus eye, his soul flies from the place to your placelessness.

You cherish him saying, "Sorrowful one, do not grieve henceforward, for heaven itself has thundered with your loud lamentation.

"I am more compassionate in cherishing than mother and father; it was to mature you that your trial occurred.

"I will make a garden, a Paradise, a cure out of your pain; out of your smoke I will fashion a new heaven better than this.

"I have spoken all, yet I have not spoken the root of the matter, Beloved, for it is better that men should hear your secret from your own mouth."

287

Saki of the moonface, circulate the cup, deliver me out of shame and name.

Saki, I am a prisoner in your snare, for you have laid at every step a snare.

Have done with sloth, seize me! Be not slothful, for the tribe has departed.

Is not sobriety the alighting-place of every care? Is not joy banned in anxiety?

5   Fast, for fasting is great gain; the faster drinks the wine of the spirit.

It is in tradition that whoever keeps the fast sees the moon of God in the evening time.

It is not just that when I enter by the door, you should flee from me by the roof:

You flee and I crying after you, "Be patient one moment, O fleet of pace!"

Moslems, Moslems, what remedy is there? For I am con-
sumed with fire, and yet this business is unsettled.

10   There is no remedy but pure wine in cups which noble men
have circulated.

The tale of lovers has no end, so we will be satisfied with this,
and so farewell!

The answer of Mutanabbī's saying is this: "A heart which
wine cannot console."

288

There are a few dissolutes this side, hidden in the shade of
the heart, and yonder sun shines from the roof of the heart
upon their souls;

Every star became a Venus, every mote a sun, sun and stars
before them spinning like motes.

Reason and heart, gone astray, have carried all the souls to
heaven; every one of them has become a Kai-Khusrau and a
king without parasol and standard.

You have slain many a mount and gone around the world;
journey into your soul, and behold a people become altogether
soul.

5   With this divine benefaction, with this beauty and loveliness,
see the command-worshippers absorbed in the command.

Their hearts are as mirrors, those rancorless hearts of theirs;
their hearts like the field of the skies, a king entering the field.

Through their jubilees and ululations, their sugar-cracking
lips, dessert and wine and that other thing have become cheap
in our town.

If I were unselfed as last night and thought not of the distur-
bance, unselfed I would have spoken the rest of this;

But for now I close my mouth, because I am in pawn to my-
self, till the time when my heart has become drunk with him.

10   King of the kings of the soul, Shams al-Ḥaqq-i Tabrīz—
through him every soul has become a sea, every body a coral.

289

Lovers, lovers, I am mad; where is the chain? Chain-rattler of the soul, your clamor fills the world.

You have forged another chain and flung it upon my neck; you have galloped from heaven to waylay the caravan.

Rise, soul, from the world, fly from earth and earth's plot; for our sake this torch is revolving in heaven.

He who is pained at heart, how shall his way be barred by rain and mud? That man is quit of love for whom mountain has not become a mustard grain.

5   One day a hermaphrodite cried, saying, "Wicked shepherd, why, that goat is biting me, he looked at me from the flock."

The shepherd said, "He bites the hermaphrodite and perhaps slays him underfoot, but should that trouble a real man?" "You have spoken well," said the other.

Where is your reason, if you speak? Where your foot to go running, to go from dry land to sea and become secure from the earthquake?

Then you will become king of kings, enter the ternal kingdom, rise higher than the heaven, depart from this dunghill;

Active like the Universal Reason, surging like a sea of honey, like the sun in Aries, like the moon in Virgo.

10   A hundred crows and owls and doves are making melody in your ears; if only this clamor were less, you would hear the sounds of the heart.

If you are a man of heart, become without heart; if you have reason, become mad, for this partial reason is becoming a stye in the eye of your love,

So that the unseen form may arrive and draw you out of form—for this problem has become difficult through its tangled locks.

But on this road you must trail the skirt of joy because the stage is drenched with lovers' blood.

Go, go, heart, with the caravan; go not alone on the stage because this pregnant age is giving birth to troubles;

15 There you will be freed from pains, and go in the protection of God; go in the sea like a skiff. Heart, you have gone; go without complaining.

When you have removed heart from soul, you have escaped from war and peace; you have become free and unconcerned with both shop and grain.

Your soul has escaped from anxiety, the road to dangers is barred; he who is attached to you, is always in forty day seclusion.

Since by day you have become secure from this uproarious Rumi, by night too do not worry about this jangling Zangi.

Be silent, sweet of presence; saki, bind up your waterskin, because the waves are not contained in pitcher and flagon.

290

Happy-cheeked saki of mine, give the cup like pomegranate blossom; if for my sake you will not give for the sake of the heart of the Beloved.

Saki, you are the darling, you are the sick man's cure; quick, give the draft of gladness and healing to the sick.

Pour wine out in this bowl, smite the neck of anxiety; now, do not break my heart, my heart and sweetheart, and give.

Open that tavern, abandon this rowdiness; give to the thirst-stricken lover from the vintner's vat.

5 You are the soul of spring and garden, the glory of cypress and jasmine; now make no excuses, roguish idol, but give!

When you set foot on trickery and start away from the drunkards' hands our enemy will rejoice; despite strangers, give!

Give not grief and sighing, open the way only to joy; a sigh proceeds from the wayless; open the way; give audience.

We are all intoxicated of the encounter, athirst for the bumper of immortality; as pawns, give robe and turban before the saki.

I am athirst of old, hot of heart and breast; break the beaker and cup, give much, without measure.

10   You are both moon and moonshine, I am the fish of this water; the moon cannot reach the fish, so give generously of the moonshine.

291

I am seeing a moon outside the eye in the eye, which neither eye has seen nor ear heard of.

I do not see tongue and soul and heart save without myself, from that moment that I stole a glance at that cheek.

Had Plato seen the loveliness and beauty of that moon, he would have become even madder and more distressed than I.

Eternity is the mirror of the temporal, the temporal the mirror of pre-eternity—in this mirror those two are twisted together like his tresses.

5   A cloud beyond the senses whose rain is all spirit; sprinkling on the dust of the body—what rains he has rained!

The moonfaced ones of heaven, seeing the picture of his face, have become ashamed before that beauty and scratched the back of their necks.

Posteternity took the hand of pre-eternity and took it towards the palace of that moon: having seen both, it laughed in jealous pride at the two.

About and around his palace what lions there are, roaring jealously, aiming at the blood of the self-sacrificing, adventurous men.

Suddenly the word jumped from my mouth, "Who is that king? Shams al-Dīn king of Tabriz"; and at those words my blood surged.

292

Undaunted you are coming from my breast into my sight, chanting a potent spell and confused stories.

With one breath you bring into whirling the heavens and firmament; what would one rotting perception be before your spell?

You wash away the sins of both worlds at a single penitence; why have you tightened my slip around your finger?

You have a Job in every corner, a Jacob on every side; love has broken their door and stolen their cloths from the house.

5   Parade forth to the cemetery and in that garden proclaim, "Rise, ancient dead, dance, crumbled body!"

At once the whole cemetery becomes populated like a city, all dancing, all happy, fate turning back from all.

I do not boast of this at random, I am not weaving a fantasy; I have seen this a hundred ways, I am not speaking of what I have not seen.

If anyone says, "I have fled from the people, I have gone," say, "He speaks the truth if his shirt is torn from behind."

Be silent; listen, speaker, to the sorrow of the beloved with the lover; the {object} of the quest is obstinate, so long as the questor is a seeker.

293

Suddenly, having eaten nothing and taken away nothing, I fell from the garden palace and pavilion into the depths of such a well.

The world was no festival for me; I beheld its ugliness, that yellow wanton puts rouge on her face.

How does rouge beautify that thorn of evil root? That thorn which has sunk into every liver and kidney?

She came, that blind crone, with a crown of roses, her black ribbon let loose, having blackened her eyebrows with indigo.

Look not at her anklets, regard her black legs; puppetry is very pretty—when behind a screen!

Go, wash your hands of her, Sufi of well-washed face; shave your heart of her, man of the shaven head!

Unlucky and heavy of soul is he who seeks fortune from her; he is gone in bondage to greatness, and burns like a chip.

Come to our aid, Beloved, amongst the heavy-hearted, you who brought us into this wheel out of nonexistence.

Silence! Speak only of that infinite one of sweet breath; how long will you make discourse of these numbered breaths?

294

O you whose soul had informed my soul of itself, your thought every moment has made an impression on your slave.

Whatever you think whatever enters your mind, that same instant that thing passes into your servant's mind.

My soul has become occupied with your graceful airs; your guile in secret has wrought another thing.

Every morn the reed laments, remembering your lip; your love fills the mouth of the reed with candy and sugar.

Because of your moonlike face and your stature and waist, this soul of mine has made itself like the new moon.

When I make myself like a belt, perhaps you will come to my waist, O you whose eye you have fixed on me in wrath.

In wrath you gazed and turned my heart upside down, so that this wandering heart journeyed out of itself.

295

That stranger-beloved of mine has returned to the house; today gaze about and behold strange forms!

See the faithful friends, see the brethren of purity, dancing because that treasure has returned to the ruin.

O eye, behold the garden; ear, gather the words, open your sweet lips, beloved of fair legend.

Saki today unsparingly pour the immortal wine; what does the sea diminish through those two or three measures?

5 Measure and measure in wine is not duality, if you want it to become one, break the two measures.

I am a falcon of the hunt, beloved, do not keep me in bonds; I will be no more like an owl in a ruin.

I am not content with you, patience has strayed from my heart; go, speak to another, I will not listen to your fable.

I am a grain of the skies, for a while I am in this earth; when the justice of spring comes the grain becomes green.

You are the bane of birds; of that grain which you know, you scatter a handful from a garner full of grain.

10 You who have given me lustre a hundredfold like the blue sky, beloved, answer frankly, is this so or not?

Beloved, once more shake the chain and from afar gaze upon the madmen.

This is the very rose bower of fortune, Lord, what a tree is this! A hundred drunken nightingales every moment make their nest here.

The soul comes, being dragged by the ear; the heart comes to the lovely ones, because spring has come and that stranger December has gone.

296

Every day is festival and Friday for the poor; has not yesterday's Friday become an ancient festival?

O soul, robed in festive garb like the festival moon, made of the light of the beauty of yourself, not of woolen frock;

Like reason and faith sweet outside and inside, not garlic stuffed in the heart of a walnut-sweet.

Put on such a frock and go about in this ring, like the heart clear and bright in the vestibule of the heart.

On a running river, O soul, how shall a straw stand still?
How can rancor make its dwelling in the soul and spirit?

In the eye of sanctity these words are a branch new and fresh;
in the eye of sensual perception, they are like an ancient legend.

297

O formless Beloved of the pure form-fashioner, O you who
have given the cup full of tumult to the lovers,

You have closed your mouth against uttering secrets, and
opened in the heart the door which I do not mention.

Since your beauty secretly cast off the veil, heart has gone
after saki and head after wine.

In the morning when your image drove forth riding, holy
spirits, as numerous as the sands, followed on foot;

And those who are famous in heaven for their adoration
broke their rosaries and pawned their prayer rugs.

The soul cannot endure to gaze on your face unveiled; your
beauty exceeds all that I say.

My soul runs after you like a raging camel; my body is a col-
lar bound upon the neck of that camel.

Shams al-Ḥaqq-i Tabrīz, my heart is pregnant by you; when
shall I see a child born under your auspices?

298

The dissolutes are all assembled in the Magian monastery;
give one bumper to that unique elder.

The blood-shedding master, love, has seized door and roof,
and reason is fugitive from house to house.

That most mighty beauty flung aside one veil, and all the
people of the time departed out of the veil.

The same is with the lovers who fell into this sea; what place
is there for safety and security?

5 How shall love grow cold from the voice of reproach? A lion never runs from a woman's scream.

Fill the bumper with the divine wine, leave not the "gods" of nature standing in the midst.

First give that bumper to the talkative soul, so that its speaking faculty may not utter any more legends.

Once speech is blocked, a torrent will come so that you will see not one sign left of beings and places.

What a fire Shams al-Ḥaqq-i Tabrīz has kindled! Brave, fire, congratulations, O flames!

299

This midnight who has come like moonshine? It is the messenger of love, coming from the prayer-niche.

Bringing a torch, he has set fire to sleep; he has come from the presence of the unsleepy king.

Who is this who has started all this tumult in the city, who came upon the harvest of the darvish like a flood?

Who is this? Say, for in all the world there is none but he, a king came to the door of the house of a doorkeeper.

5 Who is this who has spread such a table of bounty, who has come laughing, to lead the companions to the table?

A cup is in his hand which makes an end of the dervish; from that grape's juice the color stains his lips.

Hearts are trembling, all souls impatient—one fraction of that trembling has fallen upon quicksilver.

That gentleness and grace with which he treats his servant is the same gentleness and grace which make the ermine.

Of that lament and those tears which are the dry and wet of love, one gentle melody has reached the waterwheel.

10 A bunch of keys is under love's armpit, come to open all the gates.

Bird of the heart, if the hunter has broken your wings, yet the bird escapes from the snare when it is beaten and broken [dead].

Silence! Embodied similitudes are not mannerly, or manners have never entered your ear.

300

As it is late and raining, to home, to home! Welcome, all friends, to home, to home!

How long like owls banished about the ruins? To home, to home!

Bright-hearted companions, haste, despite all the blind ones, to home, to home!

You reasonable, sober, full of sorrow, do not disturb our hearts! To home, to home!

5   How long this loveplay with devil's forms, calling them houris? To home, to home!

You have seen the grain and not seen the harvest; even so are ants, to home, to home!

Make not how and why; friend, leave grazing to cattle, to home, to home!

In that house is the concert of the circumcision feast, with the ritually pure, to home, to home!

Shams al-Dīn-i Tabrīz has built a home for the naked; to home, to home.

301

Your heart has become like granite rock, and what can be done with granite rock?

What can glass do with granite rock, except become shattered to pieces.

You laugh like the true dawn that the star may yield its life before you.

Since love opened its bosom, thought has fled into boundary;

5   When patience perceived that flight, it too escaped on horse.

Patience and reason are gone; passion remained, weeping and in a fever.

Some men, being separated from your wine, are fallen on the road like dregs;

Though their livers have turned to blood, yet they are nimble and reckless on this path.

Because of this business we have become strangers to reason and to the busybody heart.

10   Love is the reality of command; poetry is the drum of indication.

Beware, for our prince is galloping, every morning he is on a raid.

Leave this theme of loneliness and separation, out of terror of which descriptive language breaks.

The imam has fled; muezzin, be silent, descend from the minaret.

302

What is this hurricane blowing along from heaven? Hundreds of thousands of ships staggering and reeling before it.

The ship escapes through the wind and is sunk by the wind; by the wind it is given life and is done to death.

The wind in God's command is like the breath in yours—by your command brought to cursing or reciting praises.

Know that the winds are various as fanned by the fan of predestination; by the zephyr the world is prosperous, by the pestilence it is reduced to a waste.

5   Lord, you have shown the wind, do not hide the fan; to see the fan is the lamp of the breast of the pure ones.

Whoever sees it as a secondary cause is surely a form-worshiper; whoever sees it as cause has become the reality-knowing light.

The people of form give their lives for the desire of a bead; to the eyes of people of the sea of reality, pearls have become cheap.

The imitator, becoming the dust of true men, transmits reports from them; the others keep silence, concealed behind them.

The seeker kept his eye to the path and picked up chippings; see that chipping-picker of the road has now entered the mine.

10 We tremble over our faith as a mother over her child; of what should that clever one tremble who has become entirely faith?

Like a moon you are waning in the desire for leadership; let me see you like a sun, become a king without retinue.

How long will you say that smoke is a proof of fire? Silence! Let me see you become without smoke both fire and proof.

Say how long heaven has turned and goes on turning over your head; let me see you like Messiah gone above heaven!

You who seek a portion from me—"Bring this and that!"— let me see you escape from this and that, and become that and that.

15 Enough brawling drunkard, chattering talker, let me see you become silent-speaking like the pan of the balance.

303

Ha, to and enter the sea; do not look on from afar, for the pearl is in the depths of the sea, the foam on the shore.

When you have seen the face of the king, go forth from the house like a pawn; when you have seen the face of the sun, become lost like a star.

When by that slave-cherishing you have become pure and a man of prayer, invite all like the muezzin from the minaret.

Gaze on this moon through which your heart has become bright, look upon this king who has arrived on horseback.

I will not fear and tremble when he draws the dagger of om-
nipotence; by God I will give his dagger a bribe and a portion.

What water is there that matches his grace? For he pro-
duces two hundred fountains from the breast of marble and
rock.

All day you dance for vermicelli and porridge; what do you
know of the desire of the heart for this verse and song?

Since I saw his silvery breast I flee from silver and gold, for
his breeze flees away from the hand that counts silver.

You have no fruit because you are light-laden like the willow;
you have nothing of that business because you have become a
jack-of-all-trades.

10 All the pilgrims have gone to the sanctuary and seen the
Kaaba; you have not even bought a camel with a broken bridle.

Look at your companions, all drunk and dissolute; be silent,
and become likewise, you brawler.

304

Give that spirited wine, for we are all in such a state that we
cannot tell wine from cup, head from foot.

We are all fresher than the lily and the rose branch, become
entirely spirit and spiritual glow.

All men are in the bond of passion, and passion is our slave,
for we have all escaped from this cycle of time.

Like the reed pipe we make voice at the sugar lip of the
Beloved; we sell the shop for we are all mine.

5 The light of the sun devours our bodies like a shadow, for in
form we are like being and space.

Our faces are saffron-pale out of fear for the evil eye; we are
companions of the garden and tulipbed.

We bring the Koran and swear an oath to the saki: "But from
your hand and palm we will not take wine."

Whoever has a soul catches the scent of the rose garden of
the soul; whoever has that realizes we are all that.

Our hearts are free of care like the heart of a bird, for we are all lighthearted for that heavy cup.

10 Kings yield up their crowns of gold in love for our path, for we are more belt-bestowing than youthful fortune.

Seek our souls in the front line of battle, for we go forward like arrow and lance.

We do not sit behind the veil of the shadows of mankind, for like the light of dawn we all tear veils apart.

We were evening, through the sun of the world we have become morning; we were wolves, now we are famous shepherds.

Since Shams-i Tabrīz displayed his soul-adorning cheek, we are running like the spirit towards him with heart and soul.

305

O soul, who is that standing in the house of the heart? Who may be on the royal throne but the king and the prince?

He signaled with his hand, "Tell me, what do you want of me?" What does a drunken man desire but sweetmeats and a cup of wine?

Sweetmeats hanging from the heart, a cup of pure light, an eternal banquet laid in the privacy of "He is the Truth."

How many deceivers there are at the wine-drinkers' feast! Beware, lest you fall, soft and simple man!

5 In the circle of reprobates beware lest you be eye-shut like the bud, mouth-open like the rose.

The world is like a mirror, the image of the perfection of Love; men, who has ever seen a part greater than the whole?

Go on foot like the grass, for in this rose garden the Beloved like a rose is riding; all the rest are on foot.

He is both sword and swordsman, both slain and slayer, all Reason, and giving reason to the mind.

That king is Ṣalāḥ al-Dīn—may he endure forever, may his bountiful hand be perpetually a necklace on my neck!

306

I saw my sweetheart wandering about the house; he had taken a rebec and was playing a melody.

With a plectrum like fire he was playing a sweet melody, drunken and dissolute and charming from the Magian wine.

He was invoking the saki in the air of Iraq; the wine was his object, the saki was his excuse.

The moonfaced saki, pitcher in his hand, entered from a corner and set it in the middle.

5　He filled the first cup with that flaming wine; did you ever see water sending out flames?

He set it on his hand for the sake of the lovers, then prostrated and kissed the threshold.

My sweetheart seized it from him and quaffed the wine; flames from that wine went running over his face.

He was beholding his own beauty, and saying to the evil eye, "Never has there been, nor shall there come in this age, another like me."

307

I am sprung from you and likewise you have devoured me, I melt in you since through you I froze.

Now you press me in your hand, now under your foot with grief; for the grape does not become wine until it is pressed.

Like the light of the sun, you have cast us on the earth, then little by little carried us back in that direction.

We return from the body's window like light into the orb of a sun, pure of sin and blemish.

5　Whoever sees that orb says, "He has become alive," and whoever comes to the window says, "So-and-so is dead."

He has veiled our origin in that cup of pain and joy; in the core of origin we are pure, all the rest left behind like dregs.

Source of the source of souls, Shams-i Ḥaqq-i Tabrīz, a hundred livers are on fire for you—so how many kidneys?

308

The sun has risen from the depths of the water, hear *Lā ilāha illa 'llāh* from every mote.

Why speak of motes? When the sun of the soul arrived, they robbed from the sun its very cloak and cap.

The moon of the heart like Adam has emerged from water and clay, and a hundred suns like Joseph are going down into the well.

Lift a head from the earth, for you are not less than an ant; carry to the ants the tidings of the plain and threshing floor.

5 The ant was satisfied with that rotted grain because it was not aware of our verdant ear of corn.

Say to the ant, "It is springtime, and you have hands and feet; why do you not make your way from the tomb to the open land?"

Why speak of ants? Solomon has rent the robe of yearning; punish me not, O God, for this useless image.

But they cut a gown to fit the purchaser's figure; though the garment is long, the stature is short.

Bring a long stature, that we may cut a gown before whose length the moon's bowstring is broken.

10 I keep silence hereafter, that through my silence truth and falsehood may be separated as grain from chaff.

309

Since I am intoxicated with your face, learned sage, gaze on me with those intoxicated eyes.

Through your intoxicated eyes my heart writhes (for it is

mad); drunkard and madman have a liking for each other's ways.

See my wasted heart and look fondly on me, for the sun gazes fondly upon ruins.

Go gaze, so that, by that one gaze which you gaze, marvelous trees will emerge from a single seed.

5   Your two eyes are Persian-Turk and drunk and blood-spilling; the Persian shoots Turkish arrows.

They have so plundered me and the house of the heart, that Hasanak is running with naked feet in the house.

We will come into the garden of your face and break up the house; we will manfully turn a thousand houses into a desert.

Ṣalāḥ al-Dīn, you are as the moon and have no need of this description, even as the tress-tip of houris needs no comb.

310

For a moment lay your cheek on the cheek of this drunkard, for a moment put behind your war and cruelty.

If it be hard, I bring out silver in my hand; put in this hand wine like gold.

You who have opened the doors of the seven heavens, lay the hand of generosity on my fettered heart.

All I have to offer is not-being; give the nickname of being to my not-being.

5   You are both breaker and binder of the broken; lay the balm of the soul on my broken head.

Do not put a seal on that sugar and pistachio nut; lay everlasting love upon this servant.

I have told you fifty times, O heart: do not hunt, put your foot in this net.

311

Circumambulating about your moon, the moon and sky
and Jupiter, the sun and hooplike sphere come into your
sphere—

O lord, am I seeking you or are you seeking me? O my
shame! So long as I am, I am one and you are another;

Suspending us and me, shedding the blood of both, raising
up something else, neither of man nor peri.

Let foot not remain, for foot carries us to the thorn bush;
let head not remain, for the head becomes infidel through two-
headedness.

5   One water flowing amidst the stream, one water frozen on
the bank of the stream; the former swift, the latter sluggish;
beware, swift one, lest you congeal.

The sun says to the stone, "For this reason I shone on your
stone, that you might escape from stoniness and set foot on
gemhood."

The sun of eternal love has shone in your heart; first, that
your servanthood might increase, and lastly, that you might
show mastery.

The sun says to the unripe grape, "I have come to your
kitchen so that you may not sell vinegar anymore but make a
trade of sweetmaking."

The king says to the falcon, "I bound up your eyes so that
you may break with your own kind and only regard my face."

10   The falcon says, "Yes, I am obedient; only on your beauty
I gaze, only by your image I pass, and serve you with my
soul."

The rose says to the garden, "I displayed my robes so that
you might sell all your wares and make do with me."

He who takes gold from here and makes do with another
beloved—sit awry and say truly, what is that from? From
assishness?

That is a man who gives up the ass to buy Jesus; it is of

assishness that you give up Jesus to buy the ass.

Jesus turns the drunkard into gold, and if he be gold, makes him into a jewel; if a jewel, he makes him better still, better than the moon and Jupiter.

15 You are not a Jupiter without worth, but the light of *God has purchased:* if you have anything of Joseph, you take the scent of this shirt.

To me, as to Mary, dates come forth from a withered branch without cause; to me, like Jesus, mastership comes unasked in the cradle.

See the grapes without garden and vine, the light without day and night; this glorious fortune, given by God without the process of judgment.

Through my firelike face the world's bath became hot; like children weep less for a picture painted on the bathhouse wall.

Tomorrow you will see its face become food for snake and mouse, those narcissus eyes a gateway of ants.

20 You are the moonshine driven to the moon, the wall left dark; *to Him we return* has come true—Look yonder, if you can see.

Or go to Tabriz, enjoy Shams al-Dīn, or believe the words of the truthful describers.

312

Beware, Joseph of the fair name, come not on the road without a fellow traveler; break not away from the Jacob of wisdom lest you fall into a well.

He is a dog who sleeps idly before every door; and he is an ass who comes helplessly to every tent.

See from what side this love and envy enter the breast; do you know who informs the heart but a heart-cherisher?

Wait like a bird guardian over the egg, for from the breast's egg will be born drunkenness and union and laughter.

5   Only he has a skirt; all are beggars, uncle—clutch with both your hands his royal skirt.

Like the sun go in grief for him into the fire till night; when it is night, gently turn about his roof like the moon.

On his roof these stars are keeping watch till dawn; by Allah, what a blessed presence, what an imperial court!

Those prophets who even in the earth turned their faces to heaven escaped from the snare of earth and the company of every fool;

They were snatched by that side like iron by a magnet, like a straw which flies without wings to amber.

10   Know that without His sending down no provision grows in the earth, without the society of His guiding form no substance can come into being.

The spirits are excited like camels by the cry, *"Travel!"*—like a Bedouin He cries, "Forward!" to those camels.

On the table of the heart the soothsayer casts the sand divination realities, so that through His figures the sand has become fine gold and pure.

Go more gaily, fellow travelers, for a physician has come into the world who brings to life every dead one, gives sight to all who are blind.

All these things come to pass; but when his face lifts the veil, no Venus or melody remains, no "woe, woe" to the mourner.

15   Be silent, if you are a nightingale, go, fly back to the rose-bush; the bolbol goes to the thornbed, but only rarely, from time to time.

313

Before this I sought a purchaser for my discourse, and now I wish of you to buy me from my words.

I have carved idols enough to beguile every person; now I am drunk with Abraham, I am sated with Āzar.

An idol without color and scent arrived; my hand was put out of action by him. Seek another master for the shop of idol-making.

I have cleared the shop of myself, I have thrown away the tools; having realized the worth of madness, I have become free of thoughts.

5   If an image enters my heart I say, "Depart, you who lead astray!" If it displays grossness, I destroy its composition.

Who is suitable for Lailī? He who becomes Majnūn for her. That man is at the foot of the flag whose soul is on the other side.

314

Do not fling stones at the factory of glassmaking, do not strike anew the wounded heart of the broken-hearted.

Strike all at my heart, for it is a pity and stupidity for your blows and stones to strike another's breast and soul.

Free all the captives of cruelty save me, that on your servant you may look with cruelty.

I am happy whether you are faithful or cruel; may I never journey without you, either in fidelity or cruelty.

5   If your image has not entered the eye of a particular man, the eye of a slain ibex is dark and gazes wildly.

Before the world's prison I was with you wholly; would that I had never passed by this place of snares.

How often I have said, "I am happy. I will not go on a journey"; see this hard journey, the road from the heights to the earth.

Your grace deluded me, saying "Go, do not be afraid: my generosity shall be your escort, there shall be no danger to you.

"When you go into strange lands, you will have time to become mature; then you will return to your homeland with learning and accomplishment."

10   I said, "O soul of mine, what information shall I gain without you? Who goes from you for the sake of information? Only the uninformed.

"When I quaff wine from your hand, I am unaware and drunk and happy, without danger and fear of anyone, untroubled by any man."

He spoke words in my ear like the words of highwaymen; the king rolled me off my head, he bewitched me.

The story is long indeed—alas for the cunning and deceit, if this night his generosity does not show us any dawn.

315

You have come in order to expound my secret to all, to reveal and indicate that signless king.

Last night your drunken fantasy came cup in hand. I said, "I will not drink wine"; it said, "Do not, the more loss to you."

I said, "I fear if I drink, shame will fly from my head; I will reach out to your curls, and you will withdraw from me."

It saw that I was making airs and said, "Come, it is astonishing that when someone offers you his soul, you should frown on him.

5   "With all you are deceit and cheating; with the like of me would you be the cheat too? I am the provost of secrets; do you hide a secret from me?

"I am the treasure of the heart of earth; why do you lay your head on the earth? I am the *qibla* of heaven; why do you turn your face to heaven?

"Look at the king who gives you the {light} of vision; if you angrily turn your head away, you will do the same on the day of death.

"Be pale of cheek for him who gave you the color of your cheeks; why do you saffron your face for the sake of a shadow?

"Be like a cock, time-aware and leader; it would be a pity to make your cock into a hen.

10   "Sit crookedly but tell the truth; truth has its reward. I am your soul and spirit—do you depart to another?

"If like *Lend,* you lend [God] a clipping, you will turn half a clipping of counterfeit into a treasure and mine;

"And if for two or three days you bandage your eyes with *Fear God,* you will make the fountain of your sensible eye into a sea of the pearl of vision.

"If for a moment you go straight as an arrow at my target, you will make the shaft of the arrow of heaven a bow for your string.

"Is there any generosity better than this, that with your sins and guilt I should expound how you should lament before me?

15   "Enough for those words which will be written are not contained in the mouth; if you were to open every atom, you could make a mouth."

316

The sand has become satiated with the water; I have not become, bravo! No string in this world is there to fit my long bow.

The sea is my least draft, the mountain my least morsel; what a leviathan I am. O God! Open for me a way.

I am more thirsty than death, I writhe like hell; is not any good fat morsel coming to me, I wonder?

The lean one of love has no remedy but union; none is there but your hand to feed grass to the mouth of love.

5   Reason enters your trap and loses both head and beard, though it be heavy-headed or swift to leap.

You are the implanter of sincerity in the heart of every unitarian; you likewise print images in the heart of every anthropomorphist.

Noah from the zenith of your wave becomes mate of a raft;

spirit from the scent of your street is drunk and dissolute and distraught.

Be silent, and return to the palace of the silent ones; you, cast in a village, return to the city of love.

317

Restless heart of mine, say, of what substance are you? Of fire? Of water? Of man? Of peri?

From what direction have you come? On what food pastured? What have you seen in nonexistence? Why are you flying thither?

Why do you uproot me? Why aim at my destruction? Why cut the road of wisdom? Why tear your own veil?

All animals and living beings are wary of nothingness except you, who are carrying your baggage into nonentity.

5 You are going hot and hurrying, drunk, dissolute, to whose counsel would you hearken? How long will you fall for the coquetry of men?

You are a torrent flowing, flowing from the mountaintop of this world towards the sea of no-place, faster than my breath.

Garden and spring are bewildered to know by what breeze you blow; lily and cypress are intoxicated with you: what a rose, what a narcissus you are!

The music of the tambourine whose hoop is not accompanied by tinkling cymbals, like the ravings of an unbeliever, enters not our ears.

The Moses of your love said to me "Become untouchable"; how do I not flee from all? How not run away from the Samaritan?

10 I have fled from all, though I am in the midst of men, as the Ja'farī gold coin is in the midst of the earth of the mine.

Though the gold cries out two thousand times, "I am gold," till it leaves the mine, no one will purchase it.

318

Do not heap snow on yourself, lest you congeal; your snow will make you congeal even though you be the furnace of fire.

He who does not ferment of himself destroys your ferment; and he who kindles no fire, brotherhood does not come from him.

Look for his fatness with your hand, be not deceived by his wool; don't look at his head and moustaches, his soul is lean.

If this melody is joyful, leap up and advance ardently; do not make your head so-and-so, do not listen slackly and superficially.

319

I would have shown my face to you if I were not wholly soul; the sign of me would have been seen were I not without sign.

Silver of bosom, am I not gold? Ruby of lips, am I not jewel? I would have shown my gold-essence were I not in the mine.

Your grace does not let me, else I would drive away all the people of the world in desire of you, O sugar, like a fly.

The rosebush of the soul said to your love, "Did I not fear, I would be all tongue like the lily."

5   Men say, "You are a reasonable man, for a moment come to yourself." I reply, "If I were like this, for a moment I would be like that."

If the silver-robed moon were worthy of your street, I would take him by the waist and draw him along to you.

If the wave of passion for your love let me be for a moment, I would extinguish all fires and be the salvation of lovers.

If he had not sewed up my eye of time with the arrow of jealousy, I would be openly and visibly like a bow in his hand.

This is a symbol and metonymy for Tabriz and Shams-i Dīn;
ah, how would it be if I had been an interpreter before him.

320

Passion for that Beloved brought me out of learning and
reciting so that I became mad and distracted.

Once I took my way earnestly to prayer rug and mosque; I
put on the shirt of abstinence to increase good works.

Love entered the mosque and said, "Right-guided master,
rend the bond of being; why are you in bondage to prayer?

"Let not your heart tremble before the blow of my sword;
lay down your neck, if you wish to journey from knowledge to
vision.

5   "Do full justice to ruffianism, if you are a dissolute and
drunkard; if you are lovely and beautiful, why do you remain
behind the veil?

"Lovely ones may not flee from exhibiting their features;
how can idols suffer not to indulge in coquetry and face decora-
tion?

"Now through your face you have bestowed love and impa-
tience on reason, now through your eyes played the Messiah to
the sick;

"Now with your tresses given the image of God's cord to
the believer, now through twisted curls given a cross to the
Christian.

"If you have beheld your beauty which excels the sun, why
have you withered and decayed in this dusty prison?

10   "Why do you not become refreshed by the graces of the
heart's springtime? Why do you not laugh like the rose and
pound ambergris?

"Why do you not ferment like wine in the vat of this world,
that the fermenting may bring you forth from this enameled
lid?

"Why is your Jacob denied the lighting of your lovely face? Joseph of the lovely ones, why do you languish in the bottom of the well?

"Behold your own beauty, ignorant one, in the light of the souls of the Pegs [*autāds*], for the believer is the mirror of the believer in time of loneliness.

"The earth sees its secrets in the face of the garden, 'What through its beauty and charm I have in my heart.'

15 "The rock sees its secret in the ruby and turquoise, 'I have a treasure in my heart yearning to emerge.'

"The dark iron sees its heart in the mirror, 'I am recipient to light, after all things bright.'

"When nonentities see how nonentities have been changed, they come into existence to enjoy a meeting.

"Would the fly have gone around to every dunghill had it known that by effort and virtue the 'Anqā comes out of its composition?

"When the Sufi has become 'son of the moment,' he does not become an idle person tomorrow; that person soon becomes idle who is a fool and a procrastinator.

20 "Sit among sweethearts if you are not immature and impotent; use yourself to lovers, my friend, do not wander about everywhere.

"Fish, it has become certain to you from the sea behind your back; turn your face round and go back, since you are a sea creature.

"Hear the call of *Return*, go to the water of life; enter the water and go gaily, why do you linger in water and clay?

"With heart and soul you have gone to a place where neither soul nor heart remain; on your own foot you have gone to a place where you bite your own hand.

"Become gold through the sun of eternity; go not to another's gold, for love of gold makes you yellow, though your face is silvery.

25 "The world says to you, 'Why have you become my slave? After all you are born of the king, it is I who should be your slave.'

"The sea says to you, 'I shall be your steed, rather than that you should be my steed, acting as porter and water-carrier.'

"Be silent, I was like you too, but I kept silence and found rest; if you listen to me, you will be silent too, and find rest."

321

Today the king in secret visited the madmen; a shout went up from the souls of the spiritual distracted ones.

Amid the cries that king recognized my voice, for my voice had become purified of animal breaths.

He signaled so royally that the madman leaped from his bonds; if I am mad, O king, you are the Solomon of the *dīvs*.

O king, you share the secrets of the birds and the spells of the *dīvs;* now if it is fitting you should recite a spell on this madman.

5   An elder approached the king saying, "Bind him in chains, for this madman is causing enough disturbance and disorder in the *dīvān*."

My king said, "This madman will accept no chain other than the chain of my tress; you do not know his character.

"He bursts thousands of bonds to fly to my hand; *to us returning* he becomes, for he is a royal falcon."

322

There entered the city of man a mighty torrent; the heavens were destroyed, and a waterwheel of pure light was set turning.

That city was simply madness, mankind therein distracted; for he had escaped from yesterday and tomorrow, when he awakened from a sleep.

The water boiled and became a wind which caused every mountain to fly like straw before a fierce wind, hot and burning.

Having cleaved through the mountains, he revealed the mines, you could see ruby on ruby shining like moonlight.

5   In that glow you behold him, a Chinese moonface, his two hands of separation full of blood like the hands of a butcher.

From the scent of the blood of his hands all the spirits are drunk with him; all the skies abject before him—bravo, the gracious Giver!

When he slays, it is like the trampling of grapes that through the perishing may become immortal, the grapes become syrup.

Though you trample hundreds of thousands of grapes, all will be one when such a door has been opened for the soul towards unification.

It is necessary that Shams-i Tabrīzī should take the hand of that soul, put the ring on his finger, bestow kingly apparatus.

323

Fire-worshiping heart of mine who spins like a ball in the fire, say to the saki, "Quick now, a glass of lees to begin with!"

Come, lip-biting saki, cook with that wine the raw ones; bravo, garden and orchard and vine from which you pressed the grapes!

I will give a hint which no one gives; the hint is this, O fair of stature, that on that night you transported me unselfed, you committed me over to that moonface of mine.

You, reason, do you remember how, when the king of reason out of love bestowed that fiery wine on me, at the first breath you died?

5   That darling brought two dishes, one of fire, one full of gold; if you take gold, it becomes fire, and if you set on fire, you win the game.

See the proud saki! Extinguish that pretty fire! What do you know of the power of the fire, for there you are a little child?

Get out of the fire, you will rise happy out of Shams al-Dīn-i
Tabrīzī; and if you flee into the gold, like gold you will have
congealed.

324

My heart came like a pen in the fingers of the Beloved;
tonight it is writing *zai*, tomorrow it will write *rai*.

He trims a pen for epistolary style, copying and the rest; the
pen says, "I am resigned, you know; who am I, lord?"

Now he blackens its face, now he rubs it in his hair; now he
holds it upside down, now he uses it for a task.

On one sheet he cancels a world and makes it headless;
on another sheet he delivers a [perilous] conjunction from
calamity.

5   The splendor of the pen is according to the dignity of
the scribe, whether it is in the hand of a king or a com-
mander.

He splits its head for the reason he knows; Galen knows best
what is best for the patient.

That pen is unable to utter by its own reason any applause;
that pen knows not of its own nature to make disapproval.

Whether I call it pen or call it flag, in it is sense and
senselessness—bravo, the conscious senseless one!

The mind can not compass its description, for in it is the
union of opposites, a composition without composition,
amazing!—constrained yet with free will.

325

By the right of old companionship and friendship, do not
repeat to the Beloved all that I uttered last night, unconscious
and sick;

But if, as God decrees, that moon hears of these things, he himself knows what a melancholy lover will say in the darkness of night.

When reason is not at home, the tale will be distorted—now low, now high, now war, now submissiveness.

If God should scatter my frenzy over the world, you will not see one man with reason; all will be stripped of their reason.

5   Reason, can it be that you pour these dark suggestions into me? Cloud, can it be you who rains upon me this troubled potion?

Moslems, Moslems, guard well your hearts; let none go about me, either to sightsee or to sympathize.

326

At dawn I said to that moon, "O I body and you soul, I am in this state that you see, and weep for what you know.

"You are beyond infidelity and faith, and drive a fast mount; what a fearless king you are! Do precisely as you are.

"Just once return and pass our way, gaze on the thicket of the souls—behold the trees wet with blood, like branches of coral."

You have heard how a raw one gets a reputation among men, not fearing that self-will may stamp its brand on his forehead.

5   Do not disapprove of the pure ones; be afraid of the blow of the fearless ones—for the patience of the soul of the suffering ones will annihilate you utterly.

You who are selfed, do not wrestle with the unselfed; you enemy of the darvishes, do not mix in fight with them with a stratagem of which you are incapable;

For Shams al-Dīn-i Tabrīzī, with life-bestowing and bloodspilling, kindles the fire to a fierceness by Divine powers.

327

O spiritual form, why are you fleeing from us? You are after all of the house, you know the state of this servant.

By the right of my hot tears, by the right of my pale cheeks, by the bond that I have with you beyond this human phase—

Though the whole world were laughing, without you it were a prison; enough this, show compassion to this deprived prisoner.

Though I am with all my very dear ones, when you are afar I am sore distraught—O God, may such distraction not be the lot of anyone.

5   What shall I tie to that fleeing foot of yours so that you may not flee? You resemble an unfaithful soul; you are fleeing like our Beloved.

Though you gallop up out of the nine spheres and set fire to the seven seas, I will rend to pieces spheres and seas with love and patience and strength.

Even if like the sun you surmount the fourth heaven, I will still come secretly to your stirrup like a shadow.

328

The physician of the soul brought a tray as a present; if you are a doting old man you will become fair and youthful.

It gives life to the body, intoxication to the soul; it takes away from the heart's slackness, from the cheeks' pallor.

That was the tray of Jesus, it became the inheritance of the physicians; you will find in it the antidote, if you have swallowed the poison of death.

You who seek that tray, turn your face to this *qibla*; when you turn your face thither, you will become the moonfaced of the world.

There is a pill hidden there which touches not the teeth, neither wet nor dry, neither hot nor cold.

Through that pill smaller than a grain you will come to the top of that dome, for that has become the dwelling place of Jesus; and that grain, for all its smallness,

Has become a protection, and every powerless man seeks the protection of your generosity; never will he whom you have nourished become lean.

I said to the physician of the soul, "Today in thousands of ways there is a sure footing, since you have trodden firmly."

He to whom you have given a place will never be by aught displaced; grief will not pare that heart which you have pared of grief.

10   Be silent and hush your words now that the test has befallen you; say farewell to pledges, you are free of those pledges.

329

My soul, why do you tarry so long in the land of exile? Return from this exile; how long will you be dispersed?

I sent a hundred letters, I signaled a hundred ways; either you do not know the way or you do not read the letter.

If you do not read the letter, the letter itself reads you; and if you do not know the way, you are in the grip of Him who knows the way.

Return, for in this prison no one knows your worth; sit not with the stonyhearted, for you are a gem of this mine.

5   You who have escaped from heart and soul, washed your hands of heart and soul, leaped forth from the snares of the world—return, for you are one of the falcons.

You are both water and stream and are seeking for water; you are both lion and deer and are better than they.

How far is it from you to the Soul? Are you more remarkable than the Soul? Are you commingled with the Soul, or a ray of the Beloved?

You are the light of the moon in the night, candy and sugar on the lip; dear lord, what a person you are! Dear lord, you are a divine marvel!

Every moment you bestow beauty and splendor, and we bestow heart and head and soul. Such a market is very fine—you give and take splendidly.

10   It is of your love to take away the life, of us to die like sugar; to eat poison from your hand is the very fountain of life.

330

Become of one hue with the community, that you may feel spiritual delight; enter the street of the tavern, that you may behold the dregs-drinkers.

Drain the cup of passion, let it be that you become a disgrace; close up the eyes of your head, that you may see the secret eye.

Open your two hands if you desire an embrace; break the idol of clay, that you may see the face of the idols.

How long for the sake of an old woman will you endure such a dowry? How long for the sake of three loaves will you face sword and spear?

5   Lo, the saki who is no tyrant, in his assembly there is a circle—enter and sit in that circle; how long will you gaze on the circling of fate?

Here is a good bargain—give a life and receive a hundred; cease to act the wolf and dog, that you may behold the shepherd's love.

By night the Beloved goes about; do not take opium tonight, close your mouth against food, that you may feel the taste of the mouth.

You say, "The enemy took so-and-so away from me"; go, abandon so-and-so, that you may see twenty so-and-so's.

Think of naught but the creator of thought; thought for the Beloved is better than thinking about bread.

10   With the breadth of God's earth why have you clung to prison? Knot care less, that you may see the expanse of Paradise.

Silence this speech, that you may gain speech one day; pass away from the soul and the world, that you may behold the Soul of the world.

331

You imprisoned in air nine spheres of emerald till you brought into orbit a form of earth.

Water, what are you washing? Wind, what are you seeking? Thunder, why are you roaring? Spheres, why are you turning?

Love, why are you laughing? Reason, why are you binding? Patience, why are you content? Face, why are you pale?

What place is there for the head on the road of fidelity? What worth has life itself in the religion of manliness?

5   That man is perfect in quality who is the quarry of annihilation; there is room for not one hair in the circle of uniqueness.

Whether anguish or joy, it is far from freedom; cold is that person who remains in hotness and coldness.

Where is the gleam of the charming brow if you have seen my moon? Where is the gleam of drunkness if you have drunk spiritual wine?

Has not disquietude from this purse and that bowl seized you? After all you are not a blind ass; what are you circling around?

With the breast unwashed what profits it to wash the face? From greed you are like a broom, you are always in this dust.

10   Every day for me is Friday, and this sermon of mine is perpetual; this pulpit of mine is high, my screen is true manliness.

When the steps of this pulpit become empty of men, the spirits and the angels will bring a present from God.

332

Garden, do you know in whose wind you are dancing? You
are pregnant with fruit, intoxicated with the rose bower.

Why do you possess this spirit, if you are this body? Why do
you paint this image, if you are all soul?

What offering is life to you? Dates brought to Baṣra! How
can I speak of you as a pearl, since you are the envy of Oman?

Reason, wag your chin this wise by your own analogy;
what do you know of that wise, being fascinated by [human]
chins?

5   It is difficult to play the lute for the deaf, or to sprinkle sugar
over the head of one suffering from the bile.

Faith borrows a hundred eyes to see him, until faith becomes
drunk with that wine divine.

I fall at the foot of the heart; every day I say, "Your secret
will be hidden unless you cause it to leap forth."

That six-sided dice is appropriate to that checkerboard; how
shall the human dice be contained in any bowl?

Shams al-Ḥaqq-i Tabrīzī, why do I return every instant to
your hand, if you are not the king?

333

How happy the day when you return from the road and
shine in the window of the soul like the moon from above!

With that moon ever-waxing, devoid of all ornaments, you
will adorn like the empyrean this earthly floor.

Many a fettered man of reason, who is escaped out of self;
many a soul, which begins anew the rule of sugar-cracking,

Many a caravan without mount and provision will find,
out of this six-cornered abode, the road into the placeless
world.

5   Illuminate my soul, so that my soul says to my body, "Today regard me, you master of tomorrow!"

You are water, I am a stream; how should I seek to join you? The stream has no luster if you do not open the water.

You who are happy with being before—that is, being more than all; by Allah, so long as you are with self, you will not find repose from self.

I was seeking the heart; on the road I saw it fallen into this melancholy passion, itself like a man suffering from the bile.

Shams al-Ḥaqq-i Tabrīzī, your separation has filtered me; you will see nothing but love, though you filter me a hundred times.

334

If the knowledge of the tavern were your intimate companion, this [formal] knowledge and science would be mere wind and caprice in your eyes;

And if the bird of the unseen cast its shadow upon you, the Sīmorḡ of the world would be but a fly in your sight.

If the concourse-splendor of the king of reality displayed itself, this drum of the kings would be for you a jingling bell.

If the dawn of true felicity showed favor to you, how would your skirt and beard be in the hand of the night patrol?

5   If the leaders cast their protection on you, the thought that is before the heart would be behind.

If your heart's ear did not hear things contrariwise, one letter of the book of lovers would be enough.

He says, "All are dead, not one has returned"; if that fool saw one who had returned, he would be a somebody.

The flame of your soul is trembling at the cold wind of death; it would not be trembling if it had borrowed fire from immortality.

If your worthless nature were not a fellow traveler of the worthless, this fatal draft would be in your throat like a choking straw.

10   This child of your intelligence would have reached "*Blessed is He*"; in the school of happiness why are you stuck at "*he frowned?*"

Silence, for all these things are dependent on the "moment"; if the "moment" were here, summons would come to your aid.

335

Become a lover, become a lover and bid groaning be gone; you are after all a king's son, how long will you be a prisoner?

To the king's son, the commandership and vizierate is all a disgrace; beware that you take nothing but love.

That one is not the commander of death, he is the prisoner of death; the whole passion for viziership is naught but a boredom.

If you are not a picture on the bath, seek after the spirit; so long as you are in love with form, whence will you receive spirit?

5   Do not mingle with dust, for you are a pure essence; do not mingle with vinegar, for you are sugar and milk.

Though on this side people do not recognize you, on that side where side is not, how matchless and incomparable you are!

This world is death, and in this perishing world if you are not a prince, is it not enough that you do not die?

You are the lion of God in the form of man; that is evident in your attack and stateliness and courage.

Since I saw your learning and station and graces, I have become indifferent to the learning of the *Maqāmāt* of Ḥarīrī.

10   This life has become untimely; but since you exist in the light of God, what matters timely or late?

The measure of the beloved is the glory of the lover; helpless lover, behold of what grandeur are you and I.

The beauty of the moth is according to the measure of the candle; after all, are you not a moth of this light-living candle?

Shams al-Ḥaqq-i Tabrīz, this is why you are invisible, because you are the very source of sight, or the essence [eye] of the All-Seeing.

336

I found in my house a token of the king, a ring of ruby and a belt particular of the mine.

Last night I was asleep and he came, that heart-comforting king and spiritual confidant.

Last night my king broke two hundred cups and pots in rowdy, drunken fashion in the manner you know about.

You might say that out of drunkenness he chose my rook, for my rook is engaged on a secret business of the king.

5   Today the scent of the beautiful one is in this house, from this scent in every corner a beauty is visible.

The blood in my body is pure wine from that scent; every hair of me is a drunken pitch-black Hindu.

Give ear and listen to the drunken shout, these melodies of song from my lutelike stature.

Fire, wine and tent are as cash; the elders of the path receive their youth.

In the mirror of Shams-i Ḥaqq va Dīn, King of Tabriz; both the form of the whole is published and the sea of realities.

337

I grant that you do not see the face of that Chinese girl; do you not see the moving of this veil proceeds from her moving?

Through the luster of that moon which is hidden in the skies, you have seen a hundred moons in earthly particles.

O leaf, scattered in the contrary wind, if you do not see the wind, do you not see that you are so?

If the wind is not stirred by thought, you do not stir; and if that wind does not sit still, you do not sit still.

5   The empyrean, heaven and spirit in this revolution of states are camels in file, and you are the hindermost.

Move upon yourself and drink of this blood, for in the womb of heaven you are a fetus-child.

In the sphere of your heart suddenly a pain arises; if you raise your head from the sphere, you know that you are not this.

Your ninth month is the face of Shams al-Ḥaqq-i Tabrīz, O you who are the trustee of the trust of both worlds.

O heart, be patient in this blood until the ninth month; you are that month [moon], O king, for you are Shams al-Ḥaqq va Dīn.

338

Heart, since you have become understanding of the mysteries, you have become useless for all other employments.

Be still mad and insane; why have you come to your senses and recovered your wits?

Meditation is all for the sake of acquiring; you have become entirely giving.

Preserve that same order of Majnūn, for you have become indifferent to all orderings.

5   If you desired to be veiled and prudent, why did you go about drunk in the market?

To sit in a corner yields you no profit once you have become the friend of the dissolutes of this path.

Go forth into the desert, that same desert where you were; you have wandered long enough in these ruins.

There is a tavern in your neighborhood, from the scent of its wine you have become intoxicated;

Seize this scent and go to the tavern, for you have become nimble-paced as that scent.

10   Go to the mountain of Qāf like the Simurgh; why have you become the friend of owl and heron?

Go like a lion into the thicket of reality; why have you become the friend of fox and hyena?

Go not after the scent of the shirt of Joseph, for like Jacob you are in mourning.

339

No interpreter of our fires, not tongue for the secrets of our hearts—

Heart and love have become naked of one hundred veils, soul and soul seated two and two—

If Gabriel himself would enter between the two, he would not have one moment's security from the fire.

Every instant union upon union, on every side vision upon vision,

5   [You] see on the roof of which kings of reality you are seated as a watchman.

The end of the thread of union with God is the Mount of Sinai which cannot endure this light for a single moment.

If you were to knot together a hundred universal reasons, there would be no ladder for this tall roof;

If I utter a sign of that signless one, the signs of all true men would bow prostrated.

This word has become for you a present from that light which transcends the reach of words.

10   Words have become a belt for Shams-i Tabrīz; come, fasten it on, if you have a waist.

340

You have flown from this narrow cage, you have escaped from this prison of cutpurses.

You have removed dust from the mirror, you have seen on the mirror what you have seen.

You have heard reports of low and high; seen on high what you have heard.

Since you have committed water and clay to water and clay, you have carried the fabric of spirit to heaven.

5   You have leaped out of the revolutions of the body, you have reached the spiritual revolutions.

You have emerged out from the mother's womb that is this world, you have run to the intelligent father.

Every moment drink wine sweeter than life in exchange for every bitterness you have quaffed for our sake.

Choose and seize whatever you desire, since you have chosen us above all the world.

You have gone forth from the cooking pot of this world like sweetmeat, because you are now cooked for the table of that world.

10   Though the egg has become empty of your bird, you have flown beyond the egg of the world.

Hereafter you are not contained in this world, fly on yonder, for every moment you are augmenting.

Silence! Depart, for your lock has been opened; death has directed the key to your lock.

341

May these nuptials be blessed for us, may this marriage be blessed for us;

May it be ever like milk and sugar, this marriage like wine and halvah.

May this marriage be blessed with leaves and fruits like the date tree;

May this marriage be laughing forever, today, tomorrow, like the houris of paradise.

5 May this marriage be the sign of compassion and the approval of happiness here and hereafter;

May this marriage be fair of fame, fair of face, fair of omen as the moon in the azure sky.

I have fallen silent, for words cannot describe how the spirit has mingled with this marriage.

342

Ho, water of life, turn me about like a mill with plenty.

So continue, that forever and ever my scattered heart may be in one place, I in another.

Twig and leaf move not save by a wind; straw-blade flies not without amber.

Since a straw moves not save by a wind, how shall the world move without desire?

5 All the parts of the world are lovers, and every part of the universe is drunk with encounter;

Only they do not tell you their secrets—it is not proper to tell the secret save to one worthy.

The grazers, whose pasture grazes on the cup and table of the sweet lord.

Did not the ants tell their secret to Solomon, did not the mountain echo back to David?

Were this heaven not a lover, his breast would not be serene;

10 And if the sun had not been a lover, there would be no radiance in his beauty.

If earth and mountain were not lovers, no blade of grass would spring from their breasts;

If the sea were not aware of love, it would finally come to rest somewhere.

Be a lover, that you may know the lover; be faithful, that you may see the Faithful.

Heaven did not accept the burden of trust, for it was in love and afraid to make a mistake.

343

I heard that you praised your servant—who am I? You have shown yourself such kindness.

You are the ruby-mine, the soul of amber; in compassion you ravished a blade of straw.

I was a worthless and valueless piece of iron; you polished me, made me a mirror.

You ransomed me from the flood of extinction, for you are both Noah and the Ark of Judi.

5   Heart, if you have burned, give scent like aloewood; if you are raw, then burn now, for you are firewood.

I slept under the shadow of fortune; you opened a way for me beside the five senses.

On that road it is possible to go to east and west, without feather, without head or foot.

On that road is no thorn of free will; no Christian is there, no Jew.

The soul, beyond the circumference of its blue sky, is escaped from blueness and blindness.

10   Why do you weep? Go to the laughing ones. Why do you tarry? Go to the same place where you once were.

From this honey, which has a hundred kinds of sting, has anything increased except boils?

344

In body you are with us, in heart you are in the meadow; you are the quarry yourself when attached to the hunt.

You are girdled here in the body like a reed, inwardly you are like a restless wind.

Your body is like the diver's clothes on the shore; you like a fish, your course is in the water.

In this sea are many bright veins, many veins too that are dark and black;

5   The brightness of the heart derives from those bright veins; you will discern them when you lift your wings.

In those veins you are hidden like the blood, and if I lay a finger, you are shy.

From those veins the voice of the sweet-veined lute is melancholy, reflecting the grace of that melancholy.

Those melodies come from the shoreless sea which thunders like waves out of the infinite.

345

The springtide brings me into laughter, a hangover keeps me headspinning.

A moon has brought me into the circle, a friend has made me friendless.

I have become as a string through the voice of a lute—the melody is audible, the string is invisible.

Like dust he stirred up the world; he has vanished like a wind in a dust.

5   That king lit up life like a spark who vanished in a spark as if burning.

That one adorned the beauty of the rose garden who vanished like a rose in the soul of a thorn.

My heart says, "Tell the saki my soul is drunk at least for that remaining one."

My heart like a mirror is silent, speaking in the hand of an amazing mirror-holder;

From whom moment by moment there shines in the mirror an amazing figure of beauty.

10 Every form is as the Sultan's falcon; itself a quarry, it seeks a quarry.

346

Do you not seek a sign of the separated ones? Where has gone that fidelity and affection?

The fishes are on this dry land of exile: come, water of the sea of life!

How long shall the fish remain out of its water? What am I to say? I do not know; you know.

Who am I to remain or not to remain? I desire you to remain in the world.

5 Let thousands of souls like me and better than me be your sacrifice, for you are the soul of the soul of the soul.

You say to me, "Be silent—have you not repented that you are leaving the road of tonguelessness?"

By the dust of your feet, I was not with myself out of drunkenness and wine and dizziness.

I am no better in silence than a vat; the wine does not remain hidden in the vat.

The wine of love is a more bubbling wine, for ordinary wine bubbles for a moment and this is ever-bubbling.

10 His face, red as the Judas blossom, does that which only a hundred jars of Judas-red wine can do.

I could describe his lips further but your mouth would burn if you were to recite it.

A strange waterfowl is the lover's soul, bringing water as a present from fire;

Through fire, athirst, he discovered the joy of his water; fire makes a ladder to his water.

347

Where are you, martyrs divine, affliction-seekers of the plain of Karbala?

Where are you, light-spirited lovers, speedier on wing than the birds of the air?

Where are you, celestial kings who know how to open heaven's gate?

Where are you, escaped from life and place? How can anyone tell reason, "Where are you?"

5   Where are you, you who have broken the door of the prison and set the debtors free?

Where are you, you who have opened the door of the storehouse? Where are you, help of the helpless?

You are in that sea whereof the world is the foam; swim a while more.

The forms of this world are the foam of that sea; leave the foam, if you are of the people of purity.

My heart foamed, which took the shape of words; let go the form and go take the heart, if you are of us.

10   Shams-i Tabrīzī, rise out of the east, for you are the source of the source of the source of every radiance.

348

Out of drunkenness and dissolution I have become such that I do not know earth from water.

I do not find anyone in this house—you are sober; come, perhaps you will find.

I only know that the assembly was set up first by you; I do not know if you are wine or kabob.

Inwardly you are the soul of the soul of the soul, outwardly you are the sun of the sun.

5   You are sweet-enchanting for you are the Messiah; you burn up *divs* for you are a meteor.

Make me happy-tempered, for you are wine; make me sweet-smelling for you are rose-water.

You are the zephyr, for you make the garden to laugh, though to the thirsty you are torture.

Come, see the numerous drunkards in the bazaar, if you are a bailiff and making a census.

Like beggars for bread now questioning, like sufferers now responding.

10   Your smile is brief as a lightning flash, so you are a prisoner in the shadows of the clouds.

Enter the assembly of the Eternal king; behold circulating the *porringers like water troughs*.

You are a lovely ruby, but you are in the mine; you are very beautiful, but you are in the veil.

If to the king you fly, you are the white falcon; if to the graveyard you fly, you are the raven.

Youthful of fortune, clap hands and say, "Youth, O youth, O youth!"

15   Say no word to anyone, if he presses you hard; only say, "God knows best what is right."

349

The garden is here, springtime, and the tall cypress—we will not go back from these surroundings.

Open the veil and close the door; here are we, you and I, and the empty house.

Today I am the special companion of love, having seized the cup of I-do-not-care.

Minstrel sweet of melody, sweet of reed, you must lament mighty sweetly.

5   Saki, joyous and happy, bring the wine forward immedi-
ately

That we may drink happily and sleep sweetly in the shadow
of eternal grace—

Drink not by way of throat and stomach, sleep not as the
result of nights.

O heart, I desire you to rub that cup upon your eyes;

When you become completely annihilated in the wine, that
hour you are perfect existence.

10   You will remain constant from *He gave them to drink,* with-
out death and annihilation and transfer.

Give up thievishness, and go around happily, secure from the
governor's tortures.

You say, "Show where security is"; go, go, for still you are
questioning!

O day of such happiness, what day are you? O day, you are
better than a thousand years.

All days are your slaves; they are separation, you are union.

15   O day, who shall behold your beauty? O day, you are
tremendous in beauty.

You behold your own beauty, and that eye whose ear you
box!

O day, you are not day from the sun; you are day through
the light of the All-Glorious.

Every evening the sun prostrates itself; it begs for quittance
of your moon.

O day, hidden in the middle of the day, O day, you abide
eternally.

20   O daily bread of days and nights, O gentleness of north and
south winds,

I will be silent from speaking of perfection, for you are be-
yond every perfection.

You become not manifest in words, for you are more mani-
fest than all discourse;

By words spoken thoughts become manifest—you are above
imagination and thought,

And that imagination and thought are athirst for you, you who have given smoothness to water.

25 Both of these are dry-mouthed in the water of spirit; in the world full, of self empty.

The rest of the ode is veiled from you behind the curtain, for you are aweary.

350

When you are aiming at brotherhood, first of all you must wash your face;

If your head is splitting with drunkenness, do not seek to split the heads of your brothers.

Either drive away the smell of your armpits, or say farewell to the beloved's embrace.

In the feast of a moon with hyacinth tresses how should it be etiquette for you to lament?

5 You want a quarry without a snare; be sure that like me you are seeking the impossible.

If your ears are hot from drunkenness, you are a Sufi of the concert of riotous ecstasy.

If your mind is unconscious of your ears, you are not single, you are a thousandfold.

351

The assembly is like a lamp, and you are like water; the lamp is ruined by water.

The sun has shone upon the gathering; depart from the midst, for you are as a cloud.

Sit not at the table, for you are raw; where is the smell of kabob, if you are kabob?

You went ahead, saying, "I am the chamberlain"; by Allah, you are not the chamberlain, you are the curtain.

Since chamberlains of doors have indications, they know to what door you belong.

You are mounted on a wooden horse and stupidly rush to the charge.

Either choose love, which is triple cash-in-hand, or choose abstinence, if you seek after the reward.

Sit and rise with the wakeful ones, for this caravan has departed and you are asleep.

Through Shams al-Dīn you will arrive at the stage, and in Tabriz you will find the way.

352

Union with you is the source of happiness, for those are but forms and this is reality.

Break not for a moment from your servant, for a ship cannot sail without water.

I am a faulty Koran but am made correct when you recite.

A Joseph alone, and a hundred wolves, yet he escapes when you are shepherd.

5 Every time you ask me, "How are you?" I am with tears and pale cheeks.

For the vulgar these two are tokens; what are signs to you who are without sign?

Unspoken you hear the discourse, unwritten you read the deed.

Without sleep you show visions, without water you drive on the ships.

Silence, have done with praises and petitions, for from the unseen has come *thou shall not see me.*

353

I said to my heart, "Why are you thus? How long will you
consort with love?"

The heart said, "Why do you not also come to experience
the delights of love?"

Even if you know the water of life, how shall you choose
aught but the fire of love?

You in subtlety have become as the wind, you are full of wine
as the bumper glass.

5   Like water, you give life to images; like a mirror, you are a
trustee of beauty.

Every mean soul that has not those properties may think that
you are the same—

O you who are the soul of heaven, even though in form you
are of earth.

O fine-crumbled as *surmeh*, you are the *surmeh* of the eye of
certainty.

O ruby, of which mine are you? Enter the ring, for you are a
fine signet.

10   A thousand compassions are ashamed before you the mo-
ment you are full of wrath as a sword.

Shams-i Tabrīz, your form is lovely, and what a sweet source
you are in meaning!

354

Bird of heart, fly not save in the air of selflessness; candle of
soul, shine not save in the palace of selflessness.

May the sun of God's grace ever shine upon lovers, so
that the shadow of the phoenix of selflessness may fall upon
all.

Though a lover may behold myriad fortunes and comforts,
naught enters his vision save the calamity of selflessness.

Look upon me, who have cast myself into affliction for the sweetnesses I have experienced in the nonentity of selflessness.

5   What a life, what a hundred lives indeed, if a man should sacrifice them in desire for selflessness and for the sake of self-lessness.

Lover, sit not with sorrowful ones, lest dust should fall on the joy of selflessness.

Use cruelly anyone who is a lover of prudence that you may find new pleasures in the faithfulness of selflessness.

When you know selflessness, leadership loses its market for you; head and leadership are as the dust of the foot of selfless-ness.

It is pleasant to get visibly on the throne of kingship over one's enemies, but these things have no worth in comparison with selflessness.

10   If you wish that Shams-i Tabrīz should be your guest, empty your house of self, O landlord of selflessness.

355

You who let a garden go for the sake of a small fig, let slip the houri for the sake of an unworthy crone.

I am rending my shirt, and repulsion comes over me from the glance that a crone cast at a youth.

A stinking-mouthed crone with a hundred clutching talons and tricks, putting her head down from the roof to snare a clever one.

Who is such a crone? A savorless deception, fold on fold like an onion, fetid as garlic.

5   A prince has become her captive, pledged his belt—she laughs in secret, "Fool of a princeling!"

No fresh blossom in the garden of her beauty, no milk in the breasts of fidelity of that whore.

When death opens your eyes, then you will behold her, her face like the back of a lizard, her body black as pitch.

No, be silent, give no more counsel. The master's bond is very strong; the chain of his love draws without the help of a miserable chain.

356

Proclaim, O crier, at the head of every market, "Have you seen, Moslems, a runaway slave?

"A slave moonfaced, musk-scented, a troublemaker—swift of pace in time of coquetry, in time of peace slow.

"A boy, ruby-robed, charming of countenance, sugar-sweet, cypress-stature, saucy-eyed, acute, perfectly poised;

"In his bosom a rebec, in his hand a plucker; he plays a sweet air, charming, well-seated.

5 "Does anyone have a fruit of the garden of his beauty? Or a bunch of roses to smell from the rose bed of his loveliness?

"A Joseph by whose price the king of Egypt was bankrupted, on every side heart-wounded ones like Jacob by his glance.

"I will give freely my sweet life as lawful to whomever brings me a sign of him, or even a veiled hint."

357

"Ah, from those lightning-casting, sweet, mischievous cheeks! A thunderbolt from its lightning has fallen on the soul of every helpless one!"

When before the row of pearls and rubies shone like fire, a sea of pearls surged out of the rock.

This heart torn into a hundred pieces gave a piece to the doorkeeper of the soul; when he emerged in the heart of the curtain, it became a better piece.

Paradise is divided into eight heavens, and one like a scroll; behold the eight scrolls contained in a sheet of a cheek.

5   What kind of bird is this heart of mine, kneeling like a camel, or fire-eating like an ostrich around a blaze!

Quarry of joy, this heart of mine shared the same shop with your love; it found a fine colleague and fellow-worker in that shop.

Through the sun of your love, the motes of the souls have become like the moon, and every moment a star of felicity comes into the sky.

Your form is invisible, yet relates every detail—like the Messiah through the light of Mary, the spirit of God in the cradle.

Shams-i Tabrīzī, what inconsistency is there in the heart's states, at once abiding in love and fugitive from love?

358

Soul of a hundred rose gardens, you have vanished from jasmine; soul of the soul of my soul, why have you vanished from me?

Since heaven through you is resplendent, what is veiled to you? Since the body through you is living, how have you vanished from the body?

Out of the perfection of God's jealousy and the loveliness of your beauty, O king of men, you have thus vanished from men and women.

Candle of the nine skies, for you have passed through the nine skies, what secret is this, that you have vanished in the candleholder?

5   O Canopus, before whose face the sun fainted, it is good, it is good that you have vanished from Yemen.

Musk of Tartary makes a sign to mankind with every breath because you are the king of Cathay and have vanished from Khotan.

What wonder, if you vanish from us and the two worlds, O selfless moon that has vanished from self?

O manifestation of souls, you have vanished in suchwise that out of exceeding hiddenness you have vanished from vanishing.

Shams-i Tabrīzī, like Joseph you have gone into the well; water of life, how have you vanished from the rope?

359

What a joyous pleasure it will be, what a charming spectacle, when such a part returns to the source of the source!

Wine will come from every side to its hand, without a cup, from every side to its eye, a darling, enchanting fair—

A darling who, did the granite rock catch scent of her ruby, the granite rock would receive life to become conscious.

The wine stole one attribute from the lips of my darling; inevitably the soul became a wine-bibber for the love of those lips.

5 In dawn a monk went along with me on the way to the monastery; I saw him a fellow-sufferer and fellow-worker with myself.

He brought to me, that auspicious companion, a bowl— from that bowl my soul became out of itself, a drunkard.

In the middle of my unselfedness the Tabriz of Shams al-Dīn displayed succor for the helpless ones in unity with Him.

360

Happy the moment when with compassion you scratch the head of lovers, happy the moment when from autumn arises the wind of spring.

Happy the moment when you say, "Come, poor lover, for you are distracted by me, you have no regard for others."

Happy the moment when he clings to the skirt of your grace and you say, "What do you want of me, wasted drunkard?"

Happy the moment when that saki of the assembly issues an invitation, when the cup of wine rides on the hand of the saki.

5 The particles of our bodies will be happy through that immortal wine; this greedy body will escape from the grief of eating at tables.

Happy the moment when the Beloved demands contributions from the drunkards, takes pledge from us with sweet and lovely cheeks.

Happy the moment when in drunkenness the tip of your tress is confused, the helpless heart passionately takes to curl-counting.

Happy the moment when the heart says to you, "I have no plantation," and you say, "Whatever you plant shall grow for you."

Happy the moment when the night of separation says, "Goodnight"; happy the moment when that springtide light shall give greeting.

10 Happy the moment when the cloud of divine grace comes in the air, from that cloud you rain pearls of grace on the desert.

This earth, which is thirstier than that black sand, shall swallow the water of life completely and make no dust.

Love has entered upon us with cups and wine; drunkenness has appeared to us from a hidden beloved.

A discourse surged like waves scattering pearls, it is necessary to silence it, since you do not let it pass into here.

361

When I reached your city you withdrew into a corner from me; when I left your city you did not give me a good-bye glance.

Whether you choose kindness or incline to rancor, you are all the soul's ease, you are all the feast's decoration.

The cause of your jealousy is that you are hidden, otherwise you are evident as the sun, for you are manifest through every mote.

If you choose to be in a corner, you are darling of the heart and a prince; and if you rend the veil, you have rent the veils of all.

5   The heart of unbelief by you is confounded, the heart of faith by your wine is happy; you have robbed all of their sense, you have pulled the ears of all.

All roses are a prey to December, all heads in pawn to wine; you have redeemed both these and those from the hand of death.

Since there is no constancy in the rose, since there is no way to the rose, on you only is trust to be put; you are the stay and support.

If a few have cut their hands on account of Joseph's face, you have deprived two hundred Josephs of the spirit of heart and reason.

You fashion the form of a person from filth and blood, that he may flee two parsangs from the odor of foulness.

10   You make him a morsel of dust to become pure herbage—he escapes from foulness when you have breathed spirit into him.

Come, heart, go to heaven, go to God's pasture, since you have grazed awhile in the pasture of cattle.

Set all your desire on that of which you have no hope, for out of original hopelessness you have reached thus far.

Be silent, that the lord who bestows words may speak; for He made the door and the lock, and He also made a key.

362

Tidings are newly arrived—do you perhaps have no news of it? The envious heart has turned to blood; perhaps you have no heart.

The moon has shown his face, opened the wings of light; borrow a heart and eyes from someone if you do not have any.

Amazing, night and day a flying arrow comes from the hidden bow; yield your life to this arrow. What can you do? You have no shield.

Has not the copper of your being been changed, like Moses, to gold by His alchemy? What care? Though you have no gold in your bag like Korah?

5   Within you is an Egypt whose sugarcane bed you are; what care, though you have no supply of sugar from without?

You have become the slave of form, like the idol-worshipers; you are like Joseph, but within you do not gaze.

By God, when you see your own beauty in the mirror you will be your own idol, you will not pass over to anyone.

O Reason, are you not unjust to call him like the moon? Why do you call him moon? Perhaps you have no sight.

Your head is like a lamp containing six wicks; from what are all six alight, if you have not that spark?

10   Your body is like a camel which travels to the Kaaba of the heart; out of assishness you have not gone on the pilgrimage, not because you have no ass.

If you have not gone to the Kaaba, felicity will draw you on; do not flee, idler, for you have no means of passing from God.

363

Ho, watchman of the dwelling, what sort of watchman are you? For the night-thief secretly carries off all our baggage.

Throw cold water on your face, rise up and make a tumult, for because of your sleepiness all our profit has been turned to loss.

Night and the sleep of watchmen are a thief's lamp; why do you not extinguish their lamp with a breath?

Give over being idle; be a night-traveler like the stars. What do you fear of earthly beings, since you are a celestial rider?

Two or three barks of a dog do not cut off the road to horse-
men; what shall a dog or a hay-fed ox snatch from a fierce lion?

What effect have the dog of wrath and the ox of lust on a
lion who rends asunder the ranks of vision in the thicket of real-
ities?

Were you not two drops of water, that now you make an
ark and a Noah to run to left and right midst the waves of the
flood?

Since God is your protection, what peril threatens the road
for you? Your cap reaches the sky, for you are the head of all
heads.

What an excellent path it is, with God as companion; the
hard journey would become like eternal Paradise.

10 Do not say, "What present shall I bring as a token?" Their
own face is enough as a present to the sun and moon.

Whether you go or not, your felicity is running, discharging
all the business in tranquillity and love.

When fortune is your slave it does you a thousand services,
for it cannot do without you, even though you drive it from the
door.

Sleep sweetly, for luck does not sleep on your account; take a
stone in your hand, for it will become a ruby of the mine.

Mount heaven like Jesus; say, *let me see* like Moses, for God
will not say to you, "Silence, thou shall not see Me."

15 Silence, O heart; yet what use, if you block the lid of the jar?
The heart of the vat will split when those truths ferment.

Every moment two thousand times you will recite this poem,
if you realize how it travels beyond realities.

364

O idol, you are so subtle that you enter into our soul; O idol,
by the right of your grace, pray enter amongst us.

You possess the true world, you have not your home on
earth; what would it be if for a time you entered our world?

You are subtle and without mark, you are hidden even from the hidden; this hiddenness of mine shines forth when you enter our hidden part.

Since you possess the speech of all birds, Solomon, what honey you impart to the lip when you enter our tongue!

5   In the world you alone are king, no one draws your bow; I will fly like an arrow if you enter our bow.

Parade forth, Shams-i Tabrīz, for you are the touchstone of God; all our copper turns to gold when you enter our mine.

365

You have the attribute of God; when you enter any breast, you display from that breast the glow of Mount Sinai.

You have the attribute of a lamp; when you enter a house by night, all the house receives light from the splendor of your brightness.

You have the attribute of wine; when you are in an assembly you kindle two thousand tumults and riots with your sweet graciousness.

When joy is fled, when passion is flown, what grasses and roses grow when you sweetly act the water-carrier!

5   When the world is frozen, when gaiety is dead, what other worlds you open out of the unseen!

From you comes this importunity in the heart of the restless ones; otherwise what acquaintance would dark earth have with brightness?

You are the sky about the earth revolving night and day; O sky, what do you want of us? Are you not the source of all light?

Now you scatter rain, now you sift the earth; you are not a seeker of filings, after all, you are all mine and touchstone.

Like men seeking filings night and day you sift the earth; why do you worship earth? Are you not the *qibla* of all prayers?

10   What wonder if a beggar seeks a gift from a king? This is the wonder—that a king begs from a beggar.

Even more amazing is this—the king has gone so far in petition that the beggar falls into error and thinks he is king.

Sky, are you not king? Is not the earth your slave? Then why are you in the air night and day serving the earth?

The sky answers me, "No one moves without reason; if a straw flies, that is due to some amber."

My words are meat to the angels; if I speak no words, the hungry angels say, "Speak, why are you silent?"

15 You are not of the angels, what do you know of angels' food? What should you make of manna? You deserve chives.

What do you know of this pottage that comes from the kitchen of the brain, where God acts the householder night and day? Tabriz, say to Shams al-Dīn, "Turn your face to us." I err—say, "O sun, all face without a back!"

366

My idol scolds, saying, "Why have you fallen in the middle of the road?" Idol, why should I not fall from such a wine as you have given me?

Idol, I fell in suchwise that even at the resurrection I shall not rise, when you held such a cup and uncovered such a flask.

I am dissolute, yet I have a little understanding, for you took up my head and placed it in your bosom.

Idol, from your drunken eye which is the wine-holder of love, you give wine without a cup—what a mighty master you are!

5 It is of your generosity, too, that the wine has swept away my reason, for if it still kept its reason, it should burst with happiness.

You gave me a bowl so that I am clapping my hands, for with one cup I escaped from one thousand undesirable things.

By your two ravishing drunken eyes from which joy was born, you are the primal spirit, for you were not born of any man.

367

Since it has become certain to my heart that you are the soul of the soul of the soul, open the door of grace, for you are the stay of a hundred worlds.

When separation has become rebellious, you sweetly smite its neck in retribution for your lovers, for you are the sword of the age.

When union has become lean, nourish it with the goblet; everything before you attains nourishment gratis.

Your sun has at last entered Aries in felicity, for the ancient world discovers from you the glow of youth.

5   What concerts are in the soul, what flagons pouring, which are reaching the ear from that tambourine and harp and songs!

How full is this rose bower with the song of the nightingale, so that from the riotous shouts of the drunkards you cannot tell wine from bowl.

All the branches are in flower, the kings have seized the cup; all have departed out of themselves through the heavenly wine.

Convey my soul's greetings to those kings, but you will not find anyone sober to convey my greetings to them.

The gnat has quaffed wine and lost its head and beard [feather], and annihilated Nimrod with a dagger.

10   If the wine does this to a gnat, say, what will it do to an elephant? What shall I do? The wine of placeless land cannot be described.

From his life-granting wine the dog of the cave is his lion-seizer which does nothing but act the shepherd around the cavern of the drunkards.

If a dog has become so beside itself, consider what the raging lion, when it is faithful, discovers from the wine of those vessels.

Tabriz has become an East through the rising of Shams al-Dīn, for sparks reach the stars of spiritual truths from him.

368

Go, love, for you have become the most perfect of the lovely ones; you have smitten the necks of penitence and the penitent.

What can one rely upon with your love?—for you are such a thunderbolt. Who can associate with you?—for you are all brawling.

Neither earth nor heaven can stand or withstand you; you are not in these six directions, so whence have you come?

The eight paradises are in love with you; how beautiful is your face! The seven hells tremble at you; what a fire temple you are!

5 Hell says to you, "Pass, for I cannot endure you." You are the Paradise of Paradise and were the Hell of Hell.

Lovers' eyes are wet on their skirts because of your sweet eyes; you are the provocation and brigand of every ascetic man and woman.

To be without you in the cloister is nothing but madness, for you are the very life of the cloister and temple.

Give justice to my ruined heart, O judge of love!—for you have taken tribute from my ruined village.

Simple heart of mine, from whom do you seek justice? It is lawful to love to shed blood, if you are of this guild.

10 Justice for lovers is beyond the bounds of the soul; you are engaged in useless thought and fancy.

Only the angels' attributes are privy to love for sure; you are a prisoner of the attributes of donkey and *dīv* and wild beast.

Enough, practice not magic; first deliver yourself, for you are the prisoner of the passion for magic and jugglery.

369

Gaze on the cheeks of love that you may gain the attributes of true men; sit not with the cold ones so you will not be chilled by their breath.

From the cheeks of love seek something other than the form; your business is to be a fellow sufferer with love.

If you have the attributes of a clod, you will never fly in the air; you will fly in the air if you break to pieces and become dust.

If you do not break to pieces, he who composed you will break you; when death breaks you, how will you become a unique pearl?

5 When a leaf becomes yellow, the fresh root makes it green; why are you content with a love from which you turn yellow?

370

Go, nimble-rising soul go on a strange journey to the sea of meanings, for you are a precious pearl.

If you remember, you have passed through water and clay; do not be vexed that you are passing from this terrace too.

Wash your wings of this water and clay, and become light and nimble; what are you doing not to fly in the wake of your friends who have flown?

Ho, break the pitcher and enter the river, O water of life; before every pitcher-breaker how long will you be the potter?

5 From this mountaintop go like a torrent towards the sea, for this mountain to no one's body offers an abiding-place.

Enough, cut not away from the Sun either to East or West, for through him you are now a crescent, now as a moon at the full.

371

By the right and sanctity of that, that you are the soul of all men, fill a cup with that whose description you know well.

Turn everything upside down, leave neither up nor down, so that men may know that today you are in this maidan {arena, square}.

Strike the fire of wine in the chattel of shyness and shame; the drunkards' hearts are weary of secret joy.

The time has come for you to bring back to us that departed heart, that you should set aflying our reasons like young doves.

5   You are speaking subtleties in the ring of dissolute drunkards; it is fine when the treasure shines out in a ruin.

Circumambulate the fermented wine among these consumed ones; place before the raw ones that fricassee and eggplant concoction.

What has become of me? You tell me, for how should I know what has become of me, your lips utter [those] words so easily.

372

With such a gait, when will you reach the station? With such a habit, how will you gain the goal?

You are very heavy of soul and camel-hearted; how will you arrive among the nimble-spirited?

With such grossness how will you be modest? With such a joining [attachment for the world], how will you reach the joiner?

Since there is no opening (readiness) in your head, how will you achieve the solving of the difficult secret?

5   You are like water left in this clay; so how will you attain the pure from water and clay?

Disregard the sun and moon like Abraham, else how will you attain the perfect sun?

Since you are weak, go, flee to the grace of God, for without the Gracious how will you attain the excellence?

Without the tender care of that sea of loving kindness, how will you reach the shore of such a wave?

Without the Burāq of love and the labor of Gabriel how will you like Muhammad attain all the stages?

10   You take shelter in those who are without shelter; how will you attain the shelter of the welcoming king?

Before *bismillāh* sacrifice yourself utterly; else, when you lie dead, how will you attain the Name of God?

373

Once more you have resolved to go, once more you have made your heart like iron.

No, do not extinguish the lamp of our friendship; you have poured oil into our lamp.

By Allah, you have filled this world with rose and eglantine and lily of your own face.

By Allah, let no enemy say you are a friend who did the enemy's work.

5   By Allah, keep your servants together, you who have brightened the world.

Once more you are laying on one side the love-plays you did with me.

By Allah, you have purified the skirt of the evil spirit by the scatter of your sleeves.

Mine of goldminters, Ṣalāḥ al-Dīn, like the moon you have made a harvest of silver.

374

O, you who have shaken a whole world, the voice of the reed, the voice of the reed, the voice of the reed.

What is the reed? To that beloved of the sweet kiss the place to kiss, the place to kiss, the place to kiss.

That reed without hand and foot fetches from men hand and foot, hand and foot, hand and foot.

The reed is a pretext; this is not the responsibility of the reed, this is nothing but the sound of the wing of that phoenix.

5   God Himself it is; what is all this veil? It is drawing the people of God to God.

We are beggars, *God is the All-Sufficient;* know, what you see of the beggar is due to the rich.

We are all darkness and *God the light:* from the sun came the rays of this abode.

Since the light in the house is mingled with shadow, if you desire the light, come out of the house to the roof.

Now you are happy, now depressed; if you do not want a depressed heart, depart out of this depression.

375

You are putting me on trial; O love, you know my weakness, yet you go on doing so.

You are becoming the interpreter of the enemy's secret; you implant mistaken thoughts in his heart.

You are setting fire to the thicket, and at the same time uttering complaints.

It may be thought that you have been cruelly wronged, you are making uproar and complaint like the weak.

5   You are the sun—who will oppress you? You do whatever you desire from on high.

You make us envious of one another; you make our quarreling into a fine spectacle.

To the gnostics you give wine as cash-in-hand; the ascetics you make drunk with tomorrow.

You give sorrow to the death-meditating bird; the bolbols you make drunk and singing.

You make the raven desirous of dung; your parrot you make sugar-cracking.

10   The one you draw into mine and mountain, the other you set face to the sea.

You lead us to happiness by way of suffering, or else you recompense our slip.

In this sea all is profit and justice; you dispense all beneficence and kindness.

This is the head of the subtlety; you speak its end, though you make us be without foot and head.

376

Welcome, melody—you are that melody which has brought a sign from the spiritual world.

Pass by the ear and strike upon our souls, for you are the life of this dead world.

Ravish the soul and go aloft into that world where you have carried the heart.

Your laughing moon bears evidence that you have quaffed that heavenly wine.

5   Your sweet soul gives a sign that you were nourished in honey from *Alast*.

Blades have begun to sprout from the earth to show the sowings that you have made.

377

You are both candle and fair one and wine, likewise spring in the midst of December.

Every side through love of you is one with feathers ablaze, the sun, and myriads like him.

Since your fire always falls upon the reed, sugar has gone through this passion into the soul of the reed.

You have beheaded myriads with love so that the soul has not the strength to say, "Ah, alas!"

5   The lovers have built from the evil of the eye underground houses like the city of Rayy.

There is no worse torture than knowledge; alas for him who remains in good and evil.

Those women of Egypt in their unselfedness suffered wounds and did not utter "Woe!"

The king in unselfedness on the night of Ascension traversed a road of a hundred thousand years.

With the wind of selflessness break the prison of bone and sinew and tendon.

10   Shams-i Tabrīzī, annihilate us, for you are as the sun and we are as the shadow.

378

Do you know where you have come? From the midst of all-glorious sanctuary.

Do you not remember at all those happy spiritual stages?

Those things have become forgotten by you, so necessarily you are bewildered and distraught.

You sell my soul for a handful of dust; what kind of bargain and sale is this?

5   Give back the dust, and know your own worth; you are not a slave, you are a king, an emperor.

For your sake there came out of heaven the fair-faced ones, the sweetly hidden.

379

You who are imam of love, say *Allāh Akbar*, for you are drunk; shake your two hands, become indifferent to existence.

You were fixed to a time, you made haste; the time of prayer has come. Leap up—why are you seated?

In hope of the *qibla* of God you carve a hundred *qibla*; in hope of that idol's love you worship a hundred idols.

Fly upwards, O soul, O obedient soul; the moon is above, the shadow is low.

5   Do not like a beggar knock your hand at any door; knock at the ring of the door of heaven, for you have a long arm.

Since the flagon of heaven has made you like that, be a stranger to the world, for you have escaped out of self.

I say to you, "How are you?" No one ever says to the "how-less" soul, "How are you?"

Tonight you are drunk and dissolute, come tomorrow and you will see what bags you have torn, what glasses you have broken.

Every glass I have broken was my trust in you, for myriad-wise you have bound up the broken.

10   O secret artist, in the depths of your soul you have a thousand forms, apart from the moon and the Lady of the Moon [Mahastī].

If you have stolen the ring, you have opened a thousand throats; if you have wounded a breast, you have given a hundred souls and hearts.

I have gone mad; whatever I say in madness, quickly say, "Yes, yes," if you are privy to Alast.

380

In the battle ranks we have no shield before our face; in the concert we are unaware of reed pipe and tambourine.

We are naught in his love, dust at the foot of his love; we are love fold upon fold, we are all love, nothing else.

When we have obliterated ourselves we become altogether love; when surmeh is pounded, it is nothing but the source of sight.

Every body that has become an accident has become the soul and heart of self-interest. Melt for of all sicknesses, there is nothing worse than being congealed.

5   Out of desire of that melting and love for that cherishing the liver within me has turned all to blood; I have no liver any more.

My heart is broken into a hundred pieces, my heart has become astray; today if you search, there is no trace of heart in me.

Look at the orb of the moon, waning every day, so that in the dark period you might say there is no moon in the sky.

The increasing leanness of that moon derives from nearness to the sun; when afar, it is full-bodied, but such initiative does not belong to it.

O king, for the sake of the souls send Venus as a minstrel; this soft pipe and tambourine are no match for the concert of the souls.

10   No, no—for what is Venus when the Sun itself is powerless? To be suitable for such ardor is not in the power of any lute or sun.

381

Yesterday you made compact and repentance, today you have broken them; yesterday you were a bitter sea, today you are a pearl.

Yesterday you were Bā Yazīd and were augmenting; today you are in ruins, a dregs-seller and drunk.

Drink the dregs, O soul! Break from reason, O soul! Do not wear blue, O soul, until you worship idols.

Today you are very dissolute, you share the cup with the sun; You are not the master of the moon, nor the husband of the lady.

5   You are greater than dwellings, you are outside mines; you are not that, but you are just as you are.

One corner you were bound up, of that corner you were sick; you opened that which was bound and escaped wholly, escaped.

A beast is not a rider, it is only for the sake of labor; you are no beast, you are a living man and you have leaped from labor, leaped.

You are a heavenly messenger; how can you be like the moon until you ride aloft and are in the hand of the thumbstall?

Silence, give no sign, though you expressed everything; every wounded one you have wounded has become the salve of a world.

382

Minstrel, when you draw your plectrums over the strings, you draw into labor these idlers of the way.

Love, when you enter, you draw these tarriers in the world of separation to the Beloved.

Despite the highwaymen you make the world secure, you drag to the gallows the thieves of the heart city.

You see the cunning schemer, and cunningly blind him; when you see the friend, you draw him into the cave.

5   You bind a golden saddle on the nimble-footed horses; the evil pack-horses you draw to the baggage.

You cherish our melancholic ones every moment; our market-minded ones you drag very miserably.

To the thorn-enduring lovers you show the rose bower; you draw into the thorns the self-willed whose joy is but for a moment.

To him who enters the fire you give access to the water; he who runs to water, you drag him into the flames.

To Moses, dusty of face, you give the way to glory; Pharaoh, the seeker of pomp, you draw into disgrace.

10   This reversed horseshoe acts without how and why; Moses the stick-seeker, you draw into a serpent.

383

Yesterday I clutched his skirt saying, "O essence [jewel] of generosity, do not say goodnight, do not grieve us, for tonight you are mine."

The darling face lit up and glowed red like a spark. He said, "That is enough; draw back. How long with this beggar's ways?"

I said, "God's Messenger said: 'Seek your need of the handsome, if you desire to attain it.'"

He said, "The fair of face is self-willed and bad-tempered, for beauty permits plenty of airs and wickedness."

5   I said, "If that is so, his wickedness is the life of the soul, because whenever you try it, it is the talisman of the mine."

He said, "This is a raw talk; who is the handsome? This color and form is a snare, it is cunning and inconstancy.

"When a man possesses not the soul of the soul, know that he possesses not that; many a man delivers his soul with the form of mortality."

I said, "Pretty of cheek, bring nonexistence into existence; change our copper to gold, you who are the soul of alchemy.

"Copper must yield itself to discover the alchemy: you are a grain of corn, but you are outside the mill."

10   He said, "You are ungrateful, you are ignorant of copper; you are in doubt and conjecture from the things you show."

I began weeping wretchedly. I said, "You have the rule, come to the succor of your lover, O source of light."

When he saw his servant's tears he began to laugh; East and West came to life through that grace and familiarity.

Fellow travelers and friends, weep like a cloud, so that fair ones may bring their sweet presence into the garden.

384

Once again a melody has come from the reed pipe of fortune; O soul, clap hands, O heart, stamp feet.

A mine has become aglow, a world is laughing, a table is adorned, invitation is coming.

We are drunk and roaring in hope of the spring over the meadow, adoring one of handsome cheek.

He is the sun, we are a cloud; he the treasure, we a ruin; in the light of a sea we are as motes.

5   I am distracted, I am excused; suffer me to brag—with the light of Muṣṭafā I will split the moon.

385

You who are weary of us, we are very desirous; you who have withdrawn from the road, where is the courtesy of fellow-traveling?

You are the marrow of the world, the rest is all hay; how shall a man get fat on eating hay?

Every city which is ruined and turned upside down, that has happened because it remained far from the royal shadow.

When the sun has gone, what remains? Black night. When reason has gone from the head, what remains but idiocy?

5   Reason, the riot that has befallen, all springs from your departure: and then you attribute the fault to a body without reason.

Wherever you turn your back, there is error and war; whenever you show your face, there is drunkenness and stupefaction.

The eighteen thousand worlds are of two divisions only—half dead, inanimate matter, and half conscious.

The sea of consciousness from which all minds derive, that is the goal of all finite minds.

Swimming soul, who go in this sea, and you who leap from this wheel like an arrow—

10   By the tent of your body a world is illuminated; so how can you be, you spirit of the tent!

Spirit, eternity is intoxicated by your wine; in your hand, earth is transmuted to pure gold;

Your description evades the understanding of the vulgar, incomparable one, and transcends the likeness of the imagination of one who likens you.

If any lover through yearning assigns a form to you, the sea of transcendence would not be made impure.

If the babbling poets compare the crescent moon to a horse-shoe, the moon does not lose its moonliness.

15 How could the sea remain a barrier in the path before Moses? And could the blind remain blind in the protection of Jesus?

He is the master of all, even if he has not one slave; that cypress of his is erect, even though you count it as not erect.

You are Moses, though still the shepherd; you are Joseph, though still in the well.

You do not receive the wages for labor because you are not always engaged in this labor, but only casually.

Silence, for without God's food and wine from the unseen these words and images are but two or three empty bowls.

386

Bird-catcher, you have set a hidden snare; over the snare you have laid smoke-colored fabric.

Too many thousands of birds you have slain by this trick and laid all the feathers plucked as a sign.

The birds that are your watchmen make a great cry; what meanings you have planted in their cries!

For the thirsty birds you have placed in the taverns of your proximity vats of Magian wines.

5 That vat, the scent of which neither saki nor drunkard catches, you have laid down for the sake of the nightfarer that you know.

In patience and penitence you have compounded the immunity of the shield; in cruelty and wrath you have set a lance.

Without the danger of lance and shield, you have implanted for the pious believers a kingdom in the seven oft-repeated verses.

Under the black of the eye you have made the wave of light flow, and in that aged world you have set youthfulness.

In the breast which fashions forms out of imagination, you have placed a finger without pen and finger.

10   Though so many veils of flesh and sinew lie over the heart, you have given the heart penetration and visible passage.

Which is stranger—the glance that flies like an arrow, or the brow you have set as a bow?

Or that in vessel-like bodies you implanted various characters like wines bitter and sweet,

Or that this secret liquor distilled from the tongue you have placed on the tongue as the cream of speech?

Every essence and accident is as a mouth-shut bud which you have set as a veil over the cradle of virgins.

15   On the day when you cause them to blossom and remove those veils, O soul of the soul of the soul, what soul you will have implanted!

Restless hearts will see for what reason in separation you have placed entreaty and yearning.

Silence, that that soul may speak the spoken things; why have you implanted this long conjury?

387

You swore an oath that henceforth you would be cruel; now you break your oath and finish with cruelty.

Today we have seized your skirt and are drawing; how long will you offer pretexts and cheat?

Idol, that lip of yours is smiling and giving good tidings that you have resolved henceforward to be true.

Since without you entreaty is not proper for us, what profits it? It is only proper when you vouchsafe the need.

5   Without your sea we flounder like fish on the land—so fish do when you part them from water.

The tyrant is cruel and the prisoner terrifies him with you; God does with you what you do in our case!

When you are cruel, with whom shall anyone terrify you?
Only he who submits to whatever you demand.

Silence, do not sell the unique pearl; how do you fix a price
for that which is without value?

388

Reed, very sweet it is that you know the secrets; that one
does the work who has knowledge of the work.

Reed, like the bulbul you are lamenting for the rose;
do not scratch your neck, for you know the thornless
rose.

I said to the reed, "You share the beloved's breath; do not
steal the secret [from me]." The reed said, "Knowledge is for
your total destruction."

I said, "My salvation is in my destruction; set fire, burn, do
not leave knowledge."

5   He said, "How shall I be a brigand on this caravan? I know
that knowledge is the leader."

I said, "Since the Beloved cherished not those gone astray,
knowledge has become disgusted with itself."

You who are unaware of self, you have nine eyes; awareness is
for us the veil of eyes and sight.

You are a companion of the lip because you have been
beheaded; in this way head is a shame, and knowledge a
disgrace.

You have become empty of self and full of secrets because
you are aware of self-worshiping and unbelief.

10   What lament, when you drink of the ruby lips of the
Beloved? Let knowledge utter this bitter lament.

No, no, you do not lament of yourself, noble one; weep for
him who is aware of others.

If heaven laments, the ox is under the load; you are aware of
this reversed deceptive horseshoe.

389

You who slay like sugar the lovers, slay my soul sweetly this moment, if you are slaying.

To slay sweetly and gently is the property of your hand, because you slay with a glance he who seeks a glance.

Every morning continuously I am waiting, waiting, because you generally slay me at dawn.

Your cruelty to us is candy; do not close the way to assistance. Is it not the case that at the end you will slay me in front of the gate?

5   You whose breath is without a belly, you whose sorrow repels sorrow, you who slay us in a breath like a spark,

Every moment you proffer another repulse like a shield; you have abandoned the sword and are slaying with the shield.

390

Lion-heart, you have made a hundred thousand lion-hearts; you have outstripped the sun even in generosity.

Close your eyes, and have compassion once more; break your oath, if you have sworn by God.

See that these enemies are clapping their hands, since in this rage and warlike mood you have stamped your foot.

With whom is your inclination, O soul?—so that I may become his dust, so that I may become the servant of him whom you have reckoned somebody.

5   Body, at last stir yourself and make an effort. Effort is blessed; why are you languid?

Rise, approach the friend; set your face to the earth, saying, "Idol sweet as sugar, by what are you vexed?"

Master of the soul, Shams-i Dīn of Tabrizi, this head of mine is of your palm tree for it was nourished by you.

391

O soul, the breeze of spring is coming, so that you may raise
your hand towards the rose garden.

Grass and lily, tulip and hyacinth said, "There grows what-
ever you sow."

Buds and rose blossoms came as a helmet so that the ugliness
of the thorn may not appear.

Elevation has come to the tall cypress, it has found glory
after humiliation.

5 Spirit enters all the garden, for water displays spirit-
bestowing;

The beauty of the garden increases from water—it has come
as most blessed friendship.

Leaf has sent a message to fruit, "You come quickly, do not
scratch your ear."

That sweet grape is king of the fruits, because its tree was
emaciated.

In the winter of lust how long shall the garden of our heart
remain imprisoned and walled in?

10 Seek the way from the heart, seek the moon from the soul;
what does the earth possess but dust?

Rise, wash your face, but with a water which beautifies the
cheek of the rose.

The branch of blossoms said to the basil, "Lay down what-
ever you possess in our path."

The nightingale said to the garden, "We are the quarry of
your snare."

The rose entreats God for mercy, "Do not put winter in
command over us."

15 God says, "How does juice come out of fruit until you
squeeze it?

"Do not grieve over December and the raiding Ghuzz, and
regard this business as lying at my door.

"Thanks and praise, joy and increase do not appear except you lament.

"I will give you life unnumbered if I take away numbered life;

"I will give you wine without hangover if I take away wine that yields hangover."

20   How many pictures hath knowledge, why do you go on painting its pages?

Through you the face of the pages has been blackened; how can you read the writing of day?

Have done with smoke; look at the light from the moon of the Beloved in the dark night.

Enough, enough, come down from your horse, so that he may ride forth, the horseman supreme.

392

The Burāq of the love of realities carried away my mind and heart; ask me where it took them? Thither you do not know.

I reached that arch where I saw neither moon nor sky, that world where even world is parted from world.

Give me respite for a moment for my mind to return to me; I will describe the soul to you—give ear, for you are the soul.

But approach nearer, my master, lay your ear on my mouth; for walls have ears, and this is a secret mystery.

5   It is a loving care from the Beloved, this so strange a grace; the lamps of vision enter by way of the ear.

Accompany the khidr of reason to the fountain of life, so that like the fountain of the sun by day you scatter light.

As Zulaikhā became young through the intention of Joseph, so the ancient world recovers its youth from this star.

The Canopus of the soul swallows moon, sun and pole of the seven skies when he rises from the Yemeni pillar.

Take for a moment a clipping of faith and place it under your tongue that you may see how inwardly you are a mine of gold!

10   You have fallen into the mouths and men are chewing you; since you are a fine and well-baked bread, you are always the same.

You dance like a mote when light takes your hand; it is out of coldness and wetness that you are heavy as sand.

When the sun rises it says to the dark earth, "Since I became your companion, you are a master of double conjunction."

You are not a goat to come and play the rearing horse; you are a shepherd like a raging lion before the herd of lions.

Light up the five lamps of your senses with the light of the heart; the senses are as the five prayers, the heart like the seven oft-repeated verses.

15   Every dawn a cry comes out of the heavens, "When you settle the dust of the road, you lead the way to a sign."

So draw not back the reins of resolution like a hermaphrodite; ahead of you are two armies toward which you advance like a lance.

Sugar has come to you, saying, "Open your mouth"; why have you closed your mouth like a pistachio to the sugar's invitation?

Take the bowl of sugar; eat by the bowlful—may you enjoy it! Do not beat the drum of legend—why do you give in to the tongue?

Through Shams, Pride of Tabriz, you worship the sun, for he is the sun of spiritual sciences, the governor of the sun of place.

393

You are my heaven, I am the earth in astonishment; every moment what things have you set growing in my heart.

I am the dry-lipped earth; rain that water of grace. Of your water earth discovers rose and rose garden.

What does the earth know, what have you sown in its heart?
It is pregnant by you, and you know what it is bearing.

Every atom is pregnant by you with another mystery; for a
while you writhe with the pregnant women in agony.

5 What things are in the womb of this enfolded earth from
which are born "I am the truth" and the cry "Glory to me!"

Now it groans, and a camel is born of its womb; a staff falls
and takes the way of serpenthood.

The prophet said, "Know the believer is like a camel, always
drunk with God who looks after his camel.

"Now he brands him, and now sets provender before him;
now he binds his knees with the shackle of reason,

"And now he loosens his knees to dance like a camel, to rend
asunder the bridle and go in disarray."

10 See how the meadow can not contain itself for joy, since the
spiritual garden has given it so many forms.

See the power of the Universal Soul to impart understanding,
so that through it the dullard earth has become a spiritual shaper.

Like the Universal Soul, the whole plenum is a veil or curtain
of the Sun of Majesty who has no second,

The eternal Sun which never sets, the light of whose face is
neither of the Aquarius nor of Libra.

One by one all that He sowed is appearing. Silence, for the
oyster shells are pregnant with the divine pearls.

394

The lord of beauty and quintessence of loveliness entered the
soul and mind as a man will stroll in the garden at spring.

Come, come, for you are the life and salvation of men; come,
come, for you are the eye and lamp of Jacob.

Lay foot on my water and clay, for through your foot dark-
ness and veiledness depart from water and clay.

Through your glow stones turn to rubies, through your
searching the searcher reaches his goal.

5   Come, come, for you bestow beauty and glory; come, come, for you are the cure of a thousand Jobs.

Come, come, though you have never departed, but I speak every word to you for a desired end.

Sit in the place of my soul, for you are a thousand times my soul; slay your paramour and lover, for you are the Beloved.

If the king is not the king of the world, O melancholy world, by His life I bid you say, "Why are you in confusion?"

Now you are gay and fresh with His green banner, and now you are overturned by the heart of His army of battle.

10   Now, like the thought of an artist, you fashion forms; now you sweep carpets like the broom of the porter.

When you sweep a form, you give its quintessence angel-hood, and the wings and pinions of the cherubim.

Silence, guard the water strictly like a waterbag, for if you sprinkle it through a crack, know that you are at fault.

Your heart has reached Shams, the Pride of Tabriz, because the Duldul of the heart proved itself a nimble mount.

395

Finally you have broken away and departed into the Unseen; I wonder, I wonder—by which way did you depart from the world?

You beat your feathers and wings mightily and broke your cage; you took the air and departed towards the spiritual world.

You were a special falcon in captivity to an old woman; when you heard the falcon-drum, you departed to the placeless.

You were a drunken nightingale amongst owls; the scent of the rose garden arrived, you departed to the rose garden.

5   You suffered much crop sickness from this sour ferment; finally you departed to the eternal tavern.

You went straight as an arrow to the target of bliss; you flew to that target and departed from this bow.

This world like a ghoul gave you false clues; you took no heed of the clue and departed to the clueless.

Since you have become the sun, what have you to do with a crown? Since you have departed from the middle, why do you seek a belt?

I have heard tell of gazing on the soul when the eyes are extinguished; why do you gaze on the soul, since you have departed to the soul of soul?

10   O heart, what a rare bird you are, that in hunting for the All-Grateful you departed towards the lance with two wings like a shield.

The rose flees from autumn; ah, what a bold rose you are, that you went creeping along before the autumn wind.

Like rain from heaven on the roof of the earthly world you ran in every direction and departed by the spout.

Be silent, suffer not the anguish of speech; sleep on, for you have departed into the shelter of such a loving friend.

396

Come, come, for you will not find another friend like me; where indeed in both worlds is a beloved like me?

Come, come, and do not pass your days in every direction, for there is no other market elsewhere for your money.

You are like a dry water conduit and I am like the rain; you are like a ruined city and I am like the architect.

Except in serving me, which is the sunrise of joy, men have never seen and never will see any mark of happiness.

5   In sleep you see a thousand moving forms; when sleep has gone, you see not a single creature.

Close the eye of wrong and open the eye of intelligence, for the carnal soul has fallen like an ass, and concupiscence is the halter.

Seek sweet syrup from the garden of love, for human nature is a vinegar-seller and a crusher of unripe grapes.

Come to the hospital of your Creator, for no sick man can do without that physician.

The world without that king is like the body without its head; wind round such a head as a turban.

10   If you are not black, let not the mirror go from your hand; for the soul is your mirror and the body is rust.

Where is the lucky merchant with Jupiter in ascension, that I may do that business with him and purchase his goods?

Come, think of me who gave you thought; if you are buying rubies, at least buy from my mine.

Go on foot towards him who gave you a foot, gaze on him with both eyes who gave you sight.

Clap hands for joy for him from whose sea is the foam, for there is no grief or sorrow happening to him.

15   Listen without ears; speak unto him without a tongue, for the speech of the tongue is not without contradiction and injury.

397

If you have no beloved, why do you not seek one? And if you have attained the Beloved, why do you not rejoice?

If the companion is not compliant, why do you not become him? If the rebec wails not, why do you not teach it manners?

If an Abū Jahl is a veil to you, why do you not attack Abū Jahl and Abū Lahab?

You sit idly saying, "This is a strange business"; you are the strange one not to desire such a strange one.

5   You are the sun of the world; why are you black at heart? See that you do not any more have a desire for the knot [of Draco].

Like gold you are prisoner in the furnace so that you may not be covetous of the purse of gold.

Since Unity is the bachelor's chamber of those who say "One," why do you not make your spirit a bachelor to all but God?

Have you ever seen Majnūn have affection with two Lailīs? Why not desire only one face and one chin?

There is such a moon in hiding in the night of your being; why do you not pray and petition at midnight?

10   Though you are an ancient drunkard and not new to the wine, God's wine does not suffer you not to make turmoil.

My wine is the fire of love, especially from the hand of God; may life be unlawful to you, since you do not make your life firewood.

Though the wave of discourse is surging, yet it is better that you should expound it with heart and soul, not with lips.

398

Heart, you are the phoenix of union. Fly, why do you not fly? No one recognizes you, neither man nor peri.

You are the sweetheart, not the heart; but with every device and trickery you have taken the shape of the heart so that you will ravish a thousand hearts.

For a moment faithfully you mingle with earth, and for a moment you pass beyond empyrean and firmament and the bounds of the two worlds.

Why does not spirit find you, for you are its wings and feathers? Why does not sight see you who are the source of sight?

5   What power has penitence to repent of you? What is consciousness that it should remain conscious along with you?

What shall be that poor copper when the alchemy comes? Will it not pass away from copperhood into the attribute of gold?

Who is that poor seed when the springtime comes? Does not its seedhood pass away into treehood?

Who is poor brushwood when it falls into the fire? Is not the brushwood transformed into a spark by the flame?

All reason and science are stars; are you the sun of the world who tear asunder their veils?

10   The world is like snow and ice, and you are the season of summer; when you, king, are on its track, no trace of it remains.

Say, who am I to remain along with you? I and a hundred like me will pass away when you gaze towards me.

The perfection of the description of the lord Shams-i Tabrīzī surpasses the imaginations of predestinator and free-willer.

399

We have come once again to a lord to whose knee no sea reaches.

Tie together a thousand minds, they will not reach Him; how shall a hand or foot reach the moon in heaven?

The sky stretched out its throat eagerly to Him; it found no kiss, but it swallowed a sweetmeat.

A thousand throats and gullets stretched towards His lip. "Scatter too on our heads manna and quails."

5   We have come again to a Beloved, from whose air a shout has reached our ears.

We have come again to that sanctuary to bow the brow which is to surpass the skies.

We have come again to that meadow to whose bolbol 'anqā is a slave.

We have come to Him who was never apart from us; for the waterbag is never filled without the existence of a water-carrier.

The bag always clings to the body of the water-carrier, saying, "Without you, I have no hand or knowledge or opinion."

10   We have come again to that feast with the sweet dessert of which the sugarcane chewer attained his desire.

We have come again to that sphere, in whose bent the soul roars like thunder.

We have come again to that love at whose contact the *dīv* has become peri-like.

Silence! Seal the rest under your tongue, for a jealous tutor has been put in charge of you.

Speak not of the talk of the Pride of Tabriz, Shams-i Dīn, for the rational mind is not suitable for that speech.

400

Leap, leap from the world, that you may be king of the world; seize the sugar tray that you may be a sugar plantation.

Leap, leap like a meteor to slay the *dīv*; when you leap out of stardom, you will be the pole of heaven.

When Noah sets out for the sea, you will be his ship; when the Messiah goes to heaven, you will be the ladder.

Now like Jesus of Mary you become the soul's physician; and now like Moses of 'Emran you will go forth to be a shepherd.

5 There is a spiritual fire for the sake of cooking you; if you leap back like a woman, you will be a raw cuckold.

If you do not flee from the fire, and become wholly cooked like well-baked bread, you will be a master and lord of the table.

When you come to the table and the brethren receive you, like bread you will be sustenance of the soul and you will be the soul.

Though you are the mine of pain, by patience you will become the treasure; though you are a flawed house, you will be a knower of the unseen.

I said this, and a call came from heaven to my spirit's ear saying, "If you become like this, you will be like that."

10 Silence! the mouth is intended for cracking sugar, not for you to cast slack and become a chin-wagger.

Notes

Notes in {} brackets have been added by Franklin D. Lewis
after consulting the original Persian.

ABBREVIATIONS

Ahādīs̱ = Badīʿ al-Zamān Furūzānfar, *Ahādīs̱-i Mas̱navī* (Tehran, 1955)

CB = Chester Beatty manuscript Persian 116

Dozy = R. Dozy, *Supplément aux dictionnaires arabes* (Leiden, Paris, 1927)

E.I. = *Encyclopaedia of Islam* (London, 1908–34; new edition [2]
London, 1960–)

F = edition of Badīʿ al-Zamān Furūzānfar, *Kullīyāt-i Shams,* 8 vols.
(Tehran, University of Tehran, 1336–45/1957–66)

Gauharīn = Ṣādiq Gauharīn, *Farhang-i Lughāt va taʿbīrāt-i
Mas̱navī.* 5 vols. (Tehran, 1959–60)

Gölpınarlı = *Dīvān-i Kabīr,* Turkish translation by Abdulbaki
Gölpınarlı, 5 vols. (Istanbul, 1957–60)

Lane = E. W. Lane, *An Arabic-English Lexicon* (London, 1863–85)

Math = *Mathnawī* of Rūmī, *The Mathnawi of Jalālu'ddīn Rūmī,*
8 vols. (London, Luzac & Co., 1925–40)

N = selection by R. A. Nicholson, *Selected Poems from the Dīvāni*
  Shamsi Tabrīz (Cambridge, at the University Press, 1898)
Yāqūt = *Mu ʿjam al-buldān* (Cairo, 1906)

[POEM 1   ≺   F 3]

3. "Dark thoughts": doubts of God's benevolence, as in Koran 33:10.
"Such drawing, such tasting": cf. *Math.* I:887, "This attraction (by which
God draws the soul towards Himself) comes from the same quarter whence
came that savour (spiritual delight experienced in and after prayer)."

5. CB reads *az balā* for *mar turā*, which it notes as a variant.

6. It is God who puts fear into the hearts of sinners to induce them
to repent; see Koran 17:61.

8. "The light of the form of Muṣṭafā": the *nūr-i Muḥammadī*,
equivalent to Universal Reason, which has inspired all the prophets and
saints, see Nicholson on *Math.* II:909 and Massignon in *E.I.* III:961.

11. The story of Shuʿaib, prophet to the Midianites, is told in Koran
7:83–91, 11:85–98.

15. This verse is cited by Aflākī, *Manāqib al-ʿārifīn* 397. The source of
the story of Shuʿaib weeping was evidently ʿAṭṭār, *Ilāhī-nāma* 6140–56.

21. Bā Yazīd (Abū Yazīd-i Bisṭāmī), the famous mystic of Khorasan
(d. 261/874 or 264/877), is the hero of many spiritual anecdotes; see
Ritter in *E.I.*² I:162–63. The point of this anecdote is the pun between
kharbanda (ass-driver) and *banda-yi Khudā* (slave of God).

[POEM 2   ≺   F 14]

4. For Moses striking the Red Sea with his staff, see Koran 20:19.

5. CB reads *bāda* (wine) for *bād* (wind).

8. CB reads *ravam* (I go) for *ravī* (you go). The CB reading
hastīm (being) is perhaps superior to *mastīm* (drunkenness).

9. For Moses on Mount Sinai, see Koran 9:138–39.

11. CB reads *bāda* for *bād*, yielding the perhaps superior meaning,
"what wine have you drunk?"

[POEM 3   ≺   F 19]

1. "Like the spirit of Muṣṭafā": a reference to the famous *miʿrāj*
(Ascension) of Muhammad. The orthodox view was that his ascension

was bodily, but Rumi is attracted by the double meaning of *ravān*
("departing" and "spirit").

2. "Confused": lit. "Latticed."

3. The posture of prostration in prayer symbolizes the subjection of
reason to spirit.

[POEM 4 ⁘ F 26]

3. Man is composed of water and clay. Rumi puns on *durd* (dregs)
and *dard* (pains).

9. Rumi puns on *charā* (graze) and *chirā* (why).

[POEM 5 ⁘ F 34]

8. Many of Rumi's poems end with a command to silence, to conceal
the *mysterium tremendum* of the ineffable experience of the Divine. God
is called *al-Sattār* because of His clemency; He veils the faults of men.

[POEM 6 ⁘ F 45]

2. Khiḍar (Khaḍir, Khiḍr) was the mysterious guide who led
Alexander (Dhu'l-Qarnain) to the Fountain of Immortality, and is
the associate of mystics; see Wensinck in *E.I.* II:861–65.

3. Rumi puns on *chashma* (fountain) and *chashm* (eye); intoxication
is the term poets use to describe the languorous eye of the beautiful
beloved.

5. Selfhood must be abandoned if the mystic would attain to union
with the Beloved.

6. Duality is the fatal impediment to unity.

8. For Moses and the Burning Bush, see Koran 20:12.

16. Rumi refers to the Table sent down by God in response to
Jesus, see Koran 5:114–15. Onions and chives were preferred to the
heavenly ambrosia by the unbelieving Jews.

17. There is a play on *shūr* (riot) and *shūrbā* (broth).

18. A pun on *zabāna* (flame) and *zabān* (tongue).

[POEM 7 ⁘ F 58]

1. "The fair one of Canaan": Joseph (here as often symbol for the
Divine Beauty), in wonderment at whose loveliness the women of
Egypt cut their hands; see Koran 12:31.

3. A play on *kūhī* (a mountain) and *kāhī* (a straw).

6. The hoopoe was the Queen of Sheba's messenger to Solomon, see Koran 27:21–30.

7. Solomon was given knowledge of the speech of the birds, see Koran 27:16. Rumi doubtless knew 'Aṭṭār's mystical epic the *Manṭiq al-ṭair*.

8. Solomon had dominion over the winds, see *E.I.* IV:520.

[POEM 8 ⋅⋅ F 64]

2. Vāmiq and 'Adhrā were lovers famed in Persian legend; their romance was the subject of a lost epic by 'Unṣurī. The poet puns (pardon) on the name of 'Adhrā.

6. When Abraham was cast by Nimrod's orders into the flames, the fire was miraculously changed into roses; see Koran 21:69 and Nicholson on *Math.* 1:547.

9. Kauthar is a river in paradise, Riḍwān the angel-gardener who holds the key to the heavenly gate.

11. The legendary 'Anqā nests in the mountain of Qāf on the edge of the world.

12. "Neither of the east nor of the west": see Koran 24:35.

[POEM 9 ⋅⋅ F 69]

6. "Who brings the dead to life": see Koran 7:55.

[POEM 10 ⋅⋅ F 80]

9. For Goha the fool and jester, see Nicholson on *Math.* II:3116. For Bū Bakr the Lutanist, see Nicholson on *Math.* II:1573.

[POEM 11 ⋅⋅ F 84]

[POEM 12 ⋅⋅ F 100]

3. "The bowl has fallen again from the roof": "a metaphor conveying the idea of divulgation, exposure, and notoriety" (Nicholson on *Math.* II:2061).

5. In sleep the soul is liberated from the body; see Nicholson on *Math.* 1:400.

7. The miracle of Moses' staff, see Koran 7:110–14, 20:68–69.

[POEM 13 ∿ F 110]

2. A play on the two meanings of *chang* (clutches, harp).

[POEM 14 ∿ F 115]

1. A play on the two meanings of *ravān*.

3. Conventional images of human (material) beauty.

6. A play on the two meanings of *miyān* (midst, waist).

11. "The sugar-sprinkler": the divine source of all sweetness and joy.

13. I.e. do not expose our romance to idle gossip.

[POEM 15 ∿ F 122]

9. God is the All-rich, needing nothing in His perfection: Koran 2: 265, etc.

10. The reference is to Koran 19:25.

[POEM 16 ∿ F 132]

1. The sufferings of love lead to incomparable joy.

2. Love knows to transcend the physical universe of Reason.

4. The reference is to Ḥallāj, the martyr-mystic, executed in 309/922.

6. "The courtyard": perhaps "annihilation (*fanā*)." {Arberry's translation reads: Love says, "these thorns belong to the reason which is within you." It is also possible to construe this as: Love says to Reason, "these thorns are within you."—Ed.}

[POEM 17 ∿ F 143, N 3]

5. This verse is cited by Aflākī, *Manāqib* 743, with the readings *jān* (soul) for *dil* (heart), and *girya-sh* ("its weeping," so Nicholson also) for *gardish* ("turning about," perhaps rather, "its dust," i.e. distress).

7. The eye of the Beloved is intoxicating as well as intoxicated. Nicholson reads and translates differently.

[POEM 18 ∿ F 163]

1. This poem was probably composed after Shams al-Dīn's first disappearance from Konya.

7. The rubies of Yemen were proverbial for excellence.

[POEM 19 ∿ F 166, N 5]

8. Muslim brides have henna painted on their hands in patterns.

11. The four elements are earth, air, fire and water.

[POEM 20 ∿ F 171]

1. Even inanimate nature is moved to ecstasy, like the whirling dervishes, by the epiphany of Divine Beauty.

6. Mirrors were made of steel, and became rusty with age.

8. Venus is the harpist leading the heavenly choir, cf. 19 line 6. After this line CB adds a ninth: "O image of his beauty, drive slowly, wait for the lame travellers."

[POEM 21 ∿ F 181]

Aflākī, *Manāqib* 370–71, relates as follows the circumstances under which this poem was composed. "One day Shaikh Ṣadr al-Dīn (Qōnawī) and Qāḍī Sirāj al-Dīn with other ulema and gnostics had gone out to visit the congregational mosque of Marām, and the Maulānā (Rumi) also graced the gathering. After a while he rose up and coming to a mill, remained there a long time, so that the company waited for him beyond measure. Then the Shaikh and Qāḍī Sirāj al-Dīn came to look for him at the mill. They saw that the Maulānā was circling about the mill; said he, 'By the right of His right, this mill-stone is saying, "Glorious and Holy is He!"' The Shaikh related: 'I and Qāḍī Sirāj al-Dīn that very moment heard proceeding from that mill-stone the sound, 'Glorious and Holy is He!' Then he commenced this poem."

[POEM 22 ∿ F 188]

2. Cf. *Math.* II:2324: "Intellect shows itself in many guises, but like the peri is leagues removed from them." See Nicholson's note *ad loc.*; the peri (= jinn) can assume at will various alien forms. For the comparison of the heart to a pond fed by streams, see Nicholson on *Math.* I:2710–14.

4. "Superintendence": reading with CB, *ishrāf* for *ishrāq*.

5. For the five inward senses, see Nicholson on *Math.* I:3576.

7. "Burnishing": i.e. making the mirror the mind clear.

8. Too much conceit of freedom of action leads to disaster.

[POEM 23   ⌖   F 196]

4. A play on *khazān* (autumn) and *khīzān* (rising).

8. A play on the two meanings of *ravān*.

10. "The treasury": the roses blooming to entrance the nightingales.

[POEM 24   ⌖   F 207, N 6]

Nicholson's text of this poem differs in numerous places.

5. "The seven oft-repeated verses": Sura I of the Koran, to be re-
cited in every prayer.

12. As God said to Moses on Sinai, see Koran 7:139.

13. Rumi has realized the Muslim Unity of God, the Christian
Trinity, and the Magian Duality.

[POEM 25   ⌖   F 211]

11. "Puckered": reading with CB *turunjīda,* punning on *turunj.*

14. This verse is in Arabic in the original.

[POEM 26   ⌖   F 213, N 1]

Nicholson's text exhibits numerous variants.

3. "That madman": Majnūn (Qais), the poet-lover of Lailā in the
famous Bedouin romance. There is a wordplay between *shaid* (wile)
and *shaidā* (wild).

5. "The spider": probably the one which spun a web hiding the
entrance to the cave in which Muhammad took refuge in his flight
from Mecca. "My Lord the Most High": cf. Koran 79:24.

6. "He carried His servant by night": Koran 17:1, the allusion to
Muhammad's *mi'rāj.*

7. Vīsa (or Vīs) and Rāmīn, Vāmiq and 'Adhrā were lovers famed
in Persian legend and epopee.

[POEM 27   ⌖   F 221]

6. Cf. Koran 73:17.

[POEM 28   ⌖   F 232]

The circumstances of the composition of this poem (and oth-
ers) are related at length by Aflākī, *Manāqib* 179–82. (F's text differs

considerably from the Ankara edition.) The date 656/1258 is given.

7. Ghūṭa was the region surrounding Damascus, abounding in trees and rivers: Yāqūt VI:314. Nairab was a village near Damascus set about with gardens: Yāqūt VIII:355.

14. Rumi uses medical images.

16. The Cadi of Kāb (on whose authority Aflākī related the anecdote) had come to pay homage to Rumi.

19. This and the verse following are in Arabic.

[POEM 29 ~ F 239, N 2]

6. See note on 7, line 6.

10. Nicholson reads *Kaivān* (Saturn) for *aivān* (portico), and then inserts two extra couplets.

12. Ṣalāḥ al-Dīn Zarkūb, who died *c.* 659/1261, was Rumi's *pīr* after Shams al-Dīn vanished; he is here hailed as an embodiment of the Spirit of Muhammad, the Perfect Man.

[POEM 30 ~ F 246]

3. For Ḥallāj, see note on 16, line 4. The "people of purity" are the saintly Sufis.

[POEM 31 ~ F 250]

3. "Splitter of Dawn": Koran 6:96. "Lord of the Daybreak": Koran 113:1.

4. See the story told in *Math.* 1:3056–64.

11. Mount Ḥirā: the hill outside Mecca to which Muhammad withdrew for meditation.

[POEM 32 ~ F 260]

5. Man is the *khalīfa* of God in the world: Koran 2:28.

8. The notion of congenerity is a favourite theme with Rumi, see *Math.* 1:745, IV:2664, VI:1175, etc.

[POEM 33 ~ F 294]

2. For Ilyās (Elias) and his association in Muslim legend with Khiḍar (Khaḍir), see Wesinck in *E.I.* II:470–71.

5. "Water of the face" is a metaphor for honour, self-respect. The poverty here mentioned is of course spiritual self-surrender.

6. "The water": of Divine Grace, the Sea of the Soul.

13. See note on 15, verse 10.

15. I.e. relapse into silence.

[POEM 34   ∻   F 304]

The circumstances under which this poem was composed are related in Aflākī, *Manāqib* 165–67. Comparison with the opening verses of the *Mathnavi* is relevant.

3. "To God": cf. Koran 3:12.

8. For the theme, see *Math.* III:3901, IV:3637 and cf. Koran 23:13.

10. See Koran 31:21.

12. The language of Divine Love is international.

15. "Speech": the Logos mediating between God and man.

20. Koran 47:4. The only course with deniers of spiritual values is, not tenderness, but outright rejection.

[POEM 35   ∻   F 310, N 7]

See Aflākī, *Manāqib* 453, 569. For a verse translation, see Nicholson, *Rūmī, Poet and Mystic,* p. 161.

[POEM 36   ∻   F 314]

4. Cf. Omar Khayyám–Fitzgerald's "Two-and-seventy jarring sects."

8. A pun on the two meanings of *qaḍā* (fate, fulfilment).

[POEM 37   ∻   F 321]

[POEM 38   ∻   F 322]

5. A pun on *gul* (rose) and *kull* (all). Many passages of the Koran open with the word "say."

6. The *Fātiḥa* is the first Sura of the Koran.

11. "I am cooking you": CB reads *pazānamat* for *parānamat.*

[POEM 39   ⸱⸱   F 329]

See Aflākī, *Manāqib* 161, on Rumi preaching to dogs at the cross-roads.

5. As on the Resurrection Day the scrolls of men's deeds will flutter over their heads.

[POEM 40   ⸱⸱   F 332, N 15]

6. After this CB adds an extra couplet: "This is the house of the soul, it is the same place as the soul is, it is neither below nor above nor the six directions, for it is the middle."

12. See note on 7, verse 1.

14. "It is inauspicious": perhaps rather, "Become intoxicated."

18. A play on *zabān* (tongue) and *zabāna* (flame).

[POEM 41   ⸱⸱   F 341]

8. Junaid (d. 298/910) was the chief of the Sufis of Baghdad. For Bā Yazīd, see note on 1, verse 21.

[POEM 42   ⸱⸱   F 359]

7. The idea seems to be that the moon's occultation is during union with the sun; the terms "united" and "separation" belong to the technical vocabulary of Sufism.

[POEM 43   ⸱⸱   F 364]

1. This and the following two couplets are a quotation from Sanā'ī, see his *Dīvān* (ed. Raḍavī) 589.

5. The Night of Power (see Koran 97:1) was the night (of Rama-ḍān) on which the Koran was first revealed; see Nicholson on *Math.* II:2935.

12. {This line is also from Sanā'ī.—Ed.}

[POEM 44   ⸱⸱   F 376]

3. The reference is to Koran 12:20. Th springtide of mystical joy is seen as Joseph delivered out of the well of the winter of exclusion.

[POEM 45 ⌁ F 381]

4. The simurgh (the fabulous griffin) symbolizes the mystic adept and leader, as in ʿAṭṭar's *Manṭiq al-ṭair*.

[POEM 46 ⌁ F 393]

3. Cf. Koran 24:39.

[POEM 47 ⌁ F 395]

5. "Drowning": on *istighrāq*, see Nicholson on *Math.* I:1111, II:305.

[POEM 48 ⌁ F 409]

4. Rumi quotes from a Tradition of Muhammad. For "and is truly full", CB reads "and carnelian and (*u ʿaqīq u*)".

16. Aḥmad-Muhammad. Rumi quotes from Koran 74:35.

[POEM 49 ⌁ F 423]

5. Badakhshan in Central Asia was famous for its rubies.

13. Cf. the story of Dhu'l-Nūn in *Math.* II:1386–1460.

[POEM 50 ⌁ F 436, N 14]

5. "Wet-skirted": i.e. defiled and impure, of course with tears of blood.

6. F has the misprint *jānat* for *jāmat*.

8. A play on *qaṣr* (palace) and *Qaiṣar* (Caesar).

[POEM 51 ⌁ F 441, N 16]

Nicholson's text exhibits numerous differences.

3. "Out of your air": N tr. "From love for thee." Here CB adds an extra couplet: "Sweet breeze blowing from Love's meadow, blow on me, for the tidings of fragrant herbs is my desire!"

7. Oman, the southern part of the Persian Gulf, symbolizes the Divine Ocean.

8. Koran 12:84.

10. The Lion of God was ʿAlī, Muhammad's cousin and fourth caliph. Rustam was the famous Iranian champion.

21. 'Uthmān: Sharaf al-Dīn-i Qavvāl the minstrel, see Aflākī 222, 223, 320, etc.

[POEM 52 ❧ F 446]
6. For the Table, see note on 6, verse 16.
9. Cf. *Math.* I:2956.
11. For Ja'farī gold, see Nicholson on *Math.* I:2778 with Appendix, IV:2060.

[POEM 53 ❧ F 449, N 11]
8. CB reads *jahān* (world) for *havā* (air).
9. Apposition between *murād* (object) and *murīd* (disciple).
10. For Kauthar, see note on 8, verse 9.
11. I.e. "I am grieving." A play on "foot," "hand," and "head."

[POEM 54 ❧ F 455, N 13]
10. I.e. "If you are not a slave, but a free man of God."
14. A reference to Koran 33:53.
15. "The steely face": the mirror.

[POEM 55 ❧ F 463, N 9]
For the circumstances, see Aflākī 266–68; quoted by Rumi on his deathbed, Aflākī 966–67. Nicholson's text includes F 464 (1), as does CB.
5. Muṣṭafā: Muhammad.
6. The miracle alluded to in Koran 54:1.
7. "Like the forenoon": Koran 93:1.
11. Alast: the day of God's primeval covenant with man, see Koran 7:171.

[POEM 56 ❧ F 478]
6. Koran 2:245.
12. Ja'far-i Ṭaiyār: heroic cousin of Muhammad, see Nicholson on *Math.* II:3565, and cf. *Math.* VI:3029–3105.

[POEM 57 ✲ F 481, N 10]

4. "Air": Nicholson translates "desire."

5. "The Master": N reads *uftādast* and translates "has fallen."

11. Presumably Niẓāmī the author of the epics (d. 599/1202).

[POEM 58 ✲ F 485]

6. See note on 26, verse 3.

10. I.e. as a son of Adam, every man is heir to his ancient disobedience.

11. "Be and it is": the Divine fiat, see Koran 2:117, etc. "Ungrudging": see Koran 41:8.

13. For Korah (Qārūn) see Koran 28:76–81.

14. *Kāf* and *nūn* are the letters making up the word *kun* (Be!).

[POEM 59 ✲ F 499]

2. Rumi quotes from Sanā'ī, see his *Dīvān* 605. Bū Ḥanīfa and Shāfi'ī were founders of schools of Islamic jurisprudence.

11. "God is sufficient": Koran 4:45.

21. See Koran 99:8.

22. Koran 99:7.

[POEM 60 ✲ F 509]

4. The reference is to the legend of the seven sleepers of Ephesus, see Koran 18:8–25.

[POEM 61 ✲ F 524]

4. Zangis: Ethiopians, black slaves—watchmen.

[POEM 62 ✲ F 526]

See Aflākī 237, on Fakhr al-Dīn-i Sīvāsī suddenly going mad.

1. For the idiom, see note on 12, verse 3.

6. The Moaning Pillar: the palm-trunk in the Prophet's mosque at Medina which moaned when the Prophet grasped it, see Nicholson on *Math.* 1:2113.

[POEM 63 ⋄ F 528]
5. See note on 8, verse 6.

[POEM 64 ⋄ F 532]
4. Rumi refers to the ancient romance, told by Niẓāmī in his *Khus-rau u Shīrīn*. Farhād sought to dig his way through a mountain to reach Shīrīn.
6. Emending *lurkand* (gully) to *lauz-qand* (almond-sweet).

[POEM 65 ⋄ F 536]

[POEM 66 ⋄ F 543]
4. See Koran 23:12–14.
8. Muhammad in his Ascension disregarded the wonders of the heavens, seeking only the Presence of God. For another interpretation of the Eight Paradises, see Nicholson on *Math*. I:3498.

[POEM 67 ⋄ F 558]

[POEM 68 ⋄ F 563]
See Aflākī 155–56.
7. I.e. surrender reason, the great impediment to love.

[POEM 69 ⋄ F 566, N 21]
6. "Be brave": CB reads with N *dilā zū bāsh*, "O heart, make haste."

[POEM 70 ⋄ F 576]
5. For Ṣalāḥ al-Dīn, see note on 29, verse 12.

[POEM 71 ⋄ F 579]
3. The angel Seraphiel will blow the trumpet on the Day of Resurrection. The body once more clothes the soul in the miracle of spring.
5. Colour is a symbol for the world of phenomena, contrasted with the unicolority of the world of spirit; see Nicholson on *Math*. I:1121–35.

[POEM 72 ❧ F 581]

4. See Koran 59:2.

5. CB reads *zaft* (rough) for *raft* (departed). The poets liked to describe the grace of the cypress in movement.

8. "Yā Hū": the cry of the ecstatic mystic, "O He (God)!"

9. "The friend of the cave": the spirit of Muhammad.

13. A play on *chu nār* (like fire) and *chinār* (plane-tree).

19. See Koran 12:25–8.

20. For Manṣūr, see note on 16, verse 4.

22. "A turnover": or, "a woman's mantle."

[POEM 73 ❧ F 594]

3. "Die": perhaps "space (of the distance between post-stations)," see Lane, 1:1387. {This word *sikka* may also commonly mean "coin."—Ed.}

9. "Why did you seek": CB reads *justam* (why did I seek).

11. This poem presumably commemorates the death of Ṣalāḥ al-Dīn Zarkūb, or perhaps his temporary absence from Rumi's circle.

[POEM 74 ❧ F 598]

3. Koran 12:94.

4. Koran 12:19.

5. Koran 20:9–10.

8. See *Discourses of Rumi* 171.

9. For the famous conversion of Ibrāhīm ibn Adham (d. 160/776), see *E.I.* II:433.

12. "Did we not open": Koran 94:1.

[POEM 75 ❧ F 605]

5. Cf. *Math.* IV:2403–5, on the sight as derived from the "fat" of the eye.

[POEM 76 ❧ F 614]

[POEM 77 ❧ F 621]

8. Hārūt and Mārūt the fallen angels dwelt in a well in Babylon: see Nicholson on *Math.* I:535.

[POEM 78 ⤳ F 622, N 18]

4. {"Crop-sickness"—see notes for poem 139, verse 17, on page 399.—Ed.}

5. The text of F is clearly superior to N, "to be quit of the furniture."

[POEM 79 ⤳ F 631]

7. This poem was evidently composed to mark the end of Ramaḍān.

[POEM 80 ⤳ F 636]

[POEM 81 ⤳ F 638]

3. Koran 54:1. "Good-for-nothing": reading *halanandīd* for *hala-pandīd,* but see F VII 461.

4. Farhād: see note on 64, verse 4. Shaddād built the paradisal Iram: see *E.I.* II 519.

6. I.e. surrender to God's will without questioning.

7. 'That self': God.

10. Reading *istīzha* ('shuttle') for *istīza* ('quarrel').

[POEM 82 ⤳ F 644]

3. See Koran 43:38.

7. Cf. Koran 17:22.

8. {*rahzan*: rather than Arberry's "footpad"; it would perhaps be better to read "highway robber."—Ed.}

11. See *Math.* IV: 3430–45 for the miracle of the Nile.

[POEM 83 ⤳ F 649, N 19]

6. 'Reason': Universal Reason, the first emanation of God.

8. 'Became spirit': or, 'departed.'

[POEM 84 ⤳ F 656]

7. 'Surmeh': eye-salve brightening the vision.

9. On the Day of Resurrection the faces of sinners will be black, those of the saved bright and shining, cf. Koran 75:22–4.

[POEM 85 ⤳ F 662]

[POEM 86 ◇ F 668]

1. Rajab is the seventh, Sha'bān the eighth month: anciently Rajab was a month of truce.

7. 'Umar was the second, 'Uthmān the third caliph.

[POEM 87 ◇ F 692]

7. A play on *auḥad* (unique) and *aḥad* (one).

9. "Pegs": the great saints of every age, receiving illumination from the "Poles," see Nicholson on *Math.* II:819.

[POEM 88 ◇ F 707]

14. "The Friend": taking F's emendation *yār* for *pār*.

[POEM 89 ◇ F 727]

[POEM 90 ◇ F 728]

4. See Koran 15:36–8.

5. See Nicholson on *Math.* I:227.

6. Azrael is the Angel of Death. For this verse, see Aflākī 591.

7. Koran 36:27.

9. A play on *rūḥ, rīḥī, rāḥ, rāḥī*.

10. See Koran 4:157.

11. Manṣūr: Ḥallāj.

[POEM 91 ◇ F 730]

[POEM 92 ◇ F 735]

1. The proverbial elephant remembering India symbolizes the mystic recalling his divine origin.

5. Kai-Qubād was an ancient king of Persia.

6. 'The brothers of purity': the Sufis.

10. A play on *dād* (justice) and *dād* (dispensed).

[POEM 93 ◇ F 745]

6. A play on *ṣāf* "staining-cloth" and *ṣāf* "unsullied."

[POEM 94   ⋌   F 762]

7. 'Uzaizī: an esteemed variety of eye-salve.

8. CB reads *maujash* (its wave) for *ābash* (its water).

[POEM 95   ⋌   F 765]

[POEM 96   ⋌   F 771]

[POEM 97   ⋌   F 779]

9. For the story, see Dihkhudā, *Amthāl u ḥikam.* A Kurd who had lost his camel found it again when the moon came out, and praised the moon as though it were God.

[POEM 98   ⋌   F 782]

11. For Jesus speaking in the cradle, see Koran 19:30–31.

[POEM 99   ⋌   F 791]

4. {Furūzānfar's Persian edition has "lasso" (*kamand-ast*), where Arberry has translated "moon." Perhaps Arberry has seen and preferred a different reading (*qamar ast ?*).}

6. CB *pastī* (low) seems better than *chustī.*

11. "This sullied cup": the physical body.

[POEM 100   ⋌   F 806]

2. "Homeland": CB reads *ṭaraf* (side) for *waṭan.*

[POEM 101   ⋌   F 809]

1. For the comparison of the world with a bath-stove, see *Math.* IV:238–56.

10. Sanjar the Saljūq ruler typifies kingship.

12. For the Moaning Pillar, see note on 62, line 6.

13. "Their eyes": CB reads *nafshā-shān.*

15. "The chatter": the meaning of *dastān* is ambiguous, and the whole verse obscure.

[POEM 102   ⌐   F 819]
7. Koran 19:25.

[POEM 103   ⌐   F 821]
9. "The Messenger": Muhammad as intermediary and intercessor between man and God.

[POEM 104   ⌐   F 824]
For the circumstances of composition, see Aflākī as quoted by F.
3. See Koran 53:9; i.e. "spiritual proximity."
13. Bū Saʿīd: the famous Persian mystic and poet (d. 440/1049).
14. A play on words: for Bū Yazīd, see note on 1, verse 21.
16. More plays on words. Sanāʾī and ʿAṭṭār were great mystical poets.
23. Rumi quotes Koran 50:16.

[POEM 105   ⌐   F 833]
1. Koran 112:1.
8. A famous tradition states that "the believer sees by the Light of God."
12. A play on *khar* (ass) and *khirad* (reason).
14. "The Pole": the supreme mystic of his age, presumably Rumi himself.

[POEM 106   ⌐   F 837]

[POEM 107   ⌐   F 841]
See Aflākī 150–51.
9. For Moses' hand, see Koran 7:105. For Khiḍar and the fish, see Koran 18:61.

[POEM 108   ⌐   F 853]

[POEM 109   ⌐   F 861, N 23]
7. Koran 93:1.

[POEM 110 ⋮ F 863]

5. "Blind and blue" is an idiom for total blindness.

7. "Expunging": the mystical term *maḥw* is used.

11. By the sun's transforming power.

16. Cf. Koran 2:178.

18. Koran 18:18.

[POEM 111 ⋮ F 873]

[POEM 112 ⋮ F 879]

3. Rumi and Zangi are white and black respectively.

10. Ḥusain, son of 'Alī the fourth caliph, was slain at the battle of Kerbela by order of Yazīd.

12. For the Night of Power, see note on 43, verse 5.

13. Koran 83:25.

15. Famous Sufis of old; Ma'rūf al-Karkhī died 200/816, Shiblī died 334/945.

[POEM 113 ⋮ F 882]

4. A play on the two meanings of *sharḥ;* Rumi has in mind Koran 94:1.

9. See Koran 100:9–10.

11. The Tablet and the Pen are Koranic terms, believed by the orthodox literally to exist in heaven.

16. Koran 27:44.

[POEM 114 ⋮ F 887]

5. Koran 5:69.

9. Koran 50:34.

10. See Koran 79:24.

[POEM 115 ⋮ F 892]

1. A poem in time of Ramaḍān.

2. Self-denial attaches the soul to God.

3. Rumi quotes from Koran 100:1–2.

4. "The bow": Koran 2:63–68.

6. Koran 2:185.

10. For Jesus and the ass, see Nicholson on *Math.* II:1850.

[POEM 116 ⋇ F 900, N 20]

[POEM 117 ⋇ F 909]

1. For Aflākī's account, see F *ad loc.*

2. Koran 53:18.

17. "Sayers of Yes": the seed of Adam, cf. Koran 7:171.

18. "Two pieces of fat": the eyes.

19. "A hole": the ear-hole, attracting sound as amber attracts straw.

[POEM 118 ⋇ F 911, N 24]

[POEM 119 ⋇ F 919]

[POEM 120 ⋇ F 927]

13. I.e. bad copper cannot be transmuted to gold; the doubters will never believe.

[POEM 121 ⋇ F 937]

10. Alast: see note on 55, verse 11.

15. Khaibar: the Jewish fortress conquered by 'Alī in A.D. 629.

16. "Five times a day": at every prayer Muhammad is proclaimed God's Messenger, and, in Shī'ite lands, 'Alī his Executor.

[POEM 122 ⋇ F 940]

[POEM 123 ⋇ F 943]

[POEM 124 ⋇ F 968]

6. This and the two following lines are in Arabic.

8. Koran 34:11.

[POEM 125 ⋇ F 981]

6. "Your own": CB reads *nau* (new) for *tū*, pairing with "old."

[POEM 126 ⋊ F 984]

11. "Signless": spiritual.

13. See Koran 105:3, a reference to the miraculous defeat of the Abyssinian Abraha's attack on Mecca in A.D. 571.

16. Koran 8:17, the miracle of the battle of Badr in A.D. 624.

[POEM 127 ⋊ F 996, N 22]

10. The "points" refer to the diacritical points (of certain letters) rather than to those of a compass (so Nicholson).

[POEM 128 ⋊ F 1001]

[POEM 129 ⋊ F 1017]

10. The five senses and the six directions.

11. {Furūzānfar's Persian edition repeats "measure" (*andāza*) where Arberry's translation reads "treasure." This is perhaps due to the typesetter's misreading of Arberry's handwriting, or perhaps Arberry has seen and preferred a different reading (*ganjīna* ?). —Ed.}

[POEM 130 ⋊ F 1022]

[POEM 131 ⋊ F 1025]

4. "This sack": this physical body-prison.

[POEM 132 ⋊ F 1037]

7. "The Veiler": God.

[POEM 133 ⋊ F 1047]

[POEM 134 ⋊ F 1052]

For the circumstances, see Aflākī 280–81. Rumi was discoursing on the tradition, "I did not see God save in a red garment."

[POEM 135 ⋊ F 1073]

[POEM 136　∿　F 1077, N 26]
3. Dhu ʾl-Faqār: ʿAlī's sword, symbolizing death.
7. The five senses and the four elements.
10. "The Root": God, the source of all being.

[POEM 137　∿　F 1082]
6. "His tug": the mystical term *jadhba* (drawing) is used.
7. Idris is the Moslem Enoch: see Koran 19:57.
8. *Qibla:* the direction of Mecca.
15. Rumi refers here to 1097, a shorter-lined version of this poem.

[POEM 138　∿　F 1092]
7. Here as elsewhere Rumi plays on words' double meanings.

[POEM 139　∿　F 1095]
5. For Dhu ʾl-Faqār, see note on 136, verse 3.
9. See note on 101, verse 1.
12. Persian baths were decorated with frescoes; the symbol is of material forms of spiritual beauty.
17. {Arberry consistently chose to translate *khumār* as "crop-sickness," which is a possible meaning, but seems very far from the usual meaning in Persian ghazal poetry and in Rumi, where *khumār* means a hangover, or wine headache. By volume two of *Mystical Poems of Rūmī*, Arberry was apparently persuaded in some instances to change "crop-sickness" to headache, as in poem 391, line 19, where Arberry originally wrote "crop-sickness" in his notes, but "headache" appears in the text.—Ed.}

[POEM 140　∿　F 1103]

[POEM 141　∿　F 1121]
1. {Literally "the Beloved's messenger" (*rasūl*) —Ed.}
2. {Arberry translates the idiomatic sense of *ai chashm v-ai chirāgh* (O eye and light!) as "my darling one."—Ed.}
3. Rumi quotes an Arabic rule of etiquette.
13. Nimrod died of a gnat-bite, see Nicholson on *Math.* I:1189.

[POEM 142 ❧ F 1126]

[POEM 143 ❧ F 1131]
5. I.e. despite the unbelief of the purblind.

[POEM 144 ❧ F 1136]
1. Koran 59:2.
5. See note on 126, verse 13.
6. {Literally, for food, a fattened bird is the same to you as scorpion or snake —Ed.}
9. Rumi refers to a tradition of Muhammad describing the Last Judgment.

[POEM 145 ❧ F 1139]
3. "A hidden enemy": the carnal soul.

[POEM 146 ❧ F 1142, N 27]
1. {This line appears to be quoted from *Dīvān* of Anvarī, (Tabriz ed., 115).—Ed.}
6. Refers to the Hegira of Muhammad. Yathrib was the ancient name of Medina.

[POEM 147 ❧ F 1145, N 25]
12. Mirrors had covers of felt.

[POEM 148 ❧ F 1151]
1. {Regarding "crop-sick" see the notes for poem 139, verse 17, on page 399.—Ed.}
16. The dust of the beloved's feet has healing properties.

[POEM 149 ❧ F 1156]

[POEM 150 ❧ F 1158]
3. Rumi quotes in Arabic a tradition on *memento mori*.
4. See Koran 9:40.

9. A well-known tradition, naming Muhammad as the prime pur-
pose of creation.

[POEM 151   ⋰   F 1185]

5. "The mad lover": Majnūn Lailā.

6. See Koran 12:31.

11. Koran 50:16.

[POEM 152   ⋰   F 1195]

8. The love of Sultan Maḥmūd and Ayāz became proverbial: see
Math. V:2858 foll.

[POEM 153   ⋰   F 1201]

6. The Night of Power: a night in Ramaḍān on which the Koran
was first revealed, when prayers are answered.

[POEM 154   ⋰   F 1211]

4. A rare reference to the Crusaders.

5. The back of the mirror does not reflect the beauty of Joseph,
symbol of the Divine Beauty.

7. Cf. *Fīhi mā fīhi* 48–49.

11. "The fire": CB reads *nār-rā* for *nā-ravā*.

12. "Cursed": Koran III:1.

13. "Brooding night": Koran 81:17. CB reads *ham-jins* (congener)
for *ham-ḥabs* (fellow-prisoner).

14. "Docked": Koran 108:3.

[POEM 155   ⋰   F 1223]

1. Hārūt and Mārūt: see note on 77, verse 8.

3. Koran 108:1.

5. Koran 1:1 and 1:7.

6. "The houses": the 28 mansions of the moon.

7. Kai-Kā'ūs: ancient king of Persia who possessed a magic cup.
{"crop-sick"—See the notes for poem 139, verse 17, on page 399.—Ed.}

9. Koran 57:23.

10. "Testimony": invite it to become a Moslem.

12. Koran 99:1.

[POEM 156 ⤙ F 1235]

7. I.e. "Shall I praise his physical or his moral excellence first?"

[POEM 157 ⤙ F 1246]

7. "Hyacinthine": the curls like clusters of ears of corn.

10. Bū Lahab was an enemy of Muhammad; Bū Huraira a promi-
nent Companion who possessed a magic food-bag which never failed
him, see Nicholson on *Math.* v:2794.

[POEM 158 ⤙ F 1254]

7. A play on the two meanings of *jauhar*.

[POEM 159 ⤙ F 1270]

[POEM 160 ⤙ F 1288]

1. Manṣūr: Ḥallāj.

[POEM 161 ⤙ F 1299]

[POEM 162 ⤙ F 1301]

1. {Arberry wrote at a time when "gay" did not yet have wide cur-
rency in the meaning of homosexual orientation; the intent of the
phrase "gay reprobates" (*rind-i ʿishratī*) is something like "carefree
libertines."—Ed.}

6. The ancients believed that the emerald was a charm against
snakes.

10. Koran 20:22.

12. Koran 19:25.

[POEM 163 ⤙ F 1304]

10. "Burnt" also means "accursed."

14. The poet plays on the shapes of letters.

16. "Description" of a thing lost: perhaps "confession."

[POEM 164 ⋅: F 1317]

[POEM 165 ⋅: F 1326]
7. {"With all my eye!" (*bi-chashm*) is an idiomatic Persian expression meaning, "I will gladly do it!"—Ed.}

[POEM 166 ⋅: F 1335, N 28]
1. Chigil in Turkestan was proverbial for its handsome inhabitants.
9. Ṣalāḥ al-Dīn Zarkūb, Shams al-Dīn's successor.

[POEM 167 ⋅: F 1353, N 29]
3. "Return": Koran 89:27.
12. Koran 17:80 and 84:6.

[POEM 168 ⋅: F 1372]
7. "Blood": CB reads *khvān* (table).

[POEM 169 ⋅: F 1380]
7. For Jesus and the ass, see *Math.* II:1850.
10. CB reads *dar dardhā ai āh-gū* (You who cry ah in pain), which seems superior.

[POEM 170 ⋅: F 1393]
9. "Impotent": i.e. "plucked clean of feathers."
18. "The seven layers": the seven heavens.
19. Joseph, after coming up from the well, waxed in beauty and power.
21. "The face": a pun on *rukh*, which also means "rook."

[POEM 171 ⋅: F 1397]

[POEM 172 ⋅: F 1414]
1. See Koran 20:10–12.
5. The miracle of the bird created from clay, see Koran 3:42.

[POEM 173 ⋅: F 1422]
3. For Jaʿfar-i Ṭaiyār, see note on 56, verse 12.

5. Adam in Moslem legend was expelled from Eden for swallowing a grain of corn. Rumi puns on *bū tīmār* ("heron," lit. "father of sorrow").

7. {Arberry apparently reads *khiḍr* twice in this line, but Furūzānfar's critical edition reads once *ḥiḍr* and once *khiḍr*, which would give an alternate reading: I am the companion of presence, foot planted and head spinning, constantly seeking the approach of Khiḍar [*Khiḍr*], as I spin like a compass.—Ed.}

13. A play on *dīnār* (gold) and *dīdār* (vision). {Arberry reads "Why do you bite my lips privily, saying..." (*chi lab rā mī-gazī pinhān ki...*). This would probably be better understood as "why do you bite your lip privily, as a signal to me..."—Ed.}

20. {Zangi—See the note in poem 61, verse 4.—Ed.}

[POEM 174　　F 1429]

[POEM 175　　F 1437]
9. "In peace and well-being": as of paradise, see Koran 56:88.

[POEM 176　　F 1447]
9. "A golden calf": cf. Koran 7:146.

[POEM 177　　F 1458]

[POEM 178　　F 1462, N 34]

[POEM 179　　F 1463]
4. "The tithe-collector": taking a tenth for providing safe-conduct, see Dozy II:131.

5. "Compressed *hamza*": from the hooklike shape of the orthographic sign.

8. A play on *pīrūza* (turquoise) and *pīrūz* (Victor).

[POEM 180　　F 1472]
This poem was composed when Rumi was sixty-two; see line 5.
9. "Blood was the food": in the womb.

11. A play on *tafsīr* (interpretation) and *taf-i sīr* ("stench of garlic," eaten by the unbelieving Jews).

[POEM 181   ⋈   F 1486]

[POEM 182   ⋈   F 1489]
5. Vā'il was ancestor of the Arab tribes of Bakr and Taghlib, protagonists in the famous War of Basūs; see Nicholson, *Literary History of the Arabs* 55–57.
12. A play on *nāṭiqa* ("rational soul," lit. "speaking").

[POEM 183   ⋈   F 1503]

[POEM 184   ⋈   F 1508]
8. For the story of Joseph and the mirror, see *Fīhi mā fīhi* 186.

[POEM 185   ⋈   F 1515]
14. A play on *Shīrīn* and *shīrīnī* (sweetness).

[POEM 186   ⋈   F 1521, N 30]

[POEM 187   ⋈   F 1531]
2. I.e. the Red Sea crossing.
4. Koran 7:105.
7. See note on 141, line 13.

[POEM 188   ⋈   F 1538]

[POEM 189   ⋈   F 1546]
3. "Six doors": the six directions.

[POEM 190   ⋈   F 1554]
3. {Arberry translates "We thresh about in dry and wet," but it is possible to interpret *bi-tābīm* as "We shine upon the dry and the wet (i.e., land and sea).—Ed.}
6. Shushtar was famous for its fine robes.

10. Sanjar the great Saljuq warrior-king.

12. A play on the two meanings of *ḥalqa* (circle, knocker).

13. {Arberry translates "sign-manual of security" for *ṭughrā-yi amān*, which might be rendered as the "royal seal of protection."
—Ed.}

[POEM 191 ⋰ F 1559]

[POEM 192 ⋰ F 1562]
4. A play on *muhr* (seal) and *mihār* (toggle).
9. "Scratch a head": i.e. cajole the Beloved.

[POEM 193 ⋰ F 1564]
9. See Koran 27:17–18.

[POEM 194 ⋰ F 1576]

[POEM 195 ⋰ F 1585]
5. "In desire for": or, "in the air (*havā*) of." {There is a play on the word *havā*, meaning both "desire" and "air," so that we can also infer that the tree lifts up its hands into the air of the One who taught me desire.—Ed.}
6. A play on *ṣibā* (passion) and *ṣabā* (zephyr).

[POEM 196 ⋰ F 1590]
3. "Meanings": spiritual realities.
9. "From his line": i.e. decree.

[POEM 197 ⋰ F 1604]
1. Ḥātim the ancient Arab was proverbial for generosity.
7. Koran 7:171. *Balā* = "Yes," *alast* = "Am I not (your Lord)?"
10. The first half of this verse is in Arabic.

[POEM 198 ⋰ F 1610]
11. "Moon of the dormitory": the physical moon.

[POEM 199　❻　F 1615]

2. {See the note for poem 139, verse 17. Instead of crop-sickness, it is better to understand *khumār* here as wine-sickness or hangover. —Ed.}

[POEM 200　❻　F 1620]

[POEM 201　❻　F 1623]

4. The literal translation of the line would be: "It was all my fault that such an art came forth from me: I purposely drew a scorpion toward my own foot."

Aflākī writes: "There was an assembly for a great *samā'* in the house of Parvāna. Mowlānā was in a great ecstasy, but Seyyed Sharaf al-Dīn and Parvāna had retired to a corner and were reproaching him. Mowlānā heard them and composed this *ǧazal*... Parvāna immediately apologized and did not give Sharaf al-Dīn such an occasion any more." *Manāqib*, 339–40.

5. {Arberry's handwritten copy of this poem was missing, and could not therefore be consulted, but we may conjecture that he intended to translate "nothing of Adam except his form." The Persian of Furūzānfar's edition reads *naqshī*, which means form.}

[POEM 202　❻　F 1628]

2. Solomon had dominion over men, Jinns, and birds, and he had a magic seal with which he exercised his influence.

[POEM 203　❻　F 1634]

[POEM 204　❻　F 1638]

1. In the original: *farah ibn farah ibn farah ibn farahām*. For the sake of the introduction or induction of a certain rhythmic mood Rumi often bursts into a repetition of a single word or phrase.

3. The Garden of Eram was the famous garden built by Shaddād in Arabia Felix, see *E.I* 2:519.

4. Ḥātim was an Arab chief whose generosity is proverbial.

[POEM 205　❻　F 1641]

[POEM 206 ❧ F 1649]

12. The Wailing Column was in the Prophet's mosque at Medina. According to tradition it moaned when he grasped it. See note 6 to 62; also Nicholson on *Math.* I:2113.

[POEM 207 ❧ F 1655]

2. In Persian literature indigo and black are two colors of mourning.

3. For Abraham see note to poem 8, verse 6.
Ibrāhīm son of Adham (d. 783?) was a famous Sufi from Balkh whose life story strangely resembles that of Buddha.

6. *Rūmī* (Roman) is white-skinned, while *Zangī* is dark-skinned. They also stand for day and night respectively, and are in turn associated with happiness and grief.

9. This is somewhat different from Arberry's original translation. Literally: "Your soul is unanchored (i.e., insecure) as is your dust-filled body." Arberry's version was: "Like the body of your earth-sack on the top of the water of your soul, the soul is veiled in the body alike in wedding feast or sorrow."

14. Zamzam: a well in Mecca.

[POEM 208 ❧ F 1663]

12. The Companion of the Cave is Abū Bakr who accompanied the Prophet in his flight from Mecca. They stayed three days in a cave outside Mecca on their way to Medina. The Koran refers to the incident in sura 9:40: "If you do not help him, yet God has helped him already, when the unbelievers drove him forth, the second of the two; when the two were in the cave, when he said to his companion, 'Sorrow not; surely God is with us.'"

[POEM 209 ❧ F 1678]

10. Abu'l Ḥikam (Father of Wisdom) was the title of 'Amr Ibn Hishām, one of the most bitter enemies of the Prophet, who was killed in the second year of the Hejra (624) in the battle of Badr. Muhammad nicknamed him Abū Jahl (Father of Ignorance) because of his uncompromising attitude towards Islam. Cf. Nicholson's notes on *Math.* I:782, 1503.

[POEM 210 ∴ F 1688]

4. To experience divine love is a spiritual regeneration or birth for a Sufi. This is why the soul in the world is compared to the embryo in the womb, and when it becomes a babe just born into a new world. Cf. *Math.* notes, 1:19, 3180. Rumi says that such a love was inborn in him and from the beginning he embarked on his Sufi mission.

"On that" refers to that love. It was a common superstition that if, while cutting the umbilical cord, one made a wish the child would attain it.

5. *Lawḥ-i ghaib* (the Unseen Tablet) seems to be the same as *lawḥ-i mahfūz* (the Preserved Tablet, Koran, 85:22) which refers to the Koran. It is said to have been in heaven before its revelation. The Sufis interpret it as the First Intelligence (*'aql-i avval)* or Logos or the Active Intellect *('aql-i fa'āl)*. See Sajjādī, *Farhang-i 'irfānī,* 405, and Nicholson's note on *Math.* 1:296.

6. Covenant of Alast: *Alastu bi rabbikum?*, "Am I not your Lord?" (Koran 7:171). Thus God addressed the future generations of men (according to the Sufis their souls). They answered "Yes," and acknowledged God's right to judge their actions and to punish their sins.

[POEM 211 ∴ F 1690, N 32]

2. Abū Lahab was the unconvinced pagan uncle of Muhammad. In 616 when the pagans decided to boycott the Prophet and his friends, Abū Lahab, who was of the Quraish, withdrew his protection from his nephew. Cf. Koran III.

6. The finest quality glass was produced in Aleppo.

12. Baṣra was well-known for its dates. Rumi says that without the Baṣra of your being (i.e., without Shams) he would not have tasted a date (i.e., spiritual experience).

[POEM 212 ∴ F 1692]

[POEM 213 ∴ F 1705]

13. Aḥmad is the title of Muhammad.

14. "The believer is prudent, sagacious and cautious," *A ḥadīs,* 67.

[POEM 214 ∴ F 1713]

4. "Street of mourning": the world, which has been called by many
similar names, such as "the infidel's paradise," and symbolized by
the false dawn, a carcass, a bath-stove and a tomb. (Cf. "world" in
Nicholson's index to *Math.*).

[POEM 215 ∴ F 1725]

1. According to Aflākī Sultan Rukn al-Dīn, Saljūqī was invited to
Āq Sarāi by his emirs to decide about the strategy to face the ap-
proaching Mongol horde. He consulted Maulānā, who said: "It is
better not to go there." But Rukn al-Dīn went and was strangled
by his own people. It is reported that before his death, he shouted:
"Maulānā, Maulānā!" Meanwhile Rumi was at *Samāʿ*. He told the
disciples of Rukn al-Dīn's death and composed this poem. *Manāqib*
I:147–48.

[POEM 216 ∴ F 1737]

9. Ḥabīb Najjār (Carpenter) is a legendary character who gave
his name to a shrine below mount Silpuis at Anṭākiya. Though not
mentioned by name in the Koran (36:12ff), Moslem tradition finds
him there under the description of a man who was put to death in
a village for urging the villagers not to reject the three apostles who
had come with the divine message. Some scholars have suggested that
Ḥabīb is the Agabus of *Acts*, II: 28, but there is not enough evidence
to substantiate this suggestion. Cf G. Vajda's article in *E.I.*

[POEM 217 ∴ F 1739]

1. A *ḥadīṯ* attributed to Moḥammad says: "The true believer re-
sembles a lute whose voice will not improve unless its belly is empty."
Aḥādīṯ, 222.

[POEM 218 ∴ F 1754]

7. In Persian poetry the abode of Jesus after his ascension is usually
said to be in the Fourth Heaven (the sphere of the sun), although Ibn
al-ʿArabī *(Futūḥāt)* places him in the Second. Heaven. See *Math.* I:649.

[POEM 219 ❧ F 1760]

1. According to Aflākī (Manāqib, 703), this *ghazal* is the fourth letter in verse sent by Rumi to Shams-i Tabrīzī during the latter's journey to Syria.

12. In the original, Rumi plays on the two meanings of *shām* (i.e., evening and Syria).

[POEM 220 ❧ F 1769]

2. *Nūn wa'l-qalam* is the beginning of sura 68. Sufis interpret *nūn* as Divine Knowledge and *al-qalam* as the Universal Reason (or *'aql-i avval*). Cf. *Math.* notes, 5:1964.

6. This line is not clear in Arberry's handwritten translation. A more literal translation is "like a strange Arabic word in Persian."

9. The Garden of Iran is a mythical city built to rival paradise. See Koran 89:6.

13. The second hemistich of this line is from a poem by the Arab poet, al-A'shā, who speaking of wine, says: "And exposed it to the wind, in its jar, and he praised its jar, (and petitioned for it that it might not become sour nor spoil)." See Lane's *Lexicon* under *irtisām*.

[POEM 221 ❧ F 1786]

3. "Seven heavens" refers to the spheres of the seven planets. According to ancient Oriental geography the seas or oceans of the earth were also seven in number.

5. For "Joseph of Canaan," see note 1 to 7.

11. The Water of Life *(Āb-i ḥayvān or ḥayāt)* is the Fountain of Life in the Land of Darkness. Niẓāmī in his *Sikandarnāma* describes how Alexander was guided by the prophet Khiḍar to the Fountain but could not reach it. See note on 6, verse 2.

12. Color and scent are symbols for the world of phenomena; see note on 71, verse 5, and Nicholson on *Math.* 1:1121–35.

13. Bodies are composed of the four elements: earth, water, fire, and air. All these originally come from God.

14. For Ṣalāḥ al-Dīn Zarkūb, see note on 29, verse 12.

[POEM 222 ⌁ F 1789, N 36]

4. Nicholson in his translation of this *ghazal* (*Selected Poems from the Dīvāni Shamsi Tabrīz,* 36) compares the image of "the inverted candles" with the line in Shakespeare's Sonnet XXI: "those gold candles fixed in heaven's air."

10. Nicholson illustrates the idea with a line from *Gulshan-i Rāz,* 165:

Each atom doth invisibly enshrine
The deep-veil'd beauty of the Soul divine.

[POEM 223 ⌁ F 1794]

9. "Do not despair of God's mercy," Koran, 39:53.

14. For the angel Seraphiel, note on poem 71, verse 3.

In the pre-Islamic Iran *Mihragān* (autumn festival in honor of Mithra) was as important as *Nau-rūz,* the beginning of the Persian calendar in the spring.

17. Indians as well as black people symbolize the night.

[POEM 224 ⌁ F 1807]

1. *Dush* and *qush* are imperative forms from the modern Turkish *duşmak* and *koşmak* respectively. The latter could be read as *Kaş* (run away) instead of *Koş* (set off). Mowlānā occasionally used Turkish words and sometimes wrote *ghazals* in Anatolian Turkish. On his Turkish poetry, see Serefeddin Yaltkaya, "Mevlâna da Türkçe kelimelar va Türkçe siirler," *Turkiyat Mecmuasi* (1934), 112–68; Mecdut Mansuroglu, "Celaluddin Rumi's Turkish verse" in *Uralaltaische Jahrbücher* 24 (1952), 106–15.

[POEM 225 ⌁ F 1823]

7. For "the water of life," see note on 224, verse 11.

The reflection of the moon in the well is likened to Joseph cast by his brothers into a dark well. Cf. Koran 12.

11. *Samā ʿ,* which here has been translated as "concert," is the mystic dance of the Mevlevi darvishes accompanied by the flute and the recital of *ghazals.* The musical quality of most of the poems in the *Dīvān-i Shams* makes them ideal for such performances, and apparently Rumi had this particular point in mind when he wrote

them (cf. p. 3 in the introduction to the *First Selection*). Here Rumi opposed those Sufis and orthodox Muslims who were against the *samā'* as a ritual. There have been numerous pro and con discussions on the subject in Islamic literature, and for instance one can refer to al-Ghazālī *(Kīmīyā-yi Sa'ādat,* Tehran, 1954, chap. 15) who considers the charms of music of great help in drawing the sensitive heart toward God.

[POEM 226 ≈ F 1826]

2. Perhaps Rumi refers to the Koran where it says: "He [God] sends down His angels with inspiration of His command, to such of His servants as He pleases," 16:2.

9. "The black and blue chest" is the sign of asceticism and the chastised carnal soul *(nafs)* without whose abasement the Sufi will not attain any spiritual elevation.

12. "Hū" or "Yā Hū" are the ecstatic cries of the Sufis and mean "He" [God] or "O God!" The scent of the Beloved from His divine city is likened to the perfume of Joseph's vest which, coming from afar to the blind Jacob, gave him his sight. Cf. Koran 12:94.

[POEM 227 ≈ F 1837]

6. Arberry's translation was: "you are . . . my only one and my thousand times."

11. "The house of water and clay" symbolizes the human body where the soul, coming from a spiritual land, must sojourn and the original abode back to which it wishes to fly.

[POEM 228 ≈ F 1845]

3. Moses' face was illuminated by divine glory. One of the signs of his prophethood was his White Hand *(yadd-i bayḍā)*. See Koran 7:105 *et seq.).* 'Imrān was the father of Moses.

4. Hāmān was the minister of Pharaoh (Koran 28:6).

5. Another sign of Moses' prophethood was his rod which changed into a serpent (Koran 7:108).

6. For Abū Huraira's magic bag, see *First Selection,* note 10 to 157, and *Math.* 5:2794.

10. After casting Joseph into the well, they told Jacob that he had been eaten by a wolf. For Abū Jahl, see note to poem 209, verse 10.

11. The hatred of the black beetle for sweet scents is proverbial.

17. The reference is to a tradition which says: "Consult women and do the opposite," *Aḥādīs*, 30.

18. *Qibla* is the direction of Kaaba towards which the Muslims turn their faces while praying.

19. Arberry's translation was: "it fills from its lip with sweets from the floor of the house to the attic."

22. Koran 54:55.

[POEM 229 ～ F 1850]

3. "And the earth—We spread it forth." Koran 51:48. *Farrāsh* is a servant.

5. Abraham: note on poem 8, verse 6.

8. A *ḥadīs* attributed to Muhammad *(Jāmi'-i Ṣaghīr,* 2:49); F 4:140.

[POEM 230 ～ F 1861]

[POEM 231 ～ F 1869]

5. For Khiḍar, see note on 221, verse 11.

[POEM 232 ～ F 1876]

3. The clay of man was imbued with divine wine before his creation and this symbolizes the love of God.

7. Names: ninety-nine beautiful names of God (Koran 7:180).

8. Rumi is playing with the words which occur in the Muslim profession of faith: *lā ilāha illā 'llāh* (there is no God but *Allah). Illā* is used in antithesis to *lā.* In order to reach the kingdom of *illā* (or real existence in God) one has to undergo the Sufi experience of self-annihilation.

13. Majnūn, which literally means elf-ridden or madly in love, is the proverbial lover in Islamic literatures.

16. The Christians under Muslim rule were required to carry a distinctive girdle *(zunnār).*

18. For Khiḍar, see note on 221, verse 11.

[POEM 233 ❧ F 1888]

[POEM 234 ❧ F 1898]
3. "(O soul) return to thy Lord, well-pleased and well-pleasing."
Koran 89:28.
8. Māchīn: the lands beyond China.
15. The family of Yāsīn: the family of Muhammad.

[POEM 235 ❧ F 1904]
18. The Companions of the Elephant" were the army of the
Abyssinian Abraha who attacked Mecca in AD 571, See Koran 105, and
note on 126, verse 13.
20. According to the Koran 105, God sent large flights of birds
called *abābīl* to fling stones at the army of Abraha and destroy it.

[POEM 236 ❧ F 1910]

[POEM 237 ❧ F 1919, N 35]
3. Nicholson's version is: *mar dīda-yi khwīsh rā nadīdan*—(not to
see your own eye) "whence all objects derive their unreal existence."

[POEM 238 ❧ F 1925]
5. Luqmān seems to be Aesop in Islamic tradition. Nicholson
writes: "He appears as a sagacious negro slave in several anecdotes
related by Rumi. One of these *[Math. 1:3584 et seq.]* is identical with a
story which occurs in the fourteenth-century *Life of Aesop* by Maximus
Planudes." *Math.* 1:1961.

[POEM 239 ❧ F 1937]
6. Any object which keeps one from being absorbed in divine love
is an idol.
7. See Nicholson's commentary on 1:400–401.
8. "*Khiyāl* (fantasy or phantasm) is the same as the World of Simili-
tude (*'ālam-i miṣāl*), of which everything in the sensible world (*'ālam-i
shahāda*) is a reflection. The World of Similitude is a purgatory stage
between the worlds of souls and things." Sajjādī *Farhang-i 'irfānī*, 204.

8. According to Nicholson (*Math.* 1:2778) Ja'farī gold refers to the gold produced by the Shi'ite Imam, Ja'far-al-Ṣādiq, who was the reputed author of several works on alchemy. Also, it has been said that Hārūn al-Rashīd entrusted the coinage in Islamic domains to Ja'far the Barmecide and hence the name. In both cases it refers to pure gold.

16. Rumi plays on the two meanings of *māh* (moon and month). Thus the line also means: the festival of everyone is the time of the year (or the month) of which he is fond.

17. Koran 24:35: "God is the Light of the heavens and the earth . . . " which is "neither of the East nor of the West."

[POEM 241 ∵ F 1957]

[POEM 242 ∵ F 1958]
4. "Oil": sauce or gravy.

[POEM 243 ∵ F 1965]
6. Āzar: the father of Abraham was a famous idol-maker. Mānī, the founder of Manichaean religion, is said to have been a great painter.

[POEM 244 ∵ F 1972]
1. For the comparison of the heart to a pond fed by streams, see Nicholson on *Math.* 1:2710–14.

4. Guebre: a Zoroastrian.

5. *Khumār* (intoxicated, hazy or languid look) is used by Persian poets to describe the beautiful eyes of their beloved.

8. Water and clay: man's body, which is a cage for his soul.

12. Koran 30:72.

[POEM 245 ∵ F 1983]
10. *Talqīn* is part of the funeral ceremony in which the Muslim profession of faith is recited to the dead.

[POEM 246   ∞   F 1986]

3. For Joseph and the women of Egypt, see Koran 12:31, and *First Selection*, note on 7, verse 1.

9. God "created man out of a clot of congealed blood." Koran 96:2.

10. Water and clay: the human body. The Abode of War: the world.

[POEM 247   ∞   F 2000]

4. Referring to the well-known saying: "Everything returns to its origin."

9. The Ocean (in the original, *Qulzum*) of Light symbolizes spiritual truth, since "God is the Light of the heavens and the earth" (Koran 24:35).

10. The reference is to the epiphany *(tajallī)* of God on Mount Sinai, which shattered the mountain and left Moses in a swoon.

[POEM 248   ∞   F 2003]

6. Khotan: Chinese Turkestan which was proverbially known for its beautiful inhabitants.

9. Scattering coins over the head of the bride is still done in the East.

10. Jacob smelled from afar the perfume of Joseph's vest (Koran 12:94).

[POEM 249   ∞   F 2006]

4. *Fātiḥa*, the first sura of the Koran, is recited several times in daily prayers. Bu'l-Futūḥ seems to be a *kunya* or title meaning "father of victories." Golpinarli, following the same idea, translates the line: "If you recite *Fātiḥa* over a grave, the person will rise with the victorious ones . . . " (4:249). Otherwise, one might think that the reference is to Abu'l Futūḥ Rāžī, the celebrated commentator of the Koran, meaning a man like Abu'l-Futūḥ rises when the *Fātiḥa* is recited.

[POEM 250   ∞   F 2010]

2. Any obstacle which keeps the lover away from the divine beloved is designated as a veil.

3. "And We taught him the knowledge from Us," Koran 18:65.

5. Beginning of the sura 140.

[POEM 251 ❧ F 2015]

1. Muhammad said: "I take refuge from poverty in You (i.e., God)," and also: "My poverty is my pride." These two seemingly contradictory statements are explained by the Sufis as pertaining to two types of poverty. One which comes close to heresy is the poverty of heart, taking away from it learning, morality, patience, submission and trust in God. The other type makes man devoid of all worldly attachments for the sake of God and is a spiritual self-surrender and self-annihilation. Such poverty is the first step in Sufism. See Sajjādī's *Farhang-i ʿirfānī*, 363–66, and Ghanī's *Baḥs dar āsār va afkār va aḥvāl-i Ḥāfiẓ*, 275 *et seq*.

5. In the past rings were inserted in the ears of slaves as a sign of servitude.

[POEM 252 ❧ F 2028]

[POEM 253 ❧ F 2039]

1. According to Aflākī *(Manāqib,* 589–90) this was the last poem Rumi composed on his death bed. His son, Bahā' al-Dīn, was with him and unable to sleep and so his dying father began this *ghazal* in order to console him and make him go to bed.

For another translation of this poem, see P. Avery, "Jalāl ud-Dīn Rūmī and Shams-i-Tabrīzī with Certain Problems in Translation," *The Muslim World* 46 (July 1956), 3:250–52.

9. It is believed that the emerald has the property of blinding serpents; see Nicholson's *Commentary* on *Math.* 3:2548.

10. Bū ʿAlī is Abū ʿAlī Ibn Sīnā (Avicenna) (d. 1037) and Bu'l-ʿAlā (d. 1057) is the famous Syrian philosopher and poet. Avery in his notes to the poem writes: "Bu'l-ʿAlā was used by Maulānā to mean 'so-and-so'"; see Nicholson's *Commentary* on *Math.* 3:776, "a *konya* bestowed ironically on any foolish boaster." ʿBū ʿAlī (Ibn Sīnā) did not write

a *History*, but he did write a book in the title of which *Tanbīh* was a component. Rumi deliberately transposes the two.

[POEM 254 ∴ F 2043]

5. When Abraham was cast into the fire, God said: "O fire, be thou cool, and a safety for Abraham." Koran 21:69.

10. Ḥamza ibn 'Abd al-Muṭṭalib, the Prophet's uncle, was a dauntless warrior and called the "Lion of God" by Moḥammad.

[POEM 255 ∴ F 2053]

5. Koran 1:5.

8. The red sunset color is likened to the color of henna.

[POEM 256 ∴ F 2054, N 37]

2. God is foreign to the world, yet never absent from it, i.e., He at once transcends and pervades all phenomenal existence. Cf. *Nafaḥāt al-Uns*, 183, 1.2 (Nicholson's note).

16. After this line, Nicholson's version has an extra line which is not in F.

[POEM 257 ∴ F 2061]

8. The Turks were well known for their beauty and cruelty. *Chelebi* in Turkish means "sir."

[POEM 258 ∴ F 2071]

[POEM 259 ∴ F 2076]

[POEM 260 ∴ F 2083]

[POEM 261 ∴ F 2091]

[POEM 262 ∴ F 2092]

7. Kauthar is a river in paradise.

12. Ḥaidar (lion) was a nickname given to the Caliph 'Alī.

14. Guorjīs was a prophet who according to the Islamic traditions was slain seventy times by his people and again came to life.

[POEM 263 ❧ F 2105]

8. Perhaps a better translation would be: "With you it becomes the resident of the best tranquillity."

[POEM 264 ❧ F 2107]

[POEM 265 ❧ F 2110]

[POEM 266 ❧ F 2117]

[POEM 267 ❧ F 2120]

8. According to the Koran (34:10–11) David was a skillful maker of coats of mail.

10. Abraham asked God to show him the dead come to life. God ordered him to take four birds and cut them into pieces and place them on every hill. When Abraham called to them, the birds came to life and flew to him from every corner (Koran 2:62).

18. The rest of the poem is in Arabic.

[POEM 268 ❧ F 2130]

4. "When We said to the angels: 'Bow down before Adam.' They all bowed except Eblīs." Koran 2:33.

Hindu: slave or servant.

20. For *qibla* see note to poem 228, verse 18.

24. *Hā* and *hū* are two onomatopoetics used in calling a person. The latter could be associated with the ecstatic cries of the Sufis "Hū" (God, or He is). See note to poem 226, verse 12.

[POEM 269 ❧ F 2135]

5. During his ascension Muhammad saw four streams near the *sidra*, two of which were hidden and two of which were flowing openly. According to Gabriel the latter ones were the Nile and Euphrates and the other ones were two of the streams of paradise. See Gölpınarlı, 1:439.

6. This is a more literal translation than Arberry's. The original translation was: "How long will you respite me?"

[POEM 270 ❧ F 2142]
9. Masjid-i Aqṣā is a mosque in Jerusalem.

[POEM 271 ❧ F 2144]
9. *Ham dil u ham dast* means an associate and confidant. Arberry's translation is "my fellow in heart and hand."
12. The last part of the last line was revised. The original translation was: "What has your ecstasy to do with speech?"

[POEM 272 ❧ F 2155]
8. "O you who believe! Fear God as He should be feared, and die not except in a state of Islam." Koran 3:102.

[POEM 273 ❧ F 2157]

[POEM 274 ❧ F 2166]

[POEM 275 ❧ F 2170]

[POEM 276 ❧ F 2172]
7. "And He is with you wheresoever you may be." Koran 57:4.
8. "We are nearer to him (i.e., to man) than his jugular vein." Koran 1:16.

[POEM 277 ❧ F 2180]
2. The Abode of Security seems to be an allusion to heaven which is sometimes called "the abode of peace" *(dār al-salām)* by Rumi as against "the abode of pride" *(dār al-ghurūr)* i.e., the world. According to some commentaries in Rumi's time Bokhara was also called *dar al-salām*. See Gauharīn 4:383–84.
6. *Ṣāḥib qirān* is a person who is born under a happy conjunction of the planets.

[POEM 278 ⨳ F 2195]

[POEM 279 ⨳ F 2205]

4. *Qabqābs* are wooden shoes. This term is still used in Lebanon for slippers. See F 7:387.

5. Kai-Qubād was the second king of the legendary Kayānid dynasty. Sultan Sanjar was a Saljūq king who ruled over Iran from 1117 to 1157. Suhrāb was one of the heroes in the *Shāhnāma*.

12. *Faqīh*, a theologian.

15. Ibn Bawwāb (d. 1031) was a chamberlain to the Caliph al-Ma'mūn and a famous calligrapher who wrote in *riqā'* style. Rumi puns on Ibn Bawwāb and *bawwāb* (the Doorkeeper), and on *riqā'* and *ruq'a* (a letter).

16. Qāżi is a judge (cadi).

[POEM 280 ⨳ F 2214, N 38]

1. A different translation of this *ġazal* is given by Arberry in his *Classical Persian Literature*, 220–21.

[POEM 281 ⨳ F 2226]

6. The expression comes from a legend about the creation of the cat. The animals in the Ark of Noah complained of the mouse which was eating and destroying everything. So God ordered the lion to sneeze and the cat came out from his nose. *Ḥayāt al-Ḥayvān*, 1:17 (quoted by Furūzānfar in 7:372).

[POEM 282 ⨳ F 2232]

3. For the water of life see note to poem 221, verse 11.

[POEM 283 ⨳ F 2239, N 39]

8. "(O soul) return to your Lord, well-pleased and well-pleasing." Koran 89:28.

11. *Sar-i khar* was translated by Arberry as "donkeyhead" and has been changed into "meddler." *Sar-i khar* is someone who causes embarrassment, before whom one cannot talk openly.

[POEM 284 ⋞ F 2244]

[POEM 285 ⋞ F 2253]
2. *'Arafa* is the ninth of *Dhu'l Ḥijja*.

[POEM 286 ⋞ F 2259]
13. The reference is to this verse of the Koran: "Then He compre-
hended in His design the sky, and it had been as smoke." (41:11).

[POEM 287 ⋞ F 2266]
5. The reference might be to the *ḥadīs* which says: "Fasting in the
winter is a gain in the cold." See Ibn Aṣīr, *al-Nahāya fī gharīb al-
ḥadīs wa al-aṣar*, 3:390.
6. I could not find this particular tradition, but there are a num-
ber of *ḥadīs* which bear resemblance to this. Two of them are: "Fast
when you see the moon and break your fast when you see it again,"
and "Then fast until you see the crescent of the moon." See A. J.
Wensinck, *Concordance et indices de la tradition musulmane*, Leiden,
1955, 3:454.
12. See Mutanabbī, *Dīvān*, Beirut, 1964, 101.

[POEM 288 ⋞ F 2277]
3. Kai-Khusrau was one of the ancient kings of Iran.

[POEM 289 ⋞ F 2280]

[POEM 290 ⋞ F 2283]

[POEM 291 ⋞ F 2293]
6. To scratch the back of one's neck or ear signifies embarrassment.

[POEM 292 ⋞ F 2299]
8. Koran 12:26.

[POEM 293 ⋞ F 2303]

[POEM 294 ❧ F 2313]

[POEM 295 ❧ F 2319]

2. The Brethren of Purity (apart from its literal meaning) refers to a secret society which was formed in the eighth century to introduce Greek philosophy to the Muslim world. The treatises written by them are called *Rasā'il-i Ikhvān al-Ṣafā*.

[POEM 296 ❧ F 2322]

1. Aflākī gives the following account of the composition of this *ghazal:* "A darvish asked Maulānā: 'Who is a mystic?' He said 'A mystic is a person whose calm disposition is never disturbed by any annoyance. The mystic never becomes angry.'" *Manāqib,* 279.

[POEM 297 ❧ F 2331]

[POEM 298 ❧ F 2335]

[POEM 299 ❧ F 2336]

[POEM 300 ❧ F 2345]

[POEM 301 ❧ F 2357]

10. Verses ten, eleven and twelve are in Arabic.

[POEM 302 ❧ F 2370]

[POEM 303 ❧ F 2372]

[POEM 304 ❧ F 2379]

[POEM 305 ❧ F 2389, N 40]

1. According to Nicholson *(Dīvān-i Shams,* 238, 300) this is a reference to the *ḥadīs* of the Prophet, where God says: "My earth and heaven contain me not, but the heart of my believing servant contains me."

3. "He is the Truth," Koran 22:6.

8. Reason is annihilated in mystical love.

9. For Ṣalāḥ al-Dīn Zarkūb see note on 29, verse 12.

[POEM 306   ⋰   F 2395, N 41]

3. The air of Iraq is a Persian tune.

[POEM 307   ⋰   F 2399]

7. Islamic writers regarded the liver as the seat of the passion and anguish of love. The liver being on fire means that the lover is tormented by the fire of love.

[POEM 308   ⋰   F 2405]

1. For *Lā ilāha illa 'llāh* see note to poem 232, verse 8.

[POEM 309   ⋰   F 2412]

5. Turks were well known for their beauty and also for mistreatment of their lovers. A Persian-Turk seems to be a Turk born in Iran.

6. Hasanak is a common name for boys. Here it simply means "the boy."

[POEM 310   ⋰   F 2422]

[POEM 311   ⋰   F 2429]

15. Koran 9:111.

20. Koran 2:151.

[POEM 312   ⋰   F 2437]

5. In Persian the expression "to clutch someone's skirt" means to seek his protection or help.

6. Koran 6:11.

12. *Raml* (sand divination) was a method of divination used in the past. It made use of a board divided into sixteen sections with words on each section; these were then divided into four major parts according to the four elements. The divination would be made by

throwing grains of sand on the board and basing the prediction upon their respective situations on it.

[POEM 313   ⤳   F 2449]

2. For Āzar see note to poem 243, verse 6.

6. The love of Lailī and Majnūn is proverbial in Islamic literatures.

[POEM 314   ⤳   F 2458]

[POEM 315   ⤳   F 2465]

6. For *qibla* see note to poem 228, verse 18.

11. "Say your prayers and give charity and lend God a good loan." Koran 73:20.

12. "O you believers! Fear God and give up what remains of your demand for usury, if you are indeed believers." Koran 2:278.

[POEM 316   ⤳   F 2474]

[POEM 317   ⤳   F 2480]

2. Arberry's translation of this line is: "What have you seen in the courtyard? Why are you flying to annihilation?" In fact *fanā* has two meanings in Arabic, "nothingness" and a "courtyard," but it may be more appropriate to interpret both words as meaning "nothingness" or "annihilation."

9. Moses said to the Samaritan: "Be gone! But they punishment in this life will be that thou wilt say, 'Touch me not.'" Koran 20:97.

[POEM 318   ⤳   F 2491]

[POEM 319   ⤳   F 2493]

[POEM 320   ⤳   F 2498]

13. *Autād* (props or pegs) are the saints who are believed to be the guardians and preservers of the world. Nicholson writes in his notes to the *Math.* 2:1935: "It is well known among Sufis that every night

the *Autād* must go round the whole world, and if there should be any place on which their eyes have not fallen, next day some imperfection will appear; and they must then inform the *Quṭb,* in order that he may fix his attention on the weak spot, and that by his blessing the imperfection be removed."

18. 'Anqā or Sīmurgh is the legendary bird by which the Sufis sometimes represent the unknown God. Sīmurgh is sometimes considered to symbolize the perfect man.

19. *Ibn al-vaqt,* literally "the son of the moment."

22. "Come back thou to thy Lord, well-pleased [thyself], and well-pleasing unto Him." Koran 80:89.

23. To bite one's hand is a sign of regret.

26. Arberry had translated *markab* as "horse," but "ship" seems more appropriate in this context.

[POEM 321 ❧ F 2509]
3. It is said that Solomon had power over the *dīvs* and jinns.
7. Koran 21:93.

[POEM 322 ❧ F 2514]

[POEM 323 ❧ F 2523]
1. Perhaps a better reading is "who burns like sulphur in a fire."

[POEM 324 ❧ F 2530]

[POEM 325 ❧ F 2537]

[POEM 326 ❧ F 2546]

[POEM 327 ❧ F 2558]

[POEM 328 ❧ F 2566]

[POEM 329 ❧ F 2572]

[POEM 330 ⋅: F 2577, N 42]

1. Nicholson comments on this line: "*Jamā'a* means 'the community or brotherhood of saints and spiritual men.'"

3. "The idol of clay" is the "self" which veils man from God.

4. In Persian literature the world is often likened to an old woman who survives many bridegrooms.

10. "Was not God's land wide enough that you might take refuge in it?" Koran 4:99.

The prison refers to the earthly involvements which keep man from God.

"Knot care less": Nicholson translates this phrase "Avoid entangled thoughts" or "Do not bewilder yourself by useless thinking."

[POEM 331 ⋅: F 2589]

1. In the past it was believed that the earth was encircled by nine spheres.

[POEM 332 ⋅: F 2605]

3. For "taking dates to Baṣra," see note to poem 211, verse 12.

The Sea of Oman was well known for its pearls.

8. For a description of the game of the *nard* (an Oriental form of backgammon), see Nicholson's notes on the *Math.* 2:613. The board of this game has six sections, hence the term *shash dar* or *shashdara* is connected with it. There is an obvious analogy between this game and the world with its six spatial relations, viz., right and left, before and behind, above and below. In this line the "six-sided dice" and "the checker board" and the "human dice" seem to represent the human head (the seat of reason), and the body and the heart respectively. It means that the heart and head, or reason and intuition, cannot be reconciled.

[POEM 333 ⋅: F 2613]

[POEM 334 ⋅: F 2625]

1. This line shows the indifference of the Sufis towards the formal or traditional knowledge taught in the schools of theology.

2. For the Sīmurgh, see note to poem 320, verse 18.

10. Koran 67:1: "Blessed be He in whose hands is dominion; and he over all things hath power." This verse is connected with an incident in the life of Muhammad while he was still in Mecca. One day he was engaged in a heated discussion with the pagans of Quraish about the Koran, when an old blind man came in and kept interrupting their discussion as he wanted to learn the Koran. At first Muhammad "frowned and turned away" (Koran 80:1), but then realizing that the man might be hurt, he paid attention to him. This sura asks for more attention for anyone who seeks to know the truth.

[POEM 335   ⋰   F 2627]
4. To decorate the outside hall of the public baths with paintings on the tiles was a common practice in Iran.

5. Arberry had "essence" or "pearl."

[POEM 336   ⋰   F 2633]
9. {Possibly better than Arberry's choice of "published" (for *shuhra*) would be "broadcast," "manifested," or "proclaimed." The idea is that both the outward form and the inner meaning are revealed in the mirror of Shams.}

[POEM 337   ⋰   F 2641]

[POEM 338   ⋰   F 2647]
10. Mount Qāf is the legendary abode of the Sīmurgh, see note to verse 18 in Ghazal 320.

The legend has it that the *būtīmār* (the heron) sits on the shore of the sea but does not drink water lest it may be used up.

[POEM 339   ⋰   F 2656]
3. This might refer to the tradition which says: "There is a time for me with God that no chosen prophet or archangel can come between us." This might also be a reference to a legend about the ascension of Muhammad to Heaven. It relates that when he was about to enter

into the presence of God, he said to Gabriel, who was his guide in this celestial journey, "O my brother, why hast thou fallen behind me?" Gabriel replied, "Were I to come one fingertip nearer, sure I should be consumed." Cf. Nicholson, *Math.* 1:1066–67.

[POEM 340 ⋌ F 2664]

[POEM 341 ⋌ F 2667]
1. According to Aflākī *(Manāqib,* 726–28) this *ghazal* celebrates the marriage of the daughter of Ṣalāḥ al-Dīn Zarkūb with Niẓām al-Dīn Khaṭṭāṭ.

[POEM 342 ⋌ F 2674]
5. All the phenomenal forms are "intoxicated" with the Divine Love according to their respective capacities. Cf. *Gulshan-i Rāz*, 825.
14. The reference is to the Koran (33:72): "We indeed offer the trust to the heavens and the earth and the mountains, but they refused to bear it, being afraid of it; but man undertook it—he was indeed ignorant and unjust." The commentators of the Koran generally regard the "trust" *(amāna)* as the Faith of Islam and obedience to its laws. The Sufis say that it is gnosis *(maʿrifa)* or the inspiration of Divine Love, which only man was able to treasure. It is because of this virtue that man is the vice-regent of God and has many of His attributes.

[POEM 343 ⋌ F 2684]
4. Jūdī is the name of the mountain in the Koran (11:44) on which the Ark came to rest (i.e., the equivalent of Genesis' Ararat).

[POEM 344 ⋌ F 2693]

[POEM 345 ⋌ F 2696]
1. For *Khumār* Arberry's translation was "crop sickness."
10. This line is only in CB.

[POEM 346 ⋌ F 2703]

[POEM 347 ⋅: F 2707]

1. Karbala {Arberry elsewhere spells Kerbela} is a city in Iraq where Ḥusain, the grandson of the Prophet, fought against the Umayyad Yazīd and died with his few followers. The city was originated around the shrine of the Imam.

[POEM 348 ⋅: F 2713]
10. Koran 34:13.

[POEM 349 ⋅: F 2728]
10. "Upon them [the believers] will be garments of fine green silk and brocade, and bracelets of silver; and their Lord will give them to drink of a wine pure and holy." Koran 76:21.

[POEM 350 ⋅: F 2736]

[POEM 351 ⋅: F 2737]

[POEM 352 ⋅: F 2756]
9. When Moses asked to see God on the Mount, the answer was, "You will never see me." Koran 7:143.

[POEM 353 ⋅: F 2760]
4. In the second hemistich of this line instead of *bāda* (wine) F has *bād* (wind or air) which means: "You are puffed up with pride."
8. {*Surmeh*} is kohl, an antimony preparation used to darken the edges of the eyelids.

[POEM 354 ⋅: F 2775]

[POEM 355 ⋅: F 2776]

[POEM 356 ⋅: F 2779]

[POEM 357 ⋅: F 2788]
5. It was believed that the ostrich eats fire.

[POEM 358 ~ F 2795]

5. *Suhail (Canopus)* is mostly seen in Yemen.

6. Musk of Tartary is the best kind of musk.

[POEM 359 ~ F 2805]

[POEM 360 ~ F 2814]

[POEM 361 ~ F 2820, N 47]

4. In this verse Rumi refers to the well-known tradition which the Sufi poets often have made use of. God declares: "I was a hidden treasure and I desired to be known, so I created the creation in order that I might be known." Cf. Nicholson's notes on the *Dīvān* 4:2 and 23:7.

8. The reference is to the Koran 15:29: "[God said to the angels:] 'When I have completed him [Adam] and breathed of my spirit into him, you will fall and worship him.'" According to Nicholson *rūḥ* (spirit) is probably used here as the reasonable soul *(rūḥ-i nāṭiqa)*.

12. *When man contemplates his own evolution—from inanimate to plant and then animal life, and eventually to the state of man—he will realize that he might go further and even surpass angels in his nearness to God.* See Nicholson's notes, 47:12 and 12:6–10.

[POEM 362 ~ F 2828, N 43]

4. When Moses asked to see God (cf. note to poem 349), he only revealed himself to Mount Sinai and made it dust, and Moses fell in a swoon (Koran 7:139). Similarly the base and worldly alloy of man is transmuted by spiritual experience or God's alchemy. In Islamic literature Korah is proverbial for his riches. The Koran (27:76–81) refers to him as a man who has grown insolent and vicious because of his wealth.

5. In the past, sugar was brought from Egypt. Rumi says that within you there is a divine element which produces sweetness and love, so it is as if you have a sugar plantation within yourself.

7. If you realize your own better self, which is the reflection of the divine beauty, you will be indifferent to external beauties.

9. According to Nicholson the "six wicks" are the eyes, ears, nose and mouth.

10. The heart as the seat of love is likened to the Kaaba.

[POEM 363   ⩽   F 2830]

7. God "has created from water; then He has established relation-
ships of lineage and marriage." Koran 25:54. This also could refer to
human sperm. Man was originally one or two drops of water; now he
has become a Noah on the sea.

8. If someone's cap reaches the sky, he has attained a high position.

14. Koran 7:139, i.e., you will attain such a status that God will not
say: "You will never see me."

[POEM 364   ⩽   F 2832]

[POEM 365   ⩽   F 2838]

16. A play on the name of *Shams* which means sun.

[POEM 366   ⩽   F 2845]

7. The second hemistich of this line seems to refer to this sura
of the Koran: "Say: He is God . . . He begetteth not, nor is he
begotten."

[POEM 367   ⩽   F 2852]

9. The legend has it that by the order of God a gnat penetrated
into his brain through his nose and caused the death of this tyrant
king of Babylonia.

11. The reference is to the dog of the Companions of the Cave
(cf. Koran 28:9–22) which is the same as the Christian legend of the
Seven Sleepers of Ephesus.

[POEM 368   ⩽   F 2859]

4. According to the Muslims paradise has eight stages, whereas hell
has seven levels.

5. The reference is to the tradition which says: "The fire [of hell]
says to the pious, 'go away, your light extinguished my fire.'"

[POEM 369   ⩽   F 2865, N 46]

[POEM 370 ⤙ F 2873]

[POEM 371 ⤙ F 2880]
2. *Maidān* is a square.

[POEM 372 ⤙ F 2894]
2. "Camel-hearted" is a cowardly person or someone who holds a grudge long in his heart.

6. Koran 6:76–7: "When the night covered him [Abraham], he saw a star; he said: 'This is my Lord.' But when it set, he said: 'I do not love those who set.' When he saw the moon rising in glory, he said, 'This is my Lord.' But when the moon set, he said: 'Unless my Lord guides me, I shall surely be among those who go astray.' When he saw the sun rising in splendor, he said: 'This is my Lord; this is the greatest of all.' But when the sun set, he said: 'O my people! I am now free from your guilt of giving partners to God.'"

9. Burāq is the legendary steed of Moḥammad which carried him to his ascension.

11. *Bismillāh al-raḥmān al-raḥīm* (in the name of God, most gracious, most merciful) is repeated in the beginning of every sura of the Koran. *Bismillāh* is mentioned when a bird or animal is slaughtered, hence the word *bismil* (an abbreviated form of the same) means to slaughter. Rumi here plays on the two meanings of the word.

[POEM 373 ⤙ F 2899]
7. *Niṣār-i āstīn* (shaking one's sleeves) is a reference to dancing.

8. A play on the name of Ṣalāḥ al-Dīn Zarkūb which means Ṣalāḥ al-Dīn the goldminter.

[POEM 374 ⤙ F 2902]
6. Koran 47:38.
7. Koran 24:35.

[POEM 375 ⤙ F 2912]
13. *Bī sar u pā* (literally: without foot and head) idiomatically means a person of no importance or standing.

[POEM 376 ~ F 2916]

5. For *Alast*, see note to poem 55, verse 11.

[POEM 377 ~ F 2922]

3. Cf. the prologue of the *Math.* lines 9–10.

5. The inhabitants of the ancient city of Rayy, which now lies in the south of Tehran, used to build their houses underground or with very low doors in order to keep away the invaders. See *Rayy-i Bāstān* by Ḥusain Karīmiyān (Tehran 1971, 1:257).

[POEM 378 ~ F 2927]

[POEM 379 ~ F 2933]

1. *Allāh-u Akbar* (God is great) is the call for prayer.

10. Mahastī means "you are a moon," or "the lady of the moon," or simply a lady.

[POEM 380 ~ F 2942]

[POEM 381 ~ F 2946]

2. For Bā Yazīd see note on 1, verse 21.

3. The *Khirqa* (or the robe) of the Sufis usually was blue.

4. For Mahastī (the lady) see note to poem 379, verse 10.

[POEM 382 ~ F 2958]

9. "Dusty of face" means humble.

10. The "reversed horseshoe" is a metaphor for someone who reverses the shoes of his horse in order to confuse the trail and mislead his pursuers. Cf. Nicholson, *Math.* notes, 1:2841. The metaphor could refer to the world as well, see note to poem 388, verse 12.

[POEM 383 ~ F 2964]

2. The line is derived from the tradition which says: "Search for goodness among the handsome ones." F 6:208.

8. Arberry's translation was "Pretty of cheek, annihilate being . . . "
The revision into "Pretty of cheek, bring nonexistence into existence"
follows Furūzānfar's text.

[POEM 384   ⋏   F 2967]

5. The splitting of the moon will be the sign of the approaching
end of the world (Koran 54:1). According to Nicholson, at an early
date this passage was explained as a miracle wrought by Muhammad
in his celestial journey. Cf. notes on 1, verse 8.

[POEM 385   ⋏   F 2981]

7. According to some Sufis God has created eighteen thousand,
and according to some others fifty thousand, worlds. See Sajjādī,
Farang-i ʿirfānī, 327.

[POEM 386   ⋏   F 2984]

7. For "the seven oft-repeated verses" of the Koran, see note on
24, verse 5.

[POEM 387   ⋏   F 2998]

[POEM 388   ⋏   F 3001]

7. "Nine eyes" is a reference to the nine holes on the reed.
8. Arberry's translation was: "O shame of the head, on this way,
disgrace, knowledge."
12. According to an ancient belief, the earth was on the two horns
of an ox. The "reversed horseshoe" here seems to refer to the world.
See note to poem 382, verse 10.

[POEM 389   ⋏   F 3019]

[POEM 390   ⋏   F 3021]

[POEM 391   ⋏   F 3034]

3. This line could also be translated: "Bud and flowers came as
forgiveness so that you may not see the ugliness of the thorn."

Maghfara (forgiveness) could also be read as *mighfar-at* (your helmet)

17. The nomadic Ghuzz tribes invaded and destroyed Khorasan in the twelfth century.

[POEM 392 ᵛ F 3038]

1. For Burāq see note to poem 372, verse 6.

6. For Khiḍar, see note on 6, verse 2; also note to poem 221, verse 11.

7. *Rukn-i Yamānī* (the Yemeni pillar), a name given to the south-west corner of the Kaaba which faces Yemen. Cf. Nicholson's note 44:11.

12. For *Ṣāḥib-qirān* (Lord of the Fortunate Conjunction), see note to poem 277, verse 6.

[POEM 393 ᵛ F 3048]

7. A tradition says: "The believers are quiet and easygoing like a docile camel, when [God] binds them they accept the bond, and when He makes them sit on a rock they sit." F 6:261. Arberry had: "who makes his camel driven," a less literal translation.

[POEM 394 ᵛ F 3050]

13. Duldul was the name of a mule ridden by 'Alī.

[POEM 395 ᵛ F 3051, N 48]

3. The story of a white falcon whose beak and claws were cut by a "wicked old woman" is told in the *Math.* 2:265–325. The falcon typifies the human soul who has been separated from its divine origin. The "falcon-drum": according to Nicholson's note on the *Dīvān* (16:3), "When the huntsman wishes to call his bird back, he beats a drum: the hawk, having an affection for the drum, returns speedily."

10. *Shikūr-i shakūr* if applied to God means "in the search of or hunting for one who is All-Grateful and rewards well His servants." Nicholson, on the authority of one line from Sa'dī's *Būstān*, suggests that "the two wings like a shield" are hope and fear, since the Sufis believe that "fear and hope for man are like the two wings of a bird." Cf. Nicholson's note on this poet, verse 10.

[POEM 396   ❧   F 3055, N 45]

5. For the sleep of phenomenal existence, see Nicholson's notes on the *Dīvān* 39, verse 9 and 36, verse 5.

6. For the "eye of intelligence," see Nicholson's note on the *Dīvān* II: verse 5.

F. has *chashm-i khar* which Arberry translates literally as "the ass's eye." Nicholson has *chashm-i kaj* (the eye that sees falsely). The "eye of wrong" here replaces the former version.

10. Being black or being buried in the dark refers to man's involvement in this world.

11. *Mushtarī-ṭāli'* means a person born under the planet Jupiter which apparently brings good fortune. Another reading could be "a person whose planet is Jupiter when it is in ascension."

[POEM 397   ❧   F 3061]

5. *'Uqdat al-dhanab* in common parlance is "the knot of Draco" whereas its literal meaning is "the node of the tail" as opposed to "the node of the head" ('uqdat-al-ra's). The former refers to the intersecting point between ecliptic and lunar orbits as the moon is ascending to the north, while the latter is its descending point to the south (cf. C.A. Nallimo, *Opus Astronomicum al-Batamii*, 2:346; Bīrūnī, *The Book of Instruction in the Elements of the Art of Astrology (al-Tafḥīm)* text and translation by Ramsay Wright, London, 1934, 154. Popular imagination placed a dragon on the lunar orbit which they said devours the sun, hence the "tail" and "head."

6. *'Azab-khāna* is a bachelor's house and metaphorically means a house of loneliness. Cf. F 7:369.

[POEM 398   ❧   F 3071]

[POEM 399   ❧   F 3079]

7. For *'anqā*, see note to poem 320, verse 18.

[POEM 400   ❧   F 3090]

1. {Arberry's handwriting is difficult to read here, but it may also

be construed as "seize sugar now" rather than "seize the sugar tray" (for *shikar sitān hala*).}

2. The reference is to the Koran 67:5: "And We have adorned the sky of the world with lamps, and We have made them as missiles to drive away the evil ones."